Bridge of No Return

Bridge of No Return

The Ordeal

of

of the

No Return

U.S.S. *Pueblo*

F. Carl Schumacher, Jr. & George C. Wilson

Harcourt Brace Jovanovich, Inc., *New York*

VB
230
S34

To the crew of the U.S.S. *Pueblo*

Contents

Bridge of No Return

Prologue   *by George C. Wilson*

More than a United States Navy ship was captured on January 23, 1968, when the North Koreans hijacked the U.S.S. *Pueblo*. A whole nation was captured.

The traditions of the United States, its pride, and its sense of what is right and what is wrong were then all put on trial along with the eighty-two men from the *Pueblo*.

Kim Il Sung, the ruler of North Korea, assumed the role of public prosecutor in this international trial of an open society versus a closed society, of democracy versus Communism. He used the men of the *Pueblo* as hostages. He made them sign confessions of uncommitted acts to save their lives. His price for their freedom was a confession of guilt by their country. He said that the United States must admit it intruded into North Korean territorial waters—a national act of perjury; apologize for doing so—a national act of humiliation; and promise not to intrude again.

North Korea, compared with the United States, was no military power. It could have been virtually incinerated by American Polaris missiles. The fact that it was not provided a revealing example of the limited diplomatic power of nuclear weapons.

Just eighty-two lives—they were all that Kim needed to humiliate the United States, provided only that he could break these men—by torture, trickery, or any other means—to his purpose. The *Pueblo* men were his leverage. They were made to perform as he willed. A

3

calculated combination of physical hardship, relentless psychological pressure, and repeated bloody beatings produced what he demanded —the admissions of guilt, broadcast apologies, televised press conferences, and publicized letters to the President of the United States.

The men of the *Pueblo* knew they were being manipulated, but not one of them—not a single man from this widely varied crew of eighty-two—found a way to keep from being used. Yet the Code of Conduct for Members of the Armed Forces of the United States dictated that each member of the *Pueblo* crew resist *and* prevent such manipulation.

Lieutenant (j.g.) F. Carl Schumacher, Jr., Operations Officer on the *Pueblo,* was one of the men so used. After almost a year in captivity, he came back to discover that few, if any, Americans understood how it is in Communist North Korea. They had no feeling for the pulverizing pressures put on American captives. He worried about the limited and confused meaning that had come out of the *Pueblo*'s grim experience.

The Navy had conducted an extensive Court of Inquiry after the *Pueblo* men were returned. But its focus was almost solely on why the Captain had let his ship be captured, why he lost her without a fight. Naval traditions were stressed, but little, if any, emphasis was placed on the larger issue of what is to be expected of the men who are ordered into that gray area between all-out peace and all-out war. The Code of Conduct proved completely untenable under torture. Yet the same code is in effect today, even after the Navy examined it in the light of the *Pueblo* experience. More men are being sent out to dangerous areas where the code will not work if they get captured. Yet these Americans will continue to be judged by their compliance with that code.

Skip Schumacher is one of the men who grieved about the code and his inability to live up to it. He felt compelled to examine why he had not been able to fulfill its terms. Where was the flaw? In him? In his shipmates? In the code? In its authors? In its administrators? Some measure of response to these gravely haunting questions was essential to him. He has steadfastly sought it.

This book is the result of his search. It is, for the most part, one

4

man's eyewitness account of the first and last voyage of the *Pueblo* and the captivity that followed. It is an intensely personal book, revealing, as it must, many intimate thoughts that most men prefer to hold to themselves. It was a painful book to write, for, beyond the repeated probings into an extended sequence of brutal experiences that he would long to forget, Schumacher has reached for the standard of merciless honesty. Only through so open a recounting can he hope to explain the ordeal of the crew of the *Pueblo* in such a way that people in this nation can understand what the United States asked of the men it sent out into the Cold War and what it is still asking of other men.

A striving toward honesty may not produce accuracy in every detail. Schumacher has a remarkable memory, yet he is aware that his recollections of conversations, especially with his North Korean captors and in moments of extreme stress, may be faulty. The duration and extent of pain during torture is difficult for its victim to gauge. Moreover, the documented records reveal inconsistencies. In this collaboration, we have taken these possibilities of discrepancy into careful account. We have exercised prudence to avoid exaggeration or distortion, and we believe we have stated essential truth in all matters of fact.

The texts of the confessions, letters of apology, press conferences, and other "forced" statements quoted herein are taken from official releases made by North Korean propaganda agencies and published in controlled Communist periodicals. It may be assumed that these releases match with reasonable accuracy the statements "extracted" by force and coercion from the *Pueblo* crew members.

In matters of opinion, our collaboration remains firm. Although the Prologue and the Epilogue of this book bear only my by-line, they are the result of long discussions and full understanding between us. The opinions and conclusions in both the Prologue and the Epilogue are mutually held.

This is not a book of self-justification. Schumacher is no longer seeking a personal rationale for his failure to live up to the Code of Conduct. The Navy Court of Inquiry made no charges against him. In fact, the Navy praised him for the leadership he exhibited in captivity. With the publication of this book, he means to let the record speak for itself.

Neither is this book an argument on tactics or strategy, or of command decisions made aboard the *Pueblo*. Such matters have been dealt with in volumes specifically directed to them. They play a part in this account only as they bear on actual events, on the Code of Conduct, on the limited focus of the Court of Inquiry, and on the inconclusive action taken by the Secretary of the Navy.

This book is, instead, the story of what the *Pueblo* disaster meant to one man, who in certain poignant and critical respects reflects the essential experience of the entire crew and of other United States military men taken prisoner by sophisticatedly savage foes in the impersonal, ruthless, and ruleless Cold War.

If this book helps to relieve those who carry false guilt, if it advances by even one small step the reform of a deceptively admirable, but practically vicious code, if it alerts the public and the military departments to their full responsibilities, then it will have served its writers well.

Only Way Out

I had to kill myself.

Then I would win. The Democratic People's Republic of Korea would lose. The only catch was that I would die at twenty-four. I didn't want to die. But clearly it was the thing to do.

I came to that decision after only three days in North Korea. Those days were even more nightmarish than was the capture of our ship, the U.S.S. *Pueblo,* on the high seas off Wonsan on January 23, 1968. We had been sure that such a thing would never happen. Yet it did.

The North Koreans stole our ship at gunpoint, blindfolded and tied us, and packed us on a train for an all-night ride across country to Pyongyang, capital of North Korea. What brought me to the decision to commit suicide started at the Pyongyang train station when a Korean guard took my blindfold off and untied my hands.

It was 5:45 in the still-black morning of Wednesday, January 24. I was sitting in a double seat of a train—its wood trim and rough floors making it look like part of a set for a Western. The only light was tired and brownish-looking—matching my mood of depression. I wasn't supposed to look around the train. The guard had pushed my head down on my chest when he yanked the blindfold off. But I could still work my eyes around without moving my head much.

My blood-spattered khaki trousers—the blood from Fireman Duane Hodges, who was killed by the Korean gunfire against our ship—pressed against another pair of khaki-clad knees. I worked my eyes up the man's body until they reached his face. It was the angry face of Commander Lloyd M. Bucher, Captain of the *Pueblo.* His large black eyes were filled with pain and anger. He was grinding his teeth and kneading his fingers—a study of frustration. His ordinarily authoritative-looking commander's hat seemed to mock his impotence as he sat a prisoner in the Wild West railroad car stopped at Pyongyang. The Koreans had pushed his head down on his chest, too. There were to be no exceptions.

Next to the Captain sat Chief Warrant Officer Gene Lacy. I had last seen him when we were imprisoned by the Koreans in the forward berthing compartment of our ship. Peering around to the side, I saw Tim Harris on my right. We had shared a cabin on the ship. His reddish, freckled neck glowed even in the dull light of the railroad car. None of us tried to speak. The Koreans had forbidden it. I thought the order merciful. What was there to say?

Each of us was an island. Each of us was on his own. I had never felt so cut off, so alone, in my life. I was no longer a member of the huge American military establishment. I had been amputated from it by the Koreans.

One reassuring quality of the United States Navy is that no matter how silly a job you're doing—like being the officer in charge of Coke bottles on an aircraft carrier (there really is such a job)—you can relate it to something larger and more important. All the instructions, briefings, directives, orders, forms, and letters from the various levels of the naval command made me believe that somebody at the top had thought of everything—and that I was connected to Them. If the ship needed anything—secret publications, toothpaste, policy guidance—the request would work its way up to Them. And They were always within reach, no matter where you were.

But They could not be reached from Pyongyang. The Captain had no place to go for answers. He had to find his answers within himself. So did I. So did everybody else—at least until we got back together again and could re-establish the ship's chain of command. *If* we ever got back together again in a situation where we could communicate. The Korean guards were all around us in the train. We could not communicate there.

8

A Korean officer we later named Max, because he looked like Maximilian Schell, came alongside our double seat and looked at the four of us. He eyed us nervously, perhaps thinking that a Polaris missile was about to blow up the whole city and that we knew it.

"Now we will take you off the train," he said warily, almost questioningly. His black eyes fastened on the Captain's gold braid. "Captain," he said, "you first. Then the others."

The Captain remained seated for what to Max was obviously a suspenseful moment. He didn't move; only stared up at Max. Then, with a look of resignation and revulsion and hatred, the Captain rose and did as Max indicated. I followed the Captain down the aisle of the train and to the door on the left. Tim and Gene followed me, and I could hear the rest of the crew being lined up. I saw two dark steel steps leading to a concrete platform. The Captain was pushed down those steps. I followed.

Outside, it was still dark. Facing us was a blinding semicircle of floodlights, hemming us in. A murmur arose from behind those lights. Flashbulbs popped. I felt like an animal on public display at a trainside zoo. Max ordered the Captain to line the crew up in two rows. I turned to look at them as they shuffled into position.

Sailors ashore often look incongruous, but this crew looked particularly ludicrous. In the freezing early-morning air their breath hung in little clouds above their tousled hair. All needed shaves; all, having just come from combat, looked and smelled bad. They shoved their hands in their pockets and stamped from foot to foot to keep warm. In their eyes was fear, doubt, shock. I smiled at them. They were a good crew, but what could I say?

Cameras started their internationally recognizable whirrings, and more flashbulbs popped. I got a quick look at my watch again. It was 6:00 A.M., fifteen minutes since the train had stopped. I didn't know just where we were, though I suspected it was Pyongyang, which I found out later was correct. At the time, it didn't much matter.

The train, I realized, had been heated, for now I felt the cold rising from the platform, right through the rather unmilitary Western riding boots I had been wearing when the *Pueblo* was captured. Starting to shiver, I, too, jammed my hands into my pockets.

9

I strained to see who was behind those lights. I could see no one, could hear only the guttural hubbub. I had the impression of shifting, faceless shapes, quite a few, behind those all-too-bright lights.

Finally a man walked out from behind the lights and approached the Skipper, standing on my left. "Captain," this stranger in a green uniform and red-starred hat said in good English, "come out this way." The semicircle of lights parted slightly, and we started walking toward the opening. An order was shouted out of the dark: "Hands up!" Again we obeyed, and found ourselves walking out of the lights, not as the victims we were, but as criminals. The photographers were having a field day, and the platform was littered with power cables and the debris of their trade—empty film cartons, expended flashbulbs, and cigarette butts.

The sky was growing lighter as we marched, with hands up, toward a Czechoslovakian-made bus, which had the lines of those Mercedes-Benz tourist vans I had toured on in Europe. The bus was for civilians, a commercial bus, and we entered a world of stainless steel and plastic, an ironic witness to a barbaric scene. We were herded like animals. Guards were beside us, behind us, in front of us, and more were waiting on the bus. No American voice spoke.

I sat down in the rear with the same three officers I had been with on the train. Again we sat two facing two. When all the seats were filled, the North Koreans continued to shove and push people in, until the aisles were filled. But there was solace in this, because from the compactness came warmth. As the mob grew denser, I heard one of the crewmen hiss, "What in the hell is going on?" No one tried to answer.

The last to board were the wounded. Our Executive Officer, Lieutenant Edward R. Murphy, Jr., and one of the men carried the ship's stretcher, with Fireman Steven E. Woelk on it. Woelk had been seriously injured by the same shell that got Hodges. Then three or four of the walking wounded limped into the bus, their buddies lending a helping shoulder. Murphy did his best to comfort these men, but there was little he could do.

After all the men had been loaded into two buses—about forty in each—ten or fifteen guards pushed their way in. With their AK-

10

47's cocked and ready, they took positions around us. Three stationed themselves behind the seat I was occupying. One of them gave a command, the doors of the bus closed, and we left the parking lot.

I took advantage of the confusion to look around and try to figure out where we were. What I learned later was the Pyongyang railroad station tower dominated the scene. It had a huge clock with gold hands. The clock read 6:20. Just below the clock was a large portrait of the Beloved Leader, Comrade Kim Il Sung. The artist had given him a benevolent, pudgy face, soft eyes, and a sturdy, thick boxer's neck. A gold frame and red background set off the portrait. I knew I was in his hands now, and he did not look benevolent to me.

We went down a wide boulevard into the center of town. Even for the workers in this Communist land it was early, and I saw no passers-by. I noticed a tree—a leafless sycamore silhouetted against a bleak building by the dawning light. I could identify immediately with this tree, because I had grown up with a couple of sycamores in my neighborhood and had spent happier days climbing sycamores. I wanted to stop, to admire that tree, to ask it what it thought of this passing scene. I wanted to ask what something so familiar was doing in a place so foreign.

Whack! My survey of the scene, with head uplifted, had cost me a smashing punch on the head as a hard hand pushed my chin back down on my chest in the abject position of a prisoner. Even when the station was well behind us, I could feel the eyes of Kim on the tall tower following me. And as we passed through town I could just make out the endless walls and windows of buildings sliding by in depressing repetition.

I was starting to spin inside. The long train ride, with hands bound and eyes blindfolded, and this new trip to an unknown destination through such a sterile landscape ripped at my moorings of self-control. Sleep was tempting; so was dreaming. But I knew I had to stay in there to keep in control. I forced myself to think of what I would have been doing on other mornings at this hour.

On the ship, I would be on the morning watch. This had been my favorite watch, for I always loved the beauty of dawn at sea. No

11

matter how many times I stood on the bridge and watched the sun come up, no two mornings were ever the same. God's best poetry was written in the morning, I felt. Now, I could see no such beauty outside the bus. The North Koreans had inked over that poetry with ugly buildings, littered door stoops, and monolithically dull concrete. I saw no life. No dogs sniffed at garbage or chased the buses. No people. Dead. Dead. Everything looked dead. Is this what the other side of the Styx looks like? I thought.

Whack! Another blow on the head as Schumacher, world traveler and curious spectator, was caught peeking again. The guard kept his eye on me this time. I was limited to counting the spots of blood on my trousers.

"Now we will take you off the bus," Max said smugly. We had pulled up in front of what was to be our first prison in North Korea. We were told we could look up. What we saw was a big, four-story building faced with stucco. We came to call it the Barn. We seemed to have come in at the rear entrance, into an open courtyard flanked on two sides by identical buildings and, at the opposite end, by a garage. There was enough space here for assembling troops. I figured the buildings were probably barracks. As I looked around, I noticed we had come through a metal gate, so that the whole courtyard could be closed off and the only entrance protected by guards.

Max's eyes had none of the uncertainty detected earlier. He evidently had decided no Polaris missile was about to incinerate him. Quite obviously, here on his own army base he felt more confident. Behind him, as he stood at the doorway of the bus ready to let us out, was a mob of perhaps two or three hundred jeering guards. To them this was a dream fulfilled. The hated Americans were within clawing distance. The Koreans sounded as if they wanted our blood without delay.

The sound wasn't open shouting, with individual voices distinguishable, but more of a chant, impressive for its power, its strength. I have no doubt that it was sincere, although the only simile that fits is that of a racist lynching mob in a grade-B movie. The guards from the bus had to form a corridor for us to walk through to get into the building. They actually pushed their fellow troopers back, out of the way.

The Captain, who had bleeding shrapnel wounds in his left leg, walked off the bus toward that mob with his head tilted forward, not in depression, but in urgency, and with his jaw set, his fists clenched. He had gotten up the first two steps of the building, walking with a slight limp, when a soldier broke through the cordon and kicked him swiftly in his injured leg. The Captain, a former football halfback, and still a powerful imposing man, wheeled to face his assailant. The guards tensed, and the chantings of the mob rose. The Captain stared at that pitiful North Korean with a look of hatred and contempt—a look that said, "You son of a bitch, just let me have the chance. . . ." One of the bus guards quickly and briskly moved the assailant back into the mob, while another guard motioned the Captain forward. Reluctantly, the Captain turned and mounted the last step into the building, his gait a little slower. I was right behind him.

Max led us up concrete stairs to the third floor. There we were assigned to rooms. I was pushed into one by myself to the left of the staircase. The room had a yellow wood-frame bed, with a rice-filled mattress lying on lengthwise slats, a straight-backed chair, and a pine-colored wooden table. The floor was of uneven boards, and the walls were crumbly white plaster. Opposite the cracked, blue-painted door was a cracked double-pane window with a blue frame. A bed sheet had been tacked between the panes, so I could not see out. A silver-painted radiator was rusting on a cement platform under the window. The room was twelve feet wide and seventeen feet long, by my pacing measurements.

"Make the bed and sleep," Max ordered, pointing to the neat pile of muslin sheets and horsehair blankets folded on the bed. He slammed the door, leaving me alone. The guards, with their bayonet-tipped AK-47 rifles, stayed in the hallway. I had been up since 3:15 A.M. on Tuesday, and it was now 8:00 A.M. on Wednesday—a stretch of some twenty-nine hours. I could think of nothing better to do than follow his orders about sleep, so I pulled off my boots and jacket and put my hat on the table. I lay down on the bed with the rest of my clothes on, used the still-folded sheets as a pillow, pulled the blankets over me, and fell into a deep sleep almost immediately, hoping that when I awoke I would be back on the ship, heading into Sasebo.

"All right, come out, come out!" I heard the order as if in a dream. It was insistent. I got up, startled to see where I was, and not believing it. A guard had stomped into my room, and an interpreter was shouting at me. "Hurry up, come quickly."

I jammed my hat on my uncombed hair, pulled on my boots, and, to keep warm, put on my green Navy jacket. The guard motioned me with his handy AK-47 to get into line with the other officers. With Max leading the way, and guards on either side, we walked down the hall. It was four o'clock in the afternoon of this first day in North Korea. So much had happened already, and in such a short time since we had been boarded. The Koreans seemed to have taken us a long way just to shoot us, if that was their idea.

We were led to the end of the hall and then into a large room, apparently made by putting together several bedrooms like the one I had been in. Six straight-backed wooden chairs were arranged at the front of the rectangular room. The chairs faced a desk, with a fierce-looking officer behind it, and Max, serving as interpreter, took a chair to the officer's right. To the left of the six chairs was a long table, behind which sat four or five other North Korean officers. Guards stood behind the six chairs we were led to.

Dim light globes hung on twisted cords tufted with dust. They provided the only light, because the windows, which lined the far side of the room, were covered by sheets. The dim light gave the room an evil, almost medieval, aspect. No one spoke.

We shuffled in front of the six chairs, and I ended up in the fourth chair from the left. Max had arranged us in the line according to our rank on the ship: Commander Bucher, first; Lieutenant Murphy, Executive Officer, second; Lieutenant Stephen R. Harris, Research Officer, third; me, as Operations Officer, fourth; Ensign Timothy L. Harris, Supply Officer, fifth; and Chief Warrant Officer Gene H. Lacy, in charge of the engine room, sixth.

I sat facing a two-star general, an officer I was never to see again. He was a fat man, with jowls and chins that just melted into a thick bull neck. His eyes were deep-set, his black hair profuse and more or less combed back. From his collar peeked two gaudy silver stars set on a background of gold. His tunic was a deep yellow-green, the style Chinese, buttoned to the throat. He seemed to bob back and forth in his seat, his fat pudgy red hands resting comfortably on the rather plain wooden desk.

He let the suspense build up after we were all seated by glaring at us, one after the other, rocking silently back and forth, with a look more of amusement than of fear or contempt. He was enjoying himself, I thought, playing with us, relishing the moment.

Max, now supremely confident, displayed a leering grin. His beady black eyes darted from captive to captive. All I could hear was labored breathing around me. There was a scent of garlic in the air, and a damp mustiness to the room.

The almost jovial look left the General's face, and he began in a deep and loud voice to spout Korean at us. Gamely, Max, trying to project his master's venomous mood, translated. "You are guilty of heinous crimes against the Democratic People's Republic of Korea. You are spies. You shall be treated as spies! You have invaded the coastal waters of the Democratic People's Republic of Korea. You shall be treated as invaders!" Max's voice was working itself into the rage he wanted. His sentences came faster. "The United States," he said with contempt, "is making war against us. You are guilty of the most serious crimes against us. You shall be treated like the criminals you are!"

This opening harangue went on and on for what seemed to be at least fifteen minutes. While Max was translating, the General would glower at us one by one, to gauge the effect of his words. Our passive, almost indifferent reaction only goaded him on. At the end of his spiel the General focused on the Captain.

"What is your name and what is your job on the ship?"

The Captain started to answer, but Max cut him short.

"Don't you know to stand up when addressing a senior officer?"

He got a dumb, tired look from the Skipper.

"Stand up!"

Slowly, the Captain stood, and wearily repeated his name and title. Hurriedly, Max translated, and the General nodded with disgust and motioned to the next man. When I got up I told them my name and said I was the First Lieutenant. There was no reaction to any of the answers given, and the General went back to the Captain to start round two.

"What was your ship doing?"

"My ship," the Captain answered in a strong voice, and now obviously fed up with the proceedings, "was conducting oceanographic research on the high seas in international waters. I demand that my ship and my crew . . ." Max, while translating, motioned him curtly to stop. The General was laughing contemptuously. He put the same question to the rest of us, and we answered as had the Captain. The General wasn't even listening, but was spitting what sounded like guttural insults at us as he motioned each of us to sit down.

"You were spying—spying against the peace-loving Democratic People's Republic of Korea. Captain, will you admit to that? Will you admit you were spying, that you violated our coastal waters?"

The Captain was on his feet again, shouting right back at Max. "No. We were operating on the high seas. The nearest land was 15.8 miles away." It had never been stated, but we assumed that North Korea claimed twelve miles as its territorial waters.

"You, Executive Officer, what do you say?"

"No, sir, we were operating on the high seas. The nearest land was 15.8 miles away."

Max uttered a word of disgust, and turned to the four remaining officers. "And what do you say?"

We each started to answer, but before more than a few words were said the General was into round three.

"The United States is an aggressor against our country. You are occupying South Korea. Why are you in South Korea if you are not imperialistic, war-mongering aggressors?"

Again the Captain spoke, and this time his voice was more controlled. "It is my understanding that we are there at the specific request of the South Korean government."

Suddenly, as Max translated that statement, there was an eruption at the table to the left. A colonel, his eyes flashing with hate and anger, slammed his fist down on the table and took a savage round-

16

house swing at the Captain. The blow just missed. We were to come to know this colonel well—Super C, the officer in charge of breaking every one of us with as much torture as was required. But this confrontation was not Super C's show. He subsided as the General, playing the role of class monitor, motioned him back to his seat.

The General resumed by going down the line again with the same question: "Will you admit your ship intruded the coastal waters of the Democratic People's Republic of Korea?"

The answer was still no, all along the line of the six *Pueblo* officers.

Then he leaned forward and, with his hands spread open, palm upward, said matter-of-factly: "You will be shot before sunrise." As it was translated, we showed no reaction. There were no hysterics, no pleas for mercy. He continued. "Would you like to be shot one at a time or all at once?"

The Captain rose to his feet. "General, I demand that you shoot me and let the rest of the crew go back to the United States on their ship."

The General laughed his sarcastic laugh and turned on his look of contempt. He was obviously satisfied; he had accomplished his mission.

He waited several moments for the effect of his attitude to sink in. And then he leaned forward again, this time tapping a sheet of paper on the desk, which we hadn't noticed before. "We have the statement from your White House." Again he glared; again there was no reaction. The glare turned into a glower, and with a contemptuous wave of the hand he motioned the guards to sweep us away.

We went out in line, still without a word spoken to each other. But at least I knew, for the first time since the ship's hijacking, that all six officers were alive. I was led back to my room, and the guard slammed the door behind me. My mind reeled from the savagery of the interrogation, the strange setting, the almost unbelievable dialogue. Hatred and fear had been thick in that room, actually making it painful to breathe.

I could think of nothing better to do in the twilight of this first day than to search my barren room. Inch by inch I went over it.

17

First I looked for a hole in the sheet covering the window, but found none. I rubbed my hand over each of the dirty, random-length floor boards. I wasn't really looking for anything. It was just an impulsive, intense search to keep my mind busy. I found a short length of board lying on the beams, not nailed down, by the radiator. I lifted it out and rubbed my hand around in the darkness under the floor. I felt wood shavings and then the cool iron of a nail. A nail. A nail could be useful. Maybe a weapon. Maybe a way to do myself in if I was tortured. At the least, a nail could be my pencil. I could keep track of the days by scratching each one on the soft plaster. I didn't know what good that would do. But I wanted to do it. Some connection with that other world, any connection, would help. My mind was on a roller-coaster ride, with no end in sight. A calendar, with its semblance of order, might slow down this wild, terrifying ride.

The search completed, I replaced the loose board carefully and thought of escape. Through the vertical cracks in my door I could see the guards walking up and down the hall, with bayonet-tipped AK-47's slung from their shoulders. No exit there. Breaking the window, even if I managed to lower myself to the ground with sheets and blankets tied together to form a rope, offered no hope. Where would I go? Where would a hated white American face hide if I did break out of the compound? Would they kill the others, or torture them, to retaliate for an attempted escape? I had no way of answering these questions.

I knew from this first day that we were in cruel hands. I tried to brace myself for the worst, but, despite my efforts, my memory dredged up all the Oriental torture methods it had in stock: fingernail-pulling, ball-beating, hot irons, freezing.

There was no way out, nobody to talk to, no one to rely on, no help. Just me. And the room. And the nail.

There was a shuffling outside in the hall, and the door flew open as I was pacing the room. I spun around to face the guard, AK-47 and all. Well, this is it, I figured. Here comes the end. I'm going to be shot—as the General had said. I started to put on my jacket, but the guard motioned me to stop. Improbably, the thought of standing in the bitter-cold Korean winter waiting to be shot with just my shirt for warmth caused me to shiver. But no. This was not the time to be shot; this was the time for supper. A pudgy, all-business, I don't-give-a-damn-who-you-are-this-meal-has-got-to-be-served waitress bustled in and threw a tin bowl and a fork down on my table.

Well, if they're planning to shoot us, this doesn't make much sense, I figured. The waitress returned shortly and gave me a cup, which she promptly filled with hot water. Then she left, slamming the door behind her.

I stared down at the meager meal offered. It appeared to be some sort of vegetable cut into long strips, almost like French-fried potatoes, and then pan cooked. I tried one and found it lukewarm, but apparently digestible. In my hunger I ate about half the bowl and drank all of the sticky hot water. About fifteen minutes later, the waitress returned, picked up my bowl, gave me one of those "what's-wrong-with-the-hash-buddy" looks, and waddled out.

But not for long. Five minutes later she was back. She refilled my cup, and I figured I could keep it. Then she came back again and gave me some real presents: a bar of soap, a soap dish, a small hand towel, a tube of toothpaste, and a toothbrush. I got the export model of the last. Unevenly marked on its plain cardboard box were the words "Do not place in hot water. Made in the D.P.R.K." These were strange amenities for a man who was going to be shot before sunrise. Maybe she hadn't gotten the word. Or maybe she had and I hadn't. Or maybe the General hadn't gotten the word. No, that was improbable. Generals always got the word.

I tidied up, then lay down on the bed, trying to think of something useful to do. I stared through the clear glass of the naked light bulb hanging from the ceiling on a dirty cord. I studied the low-power filament inside as if there might be some answer there, like reading tea leaves.

The only sound I could hear was an occasional grinding of gears from a car or truck three stories below, and the shoveling of snow. Snow. The shoveling sound made me homesick. It was like hearing an American voice in a foreign country. I went to sleep in the lighted room, trying to think of the pleasant times I had spent in the snow back home. I still expected to be shot before the next day

19

dawned, just as the General had said. But because I couldn't think of any good way to prepare myself for the bullet, I did the one thing I am fairly good at: I went to sleep.

No guard shook me awake to be shot. My second day in North Korea—Thursday, January 25—started with my waking up very much alive. I had heard no rifle shots from a firing squad during the night. In fact, I had heard nothing. Could that mean they were going to torture us instead? That was the thought I awoke to. And my conviction that this was to be my fate deepened at about ten o'clock that morning when a guard came to get me. He gave me a hard shove out the door and jerked his rifle around to point the way down the hall. He pushed me to another room four doors down from mine. The room was the same size but had had the bed removed to make more space. The reception committee was waiting. Seated behind the same kind of table I had in my room were two North Korean officers. One we later named Deputy Dawg, and the other, his interpreter, I immediately dubbed Snot Nose—for obvious reasons. They had been assigned to me. I was their own special pigeon.

Deputy Dawg had three silver stars, smaller than the General's, on a gold-and-red background sewn on the collar of his green uniform, designating the rank of a junior colonel. He eyed me without interest. He seemed markedly different from the Korean stereotype. Instead of the usual round face, pudgy fingers, and brute-force gestures, he had a heart-shaped face, long thin fingers, and graceful, precise movements. The first impression I got was that of a bored, diminutive symphony conductor who must now suffer through a session with a clumsy violinist.

Snot Nose had no such grace. His nose ran like a little kid's. He had a high forehead and flushed pink cheeks. His movements were clumsy, accenting the over-all impression of sloppiness. The interrogation got underway slowly after the guard had put me in a chair facing the two officers. The guard, with his AK-47, remained standing behind me as Snot Nose asked Deputy Dawg's first question.

"What was your job aboard the ship?" The questions came right through his runny nose, making the word "job" sound like "jube," and "ship" sound like "sheep."

20

"First Lieutenant."

Deputy Dawg said something to Snot Nose in a low, threatening voice. They seemed to be in no hurry. Neither apparently had any place else to go—and they knew I didn't. Snot Nose came back to me. "No, no, no, no, no. Your jube. Your jube aburd the sheep?"

"First Lieutenant."

Another consultation, with Deputy Dawg obviously explaining why my answer was unresponsive. Snot Nose fingered his collar and slowly asked the same question again. "What was your jube aburd the sheep?"

"First Lieutenant," I said again.

"No, no, no, no, no. Not your rank. What was your jube? Your jube?"

"I was in charge of painting and maintenance."

Snot Nose translated this as best he could. While I *was* First Lieutenant, which is not a rank, but a job designation, in the Navy, I also served as Operations Officer, slightly more important, I figured, from the North Korean viewpoint.

"What were you doing at sea?" After several attempts Snot Nose finally got this one out and across.

"Conducting oceanographic research."

"What was the weather like? Wasn't it too cold for that work?"

"Yes," I replied, "we were worried about ice."

Deputy Dawg and Snot Nose talked it all over, and then they double-clutched back a step. "What was the ship doing?"

"Conducting oceanographic research."

The answer did not take. Snot Nose, pushing one hand over his shock of straight black hair, pumped himself up, pink cheeks aflame, a thick discharge running from his nose gloriously down over his chin. He brought down his hand in a pudgy little fist, slammed the table, and shouted at me, "No, no, no, no, no! You lie! You lie! You will be shot! You will be shot!"

His tirade lasted only a few moments, as I sat there with the dumbest look I could muster. Deputy Dawg gave him some more questions to ask me. They were still in no hurry. They probably had lots of tricks. Snot Nose went back to the same questions. I repeated

21

the same answers. I tried to stall, declaring time after time: "I don't understand what you are saying."

Snot Nose's English was poor, and he knew it. And Deputy Dawg knew it. So all of us half believed that I really couldn't understand him. He struggled, almost desperately, for ways to rephrase the questions, trying to recall the words from the translation book. Doubtless this was his first attempt to speak English with anyone to whom the language was native. And doubtless he was wondering if he had learned it correctly.

Deputy Dawg, while this was going on, fixed me with black eyes filled with hate. He was trying to assess whether Snot Nose was just a lousy translator or if I was just a better liar. I think he realized the game I was playing, and sensed my growing fear. I had no place to hide, and he knew it. The silences were worse than the fencing with the questions. Any moment I expected the Oriental fingernail-pulling to start. Or the ball-beating. I had been socked and kicked a few times already by the guards. But the really rough stuff had not started.

Abruptly, Deputy Dawg and Snot Nose rose from their chairs. "We'll talk to you again; now, go back." No threatening tone this time, just a matter-of-fact statement, like "Class dismissed." I rose, turned, and walked out. The ever-present guard and his AK-47 shoved me back to my room. The interrogation seemed to have no rhyme or reason—the mystical Orientals at work on a Western captive. I had expected worse.

I felt a little jubilant about that interrogation. It had all gone fairly smoothly. But back in the silence of my own room, the old fears came flooding back. My confidence that I could outwit my captors seeped away as I analyzed the interrogation. How long could I keep ahead of them?

Some amenities and new rules had come with breakfast at the start of this second day. The North Koreans had provided, as part of the morning meal, a ceramic ashtray with a flower design, a package of Kalmaigi cigarettes, and a box of matches. Frankly, this bit of consideration surprised me.

I had also been informed rather graphically by the guard right after breakfast that, no, I was not allowed to lie down on the bed whenever I wanted to. I was supposed to sit in the hard wood chair all day long, chin on chest, in abject humility. I didn't go that far, but I didn't risk lying down. That would be just asking for a beating. I sat in the chair and tried to think of something. I had no idea what the Captain or anybody else had told the Koreans, or even if any one of them was still alive.

My problem was my problem alone. I sometimes half expected to see the sudden flash and hear the deafening roar of the Bomb, as America avenged the *Pueblo*. It would have been a way out. The North Koreans would have killed me and the rest of the crew for it, but death would not have been too high a price to pay. I was dying inside anyhow, a little bit at a time, as I realized my helplessness.

Technically, in that first interrogation with Deputy Dawg and Snot Nose, I had come close to breaking the Code of Conduct for Members of the Armed Forces of the United States. Article V of that code states: "When questioned, should I become a prisoner of war, I am bound to give only name, rank, service number, and date of birth. I will evade answering further questions to the utmost of my ability. I will make no oral or written statements disloyal to my country and its allies or harmful to their cause." I had given the North Koreans more than name, rank, service number, and date of birth, though nothing they could use. The code said nothing about being allowed to fence with enemy interrogators. Yet since the United States was not fighting North Korea, was I a prisoner of war? There was nobody to ask. That was the hell of it.

Lacy had reminded the crew about the name, rank, and service number dictum of the code as the North Koreans were coming aboard the *Pueblo*. His was the last word on the subject. I felt obligated to live up to that code. So far, I had bent it, more than broken it. How much did the North Koreans know? They had the ship and all our service records intact. What would happen when they got to mine? My service jacket showed service as a Communications Officer and an Operations Officer—a far cry from being in charge of painting and maintenance. And my name was on the day-by-day narrative of the *Pueblo*'s voyage. I had written it. Did they have that?

The more I thought about what they might find, the more I worried about what they could beat out of me. I held a lot of clearances for secret information. I knew exactly what the *Pueblo* had been up to. Even worse, I knew which Communications Technicians from the ship had information of vital interest to the Communists—information that I had been told before we sailed could seriously compromise the United States. The papers the Koreans probably captured along with the ship would give them all the leads they needed for really sensitive questioning.

I worried away the rest of Thursday afternoon. The guards did not call for me again that day. The evening meal came on schedule at 7:00 P.M. The same waitress brought in the tin bowl and fork, but now something new had been added: a piece of white bread, cut in a wedge-shaped chunk, as if chopped off the loaf with an ax. Again, there was no communication: she had her job to do; I had my nothing to do. To each other we were nothing. In fact, she was probably almost as much a nonperson as I was. Government doctrine did not seem to be nourishing either of us in our circumstances.

I ate the tasteless greens and bread mechanically, and kept searching my mind for answers. There were none. I paced the room. My ties to the world where I did know some answers were the Lucky Strikes in the pocket of my jacket, my wallet, and a wristwatch my father had given me to celebrate my joining the Navy. I lit a Lucky and went through my wallet thoroughly. I took out all the papers and cards, many of which had friends' names and addresses written on them, and tore them into tiny pieces. I hid the scraps under the loose floor board. This made me feel as if I were separating my friends from the whole mess I was in. The North Koreans knew too much already. They were not going to learn the names of any friends from my wallet.

Nothing made sense. My room was a new kind of dungeon. I went to bed that night because I could not think of anything else to do. And it was an escape, the only escape open to me. The naked light bulb burned dimly over me. There was no such thing as lights-out in the Barn. I did not know whether I would be shot in my bed or shaken awake for more questioning. I went to sleep, again hoping to wake up and find that everything that had happened since Tuesday noon—when the *Pueblo* was first attacked—had been a bad dream.

But the bad dream was still there on Friday morning. I woke in the same room. Nothing had changed. I took the precious nail I had found and wrote 26 on the plaster just to the right of the door—my calendar. A new day. An old problem: how to cope. I decided on that morning to live up to the letter of the Code of Conduct. Deputy Dawg and Snot Nose, when they questioned me again, were bound to tangle me in my own web of lies. I realized, in thinking back, that they already had come close in their awkward first effort. So it was going to be by the book: name, rank, service number, and date of birth. Frederick Carl Schumacher, Junior, Lieutenant (j.g.), United States Navy, 700156, 5 May 1943. That was all Snot Nose was going to get.

The guard came for me at 9:00 A.M. He drove me with his rifle back to the same stripped-down interrogation room. It was the same set of characters, just a different script from the first one.

"Now," Snot Nose began smugly, after his night of homework and consultation with Super C about Lieutenant Schumacher, "we want to know the truth about the ship. The real purpose."

I thought to myself, Well, here goes, and replied, with my eyes riveted on Snot Nose: "Frederick Carl Schumacher, Junior, Lieutenant (j.g.), United States Navy, 700156, 5 May 1943."

"No, no!" Snot Nose screamed. "No. You are not a prisoner of war. You are a political prisoner."

I summoned my most sarcastic tone and, feeling that there was no turning back now, demanded: "Why did you shoot at our ship?" I tried to stare him down.

Snot Nose, as if nothing had happened, took it from the top once more. "What were you doing on the ship? What was your job on the ship?"

I gave him name, rank, service number again.

Deputy Dawg had had enough. "We have ways to make you talk," he said.

He said it like an expert—like an ice-water-veined officer who had presided over the breaking of many men who had more tol-

25

erance for pain than I. I stared back at him, saying nothing. I feared the worst, but hoped whatever it was would be quick.

"Do you want to die?" Snot Nose asked fiercely. He now had his cue from his superior officer: quit dawdling with this insolent American spy; get rough. The mood in the room changed. I could feel it. My insides churned. But I had to muddle through. I had decided to live up to the letter of the code if it killed me. And it looked as if that was going to happen.

"Why did you shoot at our ship?" I heard myself asking in the charged atmosphere of the room. Deputy Dawg's answer was a quick motion to two guards standing in the passageway outside the room. They joined the guard standing behind my chair. Now there were three guards, all with bayonet-tipped AK-47 automatic rifles, plus two North Korean officers in the small, sparsely furnished room, which seemed a million miles away from any help. I imagined that John Wayne would have made a heroic lunge at one of the guards and wrested his AK-47 away from him so he could shoot his way to freedom. But the impossibility of my doing anything like that was painfully clear to me. My only option was to live second by second, to try to hang on to my senses.

Snot Nose motioned me out of my chair. He ordered me to my knees and to raise my arms ramrod straight over my head. The new guards stood at each side of me, holding their bayonets about an inch from my head. I tried to keep my arms up straight but could not. My left arm sagged. The guard gave the elbow a good swift kick. The same thing happened on the other side when that arm faltered.

"What was your job on the ship?" Snot Nose asked again.

It was so stupid, so childish. Here I was, a full-grown man, on my knees and being kicked for information my tormentors knew already from my captured service jacket. But I had to play the game. It was ludicrous, outrageous. The kicking was not terrifying at that moment—just blockhead stupid. We were playing this dumb game— one of the many things beyond reason.

Snot Nose had given me my cue again, so I answered with the same question: "Why did you shoot at our ship?" I braced for the kicks and punches from the guards and half expected to feel the tip

26

of the bayonet go into me. Something was going to snap—and quick. But nothing did. They let me stay there on my knees, arms aching, while they said nothing, did nothing. A kick would have broken the tension inside me at least. I was just hanging there on a sky hook of pain. They were in no hurry. They were never in a hurry. How long was this going to last?

Finally Deputy Dawg said something curtly to Snot Nose, who then said to me impassively: "Take your hands down and stand up." I waited for the next event in their little indoor decathlon. But the guards stood stock still. Deputy Dawg evidently had decided which torture would work best on this twenty-four-year-old lieutenant who had been insolent to him. As the guards were leading me out of the room, Snot Nose let me in on the decision by asking: "How long can you go without food?"

Starvation, then, was the name of their game. Pictures of prisoners with bones sticking out and stomachs distended overwhelmed my mind as I walked back to my room. Snot Nose had asked a good question. How long could I go without food? I didn't know. I had never known hunger for any length of time. Would the starvation treatment affect my mind or just my body? I didn't know. There was nobody to ask. I didn't like the idea of pencil legs and arms. Even if I kept my sanity through starvation, these maddening bastards had plenty of other tricks to try. They were in no hurry. They had been through this before. They probably had written down the time I would break.

I didn't see how I could win. I was looking down a dark tunnel that had been cemented shut at the other end. If I started telling them what I did on the ship, they would demand to know more and more. I had to find a way to keep myself from doing this. Two facts were brutally, cruelly clear to me. Fact one: I knew too much. If they could break me, I would reveal classified information of real importance. Fact two: They would break me.

That is why, later on that Friday, after the interrogation, I concluded that I had to kill myself. It was the only patch of light in that tunnel—the only way out. I was almost glad, the longer I thought about it, that I had no other option. At least this one course of action was clear. Nothing else I had been through since noontime on January 23 made as much sense. Everything was upside down, backward, whirling, unreal. Suicide would sound crazy only to someone who was not there. To me, for the insane situation I was in, it seemed the one perfectly sane thing to do.

Suicide decided upon, I sat on the hard chair pondering the best way to accomplish it. I was like a hangman trying to find the best kind of knot for his own execution. I could jump out the window. But it would be just my luck to live through it. Living as an American cripple in North Korea seemed far worse than a quick death. I had no razor, so wrist-slashing was out. I wasn't sure I could really do it that way anyhow. I never did like the sight of blood, mine or anybody else's. Running down the hall berserk might get me shot by the guards. But more likely they would just club me down with their rifle butts and kick me back into my room. So that left the bucket of water in the corner. "Just put your head down in there and breathe in deep," I told myself. "It will all be over in a couple of minutes. Then you win; North Korea loses."

Gambling that starvation was indeed their game, and that they would let the threat of it work on me awhile, I figured I had at least a couple of hours to work myself up for the plunge. I was now out of Luckies, so I lit a Korean Kalmaigi, thinking that the same people who beat me had put the green-and-white pack of cigarettes in my room for my enjoyment.

The only things of any value I would leave behind in this room were my gold ring and my watch. Leaving the ring did not bother me too much. It had been given to me by my parents on my twenty-first birthday. My sister had found a crest that she figured must have been that of the Austrian side of the family, and she had had it made into a ring for herself. Then she had talked my parents into having a copy made for me. I wore it on the little finger of my left hand.

The watch at the moment had great sentimental value. My father, F. Carl Schumacher, Sr., had presented it to me on a special occasion for him. I remembered how ceremonious his presentation had been. It was on the night before I left home, in St. Louis, to join the Navy. He had served as a naval officer in World War II and was proud of it. He had always hoped I would serve in the Navy, and he felt that, after I finished my studies in religion at Trinity College, naval officer candidate school would be quite sensible. So when I had made my own choice for a hitch in the Navy, he was terribly proud. Over cocktails that last night, as we sat together in the living room, he talk unashamedly about the importance of flag and country. Then he handed me an elaborately wrapped gift—a bit of thoughtfulness that touched me greatly. The watch had, as he happily explained, a sweep second hand that could be stopped by pushing a little button. He said this would be useful for timing the flashes of navigational lights at sea and for timing the turns of my ship. He just assumed I was going into the Blue Water Navy. The watch was an emblem of this important fraternity.

At OCS the watch prompted some ribbing. "Hey, Schummie," a fellow prospective ensign would ask, "what the hell kind of watch is that? Let's see it." I would hand the watch over and make some gamesmanship remark about the timing hand being useful for summer sailing. Once at sea, the watch actually had won some points. The Captain of the *Vega,* a supply ship I served on before coming to the *Pueblo,* asked the officer of the deck how long it would be until we had to turn again. The OOD—like the heavily salted sailor he was—was doing the sensible thing: following the wake of the ship in front of him rather than going through all the time-to-turn drill. But just for kicks I had been timing the turns with my watch. I gave the OOD the answer by reading the watch. He passed along the answer to the Captain. A question right out of the Navy book had been asked, and had been answered in the true Navy manner. Everybody was happy. I never could figure out why the Koreans had not taken the watch from me. I wondered now if it would ever find its way back to my father. I hoped so.

Ever since I was little, I had eased a problem by pole-vaulting over it in my mind. If it was a tough exam, I would visualize myself at the end of the year getting my diploma. If it was a boring auto trip, I would show myself mental pictures of the homecoming. Now the only vaulting was into my death. I sat there visualizing what would happen when my family learned I had killed myself. Did the Navy send a telegram? Would a Western Union boy take the telegram to the door?

If he delivered it in the early morning, he would find my home at 9 Southmoor, Clayton, Missouri, a suburb of St. Louis, an impressive street. No mansions of the St. Louis barons were there. But the houses were big and comfortable. They had well-manicured lawns front and back. Even the St. Louis *Globe Democrat* was rolled and neatly bound before the newsboys dropped it on those lawns. The rolled-up newspapers in the morning light looked like so many dropped white batons.

If my family was lucky, Pop would be the one to see the telegram first. He could handle it best. Skip, he would tell the family, died in the line of duty. Pop would wonder how, and perhaps guess the truth. He would handle the whole thing with grace. The Navy would get no scene from him. The knife of pain from losing his only son would stay in his heart, but he would go on. He had a high sense of duty toward everything: his family, his country, his community, his job. Of course, he worked far too hard at his job—as president of the Hickey-Mitchell Company, a large insurance firm in St. Louis. He was obsessed with his responsibilities but claimed he was only showing everybody in the city that the man who married the boss's daughter, my mother, worked harder than anybody else in the place. He had always been a great pros-and-cons man with me. He would tell me, for instance, during my academic nose dives in high school, the pros and cons of getting the marks needed to go to college, a rundown of my options, with the analysis loaded forgivably on the side of getting good grades. He was always a most decent man. I thought golf was the silliest game in the world, especially on a stifling St. Louis afternoon. He loved it. But he let me go my own way, and never did pressure me into playing. I felt bad because it was too late now to tell him straight out how much I admired him, loved him, and how grateful I was for the independence he let me have while I was trying to grow up.

Mother would have the roughest time. I could see Pop going up to the second-floor sitting room, where she spent most of her time, surrounded by friendly books and memorabilia. This quarterdeck for the lady of the house was right off her bedroom. The furniture was relaxed, and so was she whenever she was in that room. Althea Hickey Schumacher, onetime St. Louis debutante who could laugh at her contemporaries who still tried to act that way, had plenty of wit and grit. But I knew my death would lay her low. We were on the same wave length intellectually. We delighted in throwing what we thought were outrageously funny barbs at everybody and everything, including ourselves. Her deep religious faith might pull her through. But I knew it was going to be hard on her. I hoped Pop would be able to make her understand somehow why I had had no choice.

And then there was my sister, Nancy, the high-school over-achiever who had shown a rebel streak at Smith. She was, in high school, an honor student, a class leader, a varsity tennis player. She worried more than I did about my courses at St. Louis Country Day School. But she was always smart enough not to try to lecture me. I almost felt she envied the fact that I could flunk a course without seeming to worry about it. She and Pop were alike; they had the German drive for perfection. He had built a special study room for me in the basement in the hope I would get better grades. It made a dandy place for me to smoke my way through high school undisturbed. And there was also just enough room behind the furnace down there to hide a couple cases of beer. My father enticed me down there, all right, but his special study room did not seem to improve my grades. Nancy—I began calling her Sport in high school— knew but never let on to anybody. She just kept it to herself. I loved her for this, plus her quiet understanding that I was one type of person and she another. Even though she was three years older than I, she invited me to her parties, and vice versa. We really enjoyed each other's company. When she was at Smith and I was at Trinity we saw each other often. Both of us studied religion, which gave us a lot in common. I was going to miss Sport; and she, me, I figured. Luckily John Dennis, her husband, who was a Presbyterian minister and a warm human being, would be there to take care of her.

Easily the toughest old bird in my clan was my patriarchal

grandfather, Joseph F. Hickey. He was a Scotsman with the durability of heather; a fighter, a scrambler, and a deft deflater of inflated egos, whether in St. Louis, in Washington, or any place else. Dining with Winston Churchill—which he had done the day the grand old man made his Iron Curtain speech at Westminster College, down in Fulton—was no problem. The two had a perfectly clear idea of what was right and what was wrong in the world—even if Sir Winston had managed to achieve a little wider fame. Grandfather Hickey, I was sure, had known exactly what to do after the *Pueblo* was hijacked: bomb the hell out of North Korea. That decision would have been no problem at all for him. My suicide would be a little more troublesome. He would always wonder, but not aloud, why I had done it. He dealt in black and white—not with the shadowy gray of the Cold War. But he would forgive me. I felt sure of that. He wanted top performance from every member of the Hickey-Schumacher clan, but he was magnanimous—to use Churchill's word—when he did not get it. He tried to understand young people. Although ninety years old and a working chairman in the supposedly stuffy insurance business, he closed the generation gap better than men one-third his age. He was another person I had never told how much I thought of him. I could only hope now that he knew it all along.

I would miss all of them. We were a close-knit family, almost selfish, preferring family gatherings with lots of friendly needling and laughing to more structured, and duller, parties with friends. Family jokes were our stock in trade.

Like any other conceited male, I suppose, I also read in my mind the obituary that would appear about me in the *Globe Democrat*. That was where my arch-conservative, solidly Republican family would want it to appear—not in the leftish, to them, St. Louis *Post-Dispatch*. There would be the head picture in my Navy hat and then a few paragraphs like this:

Lt. F. Carl Schumacher, 24, of 9 Southmoor, Clayton, died in prison in North Korea, the Navy reported yesterday.

Born in St. Louis while his father was serving with the Navy in 1943, Lt. Schumacher lived in St. Louis most of his life. He was the son of Mr. and Mrs. F. Carl Schumacher, Sr. The elder Schumacher is president of the Hickey-Mitchell Company here.

Lt. Schumacher was graduated from St. Louis Country Day School in 1961, and in 1965 from Trinity College, Hartford, Connecticut. While at Trinity he was a member of St. Anthony Hall and served as co-editor in chief of the yearbook. He was a member of the University Club here and the St. Anthony Club in New York.

He was sworn into the Navy August 5, 1965, enrolling in officer candidate school at Newport, R.I., the following October. After the initial 18-week course there, Lt. Schumacher attended communications school at Newport, R.I. He was assigned in June, 1966, to the U.S.S. *Vega,* a refrigerated cargo ship which operated in the western Pacific, making stops off Vietnam.

In September, 1967, Lt. Schumacher reported to the U.S.S. *Pueblo,* an intelligence-collection ship, which was captured off Wonsan, North Korea, by the North Koreans on January 23, 1968. He served as Operations Officer on the *Pueblo*.

Besides his parents, Lt. Schumacher leaves a sister, Mrs. John Dennis of Philadelphia, and his grandfather, Joseph F. Hickey, of St. Louis.

The family requests that expressions of sympathy be in the form of donations to St. Luke's Hospital.

I figured that would be a generous obit. That would be it—a lifetime wrapped up in seven paragraphs of type. I regretted that I would never have the chance to pass on what I had learned about the face of Communism these last few days.

Although the Koreans had not yet broken me, I figured they might at the next session. Then I might spill my guts. I couldn't take much pain. I knew that. So the green bucket was the answer. It was such an ordinary-looking bucket—with utilitarian green paint over metal. It was filled in the morning with clean water. I would pour water from the bucket into my porcelain washbasin for brushing my teeth and washing my face. I had to pound on the door to be allowed to dump the bucket in the head, or bathroom, down the hall. The guard would walk me there and back, making sure no two people from the *Pueblo* saw each other.

I now felt ready, that Friday night, to take the plunge into the bucket. They would never be able to say I had not lived up to the Code of Conduct for American fighting men—even though I was not sure I was one in these circumstances.

I mashed out my cigarette in that out-of-place flowered ashtray. I decided against trying to scratch a farewell note with the charcoal stub of a match or my precious nail. I felt sure that any note I wrote would be twisted for propaganda by the North Koreans.

I knelt in front of the bucket and took a last look around the miserable room—a lousy place to die. They had never mentioned this kind of thing back at OCS in Newport.

"All right, Schumacher," I told myself, "you can do it. Just stick your head in there and breathe in deep. It will all be over before you know it."

As I plunged my head in, I felt the stinging cold of the water choking me. I kept my head in—waiting impatiently for the blackness of death. Death would bring my release. I would no longer be a prisoner. I waited. There was no farewell scene of my past galloping through my mind, no instant replay of my life—just cold and suffocation.

The next thing I knew, I was on the floor of that same miserable room. I was coughing, spitting, convulsed. But I was alive. Damn it, I was still alive. I had lost again. I did not remember pulling my head out of the bucket. Some instinct of self-preservation did it for me. I had ordered my body to die. Something else had said no. I was gasping for air. I hated myself for this lack of control.

I lashed myself. "You underestimated the North Koreans. And now you have underestimated the strength of your own body and overestimated the strength of your own fortitude. You've got your own body to conquer, your own will to live."

Depression spread through me like a poison. "You failed, boy," I told myself. "You failed completely. Now where are you? Worse off than ever. You chickened out. You're weak, mushy. Is this the way the unraveling starts? Is this the way it will happen to you? Do you have any intention of living up to your decision? Are you a coward?".

"Well, no," I answered myself—struggling to catch my self-respect. "I can do it. I know I can. Maybe it takes everybody a couple of times. I can do it. I've got some more time. I'll have to rebuild the desire."

My mind, through this conversation with itself, prevailed over my body enough to get me off the dirty floor, though I was bent over with the continued siege of gasping and coughing. I forced my head up to look out the window—forgetting that all I would see was the sheet tacked between the panes.

The sheet looked grayish. The daylight trying to come through it had gotten weaker. I could tell winter dusk—yet another one—was falling fast outside. I listened for sounds of the earthly life I had tried to leave. Nothing came in. My world was still the inside of the Barn. All I could hear was the pacing of the guards—back and forth, back and forth. Had they heard me? They must have. But what did they care? Let the lousy imperialistic American choke to death. They had been taught to hate Americans. I could see it in their eyes. They would probably love to stomp me to death. I was the embodiment of all the evil deeds Americans had done to them and their country. Evening turnip time had come and gone without my being fed. What did they care? The idea was to starve me to death, to make me beg for food—to tell them anything for it.

I stumbled—still spitting up water—over to the wooden table. I picked up a cigarette. Would the prisoner like a last smoke before he dies? I was playing games with myself again. I was climbing out of the deep pit of black depression. I realized this was healthy.

Tired, I sat down in the Korean chair of thought. Then I decided that I was not taking the problem seriously enough. How could I just sit? I got up and started what I thought was the more appropriate pacing. And I talked to myself again. "What is happening? Does anybody care? Well, look at it from the Navy's standpoint. A ship gets hijacked off a hostile coast. They know all that back in Washington from our radio message. Thank God we got through. We were lucky our communications were up. At least they know definitely that we were hijacked, and that the North Koreans did it. Our commanders have the full story, so they can make a sound decision. Now what will their decision be?

"The Koreans had said, 'We have the statement from your White House.' What does that mean? Has the United States issued an ultimatum? Has it declared war? Or asked the United Nations for sanctions against North Korea? And what will North Korea do? Put us back on the ship, say it was all a dreadful mistake, and send us home? Guess again.

"Any way you look at it, there is going to be war. The United

States is not going to let these bastards get away with stealing our ship on the high seas. Look at the bombing we did of the North Vietnamese when they fired at the destroyers *Maddox* and the *Turner Joy*. And those ships got away unscathed. We were shot at, hit, and captured. The American response to our hijacking is bound to be greater than the bombing of North Vietnam to avenge the destroyers."

I stopped in my pacing to assail myself for playing Secretary of State. "This isn't getting you anywhere," I said. "How about your own problem? Here. Now. You got the word out about what happened off Wonsan. Now, what the United States should do is somebody else's problem. Your problem is to keep from blabbing. The starvation will get to you. Deputy Dawg almost broke you before. Admit it. Taking the offensive worked the last time; it might not work again. The next time you're bound to be weaker, he stronger. You were right the first time. The best move is to get out—all the way out—of this fix."

I wondered how other people convinced themselves to try suicide. I envied the Japanese military man at that moment. He probably had a regular field manual on hari-kari. What would it be called? *Thirteen Elegant Ways to Commit Suicide*? I was getting flippant. It was so hard to believe what was happening was really happening—and to me. I realized I was far from a hari-kari type. I wanted the end result but had thought little about how to do it before being locked up in the desolation of my room in the Barn.

I had never before been exposed to this side of war—or halfwar—as a man. And as a boy, I had never been one to haul a rat-a-tat-tat toy machine gun around the neighborhood, playing soldier. Military service to me was not shooting people. It was nobler than that—an obligation to my country. Then I could go on to what I really wanted to do with my life.

I was two years old when World War II ended in Europe and the United States dropped atomic bombs on Japan. I didn't feel at all involved with those events. The Big War, World War II, was something to read about, like World War I, the Civil War, the Revolution. I was too young to know anybody who had been imprisoned during World War II or had dropped the Bomb. The Bomb, though, was something I grew up with, a scorpion put in a bottle by some body way before me.

The wars after World War II were almost as remote. I was seven when the North Koreans invaded South Korea. I remembered newscasters admonishing us comfortable civilians that there was a war on. I was ten when the Korean armistice was signed. I had read a little bit about how the North Koreans and Chinese had "brainwashed" American prisoners. I wished now that I had paid more attention to those stories. Maybe they would have helped me with my own problem with the Koreans.

My problem was My War. I knew vaguely that My War had started with John Foster Dulles and brinksmanship, with Gary Powers and his U-2; then escalated on to Vietnam. Even Vietnam was not a varsity war, as far as I could tell. What the hell was a "war of attrition"? My generation seemed to be involved in a half-war, with all kinds of restrictions, no victory.

Since I had missed World War II, Korea, and had never shot or been shot at the several times the *Vega* steamed off Vietnam, my Cold War combat started when the first shot was fired at the *Pueblo*. Or was the shooting a lapse into hot war? My cold war was right here in the Barn. And, as I tried to gird myself for another suicide try, I realized that my preparation for this particular contest was pretty shaky. Nothing in my upbringing had armed me for the act of self-destruction.

I was schooled in the humanities, not the realities, in my world of St. Louis Country Day School. My objective there, of course, was to do well enough to get into college. But just as important was to have a good time along the way, which was hardly toughening for the Barn.

At home, the philosophical foundation was solid American: hard work yields worthy rewards; democracy is good, Communism is bad; the Republicans are to be trusted, the Democrats not so much. I felt secure inside the walls of my house. I read a lot, including Orwell's *Animal Farm* and *Nineteen Eighty-four*. He had sounded dead right to me.

37

The world I entered at Trinity College in 1961 was larger than the one I had left. But the hard realism of Communism had no place in it. Trinity was four years of dabbling in literature, philosophy, and the arts—with a look down the nose at those spending hour after hour in the science labs. We saw college as a chance to explore ideals and ideas, philosophers and philosophy, and to argue about anything and everything at our leisure. My college generation was not the activist generation that took on the Establishment and tried to destroy it.

And there was the Hall—short for St. Anthony Hall—half private men's club, half secret society, but, in essence, a fraternity. At the Hall I had lived in a red-brick, ivy-covered dormitory with wide chimneys. The inside was comfortable: two-bedroom suites off a common den with a refrigerator, parquet floors, fireplace, leaded casement windows. Downstairs, we ate in a paneled dining room. Sometimes we broke out of the constraints to throw food around in a sudden fight in the dining room. But ordinarily we drank cocktails before dinner and wore tuxedos to our once-a-week Hall meetings. Other students on campus used to jeeringly say that a man would join the Hall and not be seen again until graduation. This was not completely true. We regularly supplied the players for the varsity squash team and traditionally supplied both the muscle and the money for the rowing crews.

I majored in religion—one of the best of the liberal-arts departments. I liked the exploration it offered into the realm of abstract thinking. You could turn ideas over and over in your mind, test them, challenge them, accept them, reject them, argue about them. It was an enjoyable way to try to develop a personal philosophy for life ahead. I realized, though, somewhat self-consciously, that St. Louis and the people I knew there were only a thin slice of the world. My frame of reference was the comfortable life. I was looking through a crack. So I concluded that a tour in the Navy would be much more instructive than theological school and more ivory-tower pondering.

With concealed enthusiasm, I reported to officer candidate school at Newport, Rhode Island, on October 23, 1965. This is where the Navy turns out between 40 and 50 per cent of its new officers every year. The idea is to pound a little of everything into you so you don't make a complete fool of yourself on your first ship. The Navy instructors do not go into any one course in depth. It amounted to a eighteen-week cram course. Surprisingly, a lot of what we learned stayed with us.

I vaguely remember the Code of Conduct for American fighting men being mentioned in one of the lectures. But it was not one of the topics stressed. The study plan did not even require a quiz, and we did not take seriously anything we were not going to be tested on. The tests were what determined whether you went to sea as an officer or to boot camp as a bell-bottom-pants seaman.

I had no other training in the Code of Conduct after I left OCS at Newport. Nor did I, or any other officer on the *Pueblo,* receive any training in how to resist Communist brainwashing. The Navy had such a course, called SERE, for survival, evasion, resistance, and escape. But for the *Pueblo?* Why would anyone on that need SERE?

Yet I obviously needed something for My War at the Barn. Maybe I already had it, somewhere deep inside. I told myself this as I struggled alone in that awful, silent room. My position was that a man has to draw a line somewhere and say: "This I believe in enough to die for. I may be wrong; I may be right. But I believe in it."

"You have to live up to your principles by dying for them," I told myself. "Your country gave you information worth dying for. The Navy gave you a Special Intelligence clearance as a badge of mutual trust. The deepest secrets of your country were shared with you. 'Thou shalt not divulge this information' was a commandment you swore to uphold. The Code of Conduct requires no less. You always have lived up to the commandment. You must keep faith with your country, your Navy, your fellow prisoners, yourself. Eliminating yourself will preserve that part of your country you are carrying around inside your head. It is a matter of honor—as corny as that may sound."

"I'll do it, damn it. I'll do it. In a few minutes."

Cold War Ship

I had no inkling that the yellow teletype message a radioman held in his hand one evening in July of 1967 was to make me an active participant in the Cold War chess game. He obviously didn't either; he was grinning as though I had just been ordered to the Aleutians to count blankets. He waited at the door—unusual for him—to see what I would do when I read what was printed on the piece of paper.

When I read it, I could see why he stayed. The message, written in standard Navy acronyms, was ordering Ensign Frederick C. Schumacher, Jr. 700156/1105/USNR, to report to the U.S.S. *Pueblo* (AGER-2) as prospective Operations Officer not later than 30 September 1967. I was puzzled. I had not asked for a transfer off the *Vega;* I was not due for a transfer; I did not want a transfer; I was not expecting a transfer. What the hell was the *Pueblo?*

In hopes of finding out, I turned to the official volumes of U.S. Navy ships kept on board the *Vega*. There was nothing about the *Pueblo* and nothing on the designation AGER. After hours of searching, a fellow officer, as curious about my new ship as I was, found AGER translated in a directory of ship mailing addresses. The A stood for auxiliary, the G for general, and the ER for environmental research. But what did that mean?

I pondered that question for the next several weeks. Then a letter came from the Executive Officer of the *Pueblo*, which gave me my first clue that the ship was to conduct highly secret work. He wrote

40

that all he could say about the mission in an unclassified letter was that the *Pueblo* would conduct oceanographic research in the Sea of Japan. He said the ship was a converted AKL—a light cargo ship.

The prospect was tantalizing. I wanted to know more. When the *Vega* stopped at Subic Bay in the Philippines, I went to the squadron commander's flagship. The junior officers there could give me little hard information about my new assignment. But a lieutenant commander, who seemed to know something, took me aside and told me quietly that it was a good thing I was single. An AGER "spends a lot of time at sea," he said. "Better figure between 250 and 260 days a year."

"Yes, sir," I said. "But what does the ship do?"

"She'll be working directly for COMNAVFORJAPAN [Commander of Naval Forces in Japan], spends a lot of time at sea. We don't have much to do with her operations. That's about all I can tell you." Either he knew nothing more or could not tell me if he did. That was all I learned about my next assignment.

I was to fly home first, from the Air Force's Clark Field, not too far from where the *Vega* was resting for a run back to Taiwan for more fresh food. The good-byes were perfunctory. With a couple of other *Vega* ensigns, I went to the Officers' Club at Subic Bay and said good-by over beer and hamburgers. Then the bus—in the three hours it took to reach Clark—tried to help my digestion by finding every pothole in the road. The sailors on it somehow slept through this. They looked stunted by the three-foot-long wooden salad forks of carved Filipino wood they had bought for the folks back home.

I went to the Officers' Club at Clark for dinner. The drinks at such clubs all over the world tenderize the food—usually a good thing. I marveled as I sipped my drink that a Navy officer could go on like this for thirty years and then retire without having developed a stone liver. That was the enervating part of the service: most free time—what there was of it—was spent killing time in officers' clubs. The days did not seem to add up to anything much. Talk at officers' club bars was mostly ritual; no one really listened to, or cared about, what someone else was saying.

After leaving Clark at 9:00 P.M., my DC-8 flew back into the previous day, landing in Honolulu at 4:00 in the afternoon of the day before. The stop was long enough to refuel both the plane, with some JP-4, and the passengers, with Hawaiian Mai-Tai's, fruit and exotic juices masking the whisky. At 3:00 in the morning, the plane landed at Travis Air Force Base, outside San Francisco. As I walked out into the black, I knew from the operation schedules that the *Pueblo* should be somewhere in San Francisco Bay. But I thought only fleetingly of her as the bus took me over the Oakland Bay Bridge to International Airport. I would meet her soon enough, I decided. My immediate objective was St. Louis and home.

All servicemen I have talked to about it agree that telling your family what you have been doing in the Navy does not take long. Yet you do not fit in with the old home surroundings. You know it. Your family knows it. But nobody says it. After a polite interval, restlessness takes over. I soon left St. Louis for Philadelphia and New York City, winding up one Saturday evening at the St. Anthony Club for a small reunion with some old friends. Michael Lutin, an astrologist, was one of them. He looked at me with a start when he joined us at the club early in the evening, and said, "Something terrible is going to happen to you. I don't know what it is, but something terrible. And I don't know how it is going to come out." Because of what happened later, it would be nice to say that Mike's pronouncement filled me with dread. But it didn't. I recalled his premonitions only in North Korea.

I flew west to report to the *Pueblo*, and after spending a night in a motel directly across from the Anti-Submarine School, where the *Pueblo* was berthed, I drove through the gates of the base and searched for her. There were only two piers. One of them had a small ship tied up at the far end. I parked, wondering if that could really be the U.S.S. *Pueblo*. I could see her fresh paint, even from two hundred yards away, and then could make out the "GER 2" on her bow. This was it. I felt eager that Friday morning, September 30, as I walked down the pier anticipating fresh adventure.

The *Pueblo* was indeed some special kind of ship. No other her size carried so many antennas. They waved back and forth in the morning chop like supple fly rods. I was no ensign approaching his first ship this time, and I decided I was going to like the *Pueblo*. She obviously had some challenging work to do. A destroyer looks glamorous from the outside, but its work is divided up so systematically and has been done the same way for so long that the duty aboard is almost rote. The *Pueblo,* I felt sure, would not mean rote duty. I was a little worried about her smallness. Could she stand up to a blow? The doghouse compartment added on topside made her look topheavy and squat—like a pregnant trawler.

Going on board required walking *down* the gangplank—not up, as for ships of any size. I saluted the American flag as I stepped aboard. There was no commissioned officer on the quarterdeck to salute, or to tell: "Reporting aboard for duty, sir." I found only a petty officer on deck. I handed him my orders. He telephoned somebody inside.

The Executive Officer, or XO, popped into view and motioned me up a ladder near the quarterdeck where I had come aboard. Shaking my hand with a professional "Welcome aboard," Lieutenant Edward R. Murphy, Jr., made a fine first impression. He was tall, trim, studious-looking, and wore horn-rimmed glasses. He was dressed by the book: sleeves rolled down, shoes polished, black tie neatly held in place by the thin gold Navy-issue tie clip. An executive officer runs a ship for the commanding officer. He is like the foreman on a construction job. The commanding officer—to continue the construction-job parallel—stays in the trailer, involving himself directly only in really big issues. The executive officer is supposed to be the ship's face-to-face boss. This enables the commanding officer, even though he may be the one telling the executive officer to be the ship's son of a bitch, to reserve his powers for special occasions, thus making sure the impact is not softened by overuse.

"As far as anyone on the beach is concerned," Murphy said, right away, "this ship does oceanographic research. That goes for your parents, your friends—anyone." Then, after pausing, he said in a conspiratorial tone, "I've got to be sure you understand that."

"Yes, sir," I replied. "But tell me, just what is the ship up to?"

"We'll get into that some other time. Right now we've got a lecture going on about nuclear-warfare defensive measures I'd like you to attend."

The lecture, given by an officer from the Pacific Fleet Training Command in San Diego, had brought the officers and crew together in the long and narrow compartment on the port side, aft, where chow was served to the men. The room, which I learned later had been personally designed by Commander Bucher, had Formica-topped tables on a red linoleum deck. A soft-ice-cream maker stood in the middle of the room. There was a special section to the rear, with a small table and cushioned chairs, where the chief petty officers ate. I learned later that after the evening meal they and others used the table to play Monopoly. For some reason, Monopoly was the *Pueblo*'s game—not poker or acey-ducey or chess.

I studied my new shipmates. There was an unusually large number of first- and second-class petty officers in the group. Several of the enlisted men had shoulder patches depicting lightning crossed with a feather quill. This was the badge of those bright technocrats of the modern U.S. Navy, communications technicians, or CT's. They are the men who run the electronic equipment and read the black boxes for the fleet. I was to come to admire those CT's on the *Pueblo*. One of these men was CT 2 Charles W. Ayling. He represented the new breed; he was bright, well educated, clever. When he had the duty, one of his chores was to sweep the deck with a small wooden-handled broom called a foxtail. One night, shortly after I had reported aboard, the command "Now, sweepers, man your brooms" came over the 1 MC (one-megacycle) loud-speaker system. Ayling turned to me. "Ah ha," he said. "The mating call of the wood-backed foxtail. Excuse me, sir. I have to answer it."

After the lecture, the officer I was to replace, Lieutenant (j.g.) David Behr, introduced himself. The name of my billet was first lieutenant—a sort of foreman for the deck crew and deck equipment. Dave knew and liked this part of the job. He was known as one hell of a disciplinarian. Even in my introductory tour of the ship, he stopped at a rusting spot on the deck, threw his hands on his hips, and yelled: "Aw, no. That's all fouled up. Where's Boats?" This was Boatswain's Mate First Class Norbert J. Klepac. Dave, built like a

44

younger version of Vince Lombardi, short and squat, obviously had the deck crew in hand. But I learned later that he and the Captain fought a lot. That probably was why I was so immediately welcomed.

Dave was straightforward enough. When I asked him about my duties as Operations Officer, he answered: "Operations? What the hell do I know about Operations? That's about as fouled up as anything else on this boat." I was on my own, then, in that department, which didn't bother me much. My duties on the *Vega*—as communications Officer and Assistant Operations Officer—had prepared me well. I assumed I would supervise communications on the *Pueblo*, schedule when and where the ship sailed, and plan the training of the crew.

I knew that electronically, however, the *Pueblo* went way beyond my competence. That was why there were so many CT's aboard. I asked Dave about them. "Aw, those CT's. They think they're so damn smart. Not a sailor among them. Afraid to get their lily-white hands dirty. And the XO! Watch out for him. He'll sit on everything. And the Old Man! Have you met him yet? Probably still hung over, in the sack."

"Welcome aboard, Mr. Schumacher," I told myself. "You've lucked out again. So you didn't want to go on to Taiwan with the *Vega* to pick up vegetables and fruit for the boys in Vietnam. Now you've got yourself on an electrified *Reluctant,* with no Mr. Roberts between you and the Captain."

Dave filled me in on the Old Man as we headed for the wardroom for lunch. The CO's name, he said, was Lieutenant Commander Lloyd M. Bucher, a career submariner who had the misfortune to draw a surface ship for his first command. The diesel submariners hate this. They call it being "surfaced." But there are not enough subs to go around. So up the promotion ladder for submarine officers often means out of the submarine service they love—unless they go into Admiral Rickover's exclusive nuclear-submarine Navy, complete with long hours, long patrols, and virtually guaranteed divorce.

As Dave had predicted, the Captain was not yet about. I sat at the far end of the wardroom table, which was about the size of two card tables, and cater-cornered from the Captain's chair, wondering what he would be like. The conversation stiffened because of me; a new face in the wardroom, the officers' social center on a ship, always does that. I admired the compactness and neatness of the room. Whoever had installed the equipment in the small space had worked with the precision of a watchmaker. Along one bulkhead, within easy reach of the captain's chair, were two tape recorders, twin Ampex's, with a Scott tuner. Cabinets covered with wood-grain material lined the upper wall spaces, and two blue-and-white electric coffeepots perked away on the sideboard. Carpeting on the deck added warmth and softness. There was not enough space for a couch or a big TV, but it was a cozy spot just the same.

Wham! Socko! Blam! In came Batman. The Captain electrified the atmosphere in the wardroom when he made his appearance; I could sense the ozone. He sat down seemingly with one powerful motion. Murphy introduced me. The Captain's hand shot toward mine like a right jab. His nasal voice went through me like a command. "Welcome aboard. Glad to have you. Where'd you come from?"

I managed, despite feeling incoherent, to get out a few sentences on my background. My new skipper took them in along with the food he shoveled into his muscular body. Chest muscles bulged under his shirt, and thick brown hair ran wildly all over his head and down over his ears and neck. Bulging black eyes, tinged with red, swept over me and everything else in the room. He seemed constantly in motion, his arms reaching around like a long crane to pick up things. There was none of that "Please pass the salt, Mr. Schumacher" formality. While one hand fed his stomach, another shot over to the tape recorder to feed music into his mind. Johnny Cash tapes, I learned that first day, were his favorites.

The Captain projected power, lots of power. To be honest, he scared the hell out of me that first meal. I had an idea I was in for a rough time. His words conveyed the same kind of self-assurance and power as did his barrel chest, boxer's neck, and muscled arms. He completely dominated the conversation. The other officers in the wardroom might as well have been the salt and pepper shakers he never asked for. Yet what he said interested me. He was no boorish bore. He played with ideas as he talked, illuminating part of a subject you had not seen or thought about before. He could do this with topics as far apart as naval operations in Vietnam and the Chargers football team in San Diego. In between, he could throw a deft needle into one of the officers at the table for his behavior on his last liberty. He was a fascinating virtuoso. I felt his power when he turned toward me and asked, "Hey, Skip"—he had learned my nickname when we were introduced—"you a qualified OOD?"

"Yes, sir. Independent steaming." That is the Navy's polite way of saying that an officer is authorized, when officer of the deck, to drive a ship as long as there is no other ship in sight to run into.

"Good," the Captain replied. "Let's see. We go out again Monday, don't we? Why don't you take the ship out, and I'll see how you do? Stand duty with Dave for a couple of days, and then we'll work you into the regular rotation for in-port watches."

The Captain had spoken. He was obviously a show-me skipper. "You say you can drive a ship," he seemed to be saying to me; "all right, then, let's see you drive mine." He turned to other subjects for a while and then left the wardroom in the same quick way he had entered.

On Monday, I was right up there on the open bridge of the *Pueblo*. The Captain sat in a chair behind me. I managed to send the right commands to get us back away from the pier and headed in the right direction for the channel. While we were steaming out, though, I decided a slight course correction was needed. "Left five degree rudder," I called down to the boatswain's mate handling the wheel in the pilothouse below me. The *Pueblo* swung around—and then kept on going, like a Comet sailboat given full left rudder. We swung around thirty degrees, not five, and were headed dead for a mudbank—all in three seconds. The Captain leaped out of his chair to order the course corrections before I realized what was happening. Expecting a verbal keel-hauling, I braced for his blast.

"Well," he said, turning the conn back over to me, "she's settled down now. You got her. I guess that was a little unfair of me. This ship's got a rudder as large as a damn barn door. All you ever need

47

to use for this kind of maneuvering is two or three degree rudder. It's better if you give the helmsman a course to steer." He paused, then launched into a new burst of staccato. "We get out here, we'll try a little docking practice; let you get used to her."

Getting used to her, it turned out, was fun. The Captain was an excellent ship handler and instructor, and apparently considered the latter his more important job. "It's a pretty scary thing," he told me in one of those practice sessions off San Diego, "to sit here outwardly calm while some fuzzy-chinned ensign is about to run your ship aground. You know he's doing something wrong. You just hope like hell he will catch it. If you correct him ten seconds too early, you destroy his self-confidence. Ten seconds too late, and you destroy your ship."

That was the CO I came to know in those first training days in San Diego. He even admitted to pulling his share of goofs when he had been a junior officer like me. He said he learned more from his failures than from his successes. He wanted to give his officers plenty of opportunity to learn the same way—hairy for him or not.

I did learn from my mistakes on the bridge, and I became attached to the little *Pueblo*. She was responsive if handled right. I began to regard her as something special, in a warm, personal way. She was only 176½ feet long, and displaced 935 tons if fully loaded. This made her in size a lot closer to the Pilgrims' ninety-foot-long *Mayflower* than to the queen of the modern Navy's fleet, the 1,101½-foot-long *Enterprise*, a nuclear-powered aircraft carrier displacing 85,600 tons.

I was as unhappy with my orientation on the inside workings of the *Pueblo* as I was happy with my progress on the bridge under the tutelage of the Captain. I simply could not find out specifically what we were going to be doing out there in the Sea of Japan. And if I didn't know that, I didn't see how I could be an effective Operations Officer for the ship.

A man who did know was Lieutenant Stephen R. Harris, the officer in charge of the intelligence center on the ship. He called his domain the SOD Hut. The name came from Special Operations Department. The gray aluminum door to the SOD Hut had that name written on it, in dark-blue letters. But I could not go through that

48

door the whole time we were in San Diego training for our deployment. It had three separate locks: a key lock in the aluminum door handle, a combination lock, and five black buttons mounted on a brass plate just above the combination dial, which had to be punched in a certain sequence. The Captain did not bother with all that. He just pounded his big fist on the door until someone inside let him in. I could not do the same thing because I did not have the Special Intelligence security clearance required.

I told Steve Harris at every opportunity—over coffee in the wardroom and out on liberty in San Diego—that it was patently ridiculous for the officer supposedly in charge of operations and communications to be locked out of the ship's main center of operations and communications. He agreed, said he would send off the necessary papers, but warned that it would take time. And so the matter rested, with the result that my preparation time in San Diego was not as productive as it could have been.

Not knowing the details of our mission handicapped me on the little things as well as the big things—like ordering supplies and ship-recognition manuals. Various naval headquarters prepare and send out lists for the various types of ships. Destroyers get one allowance list, for instance, aircraft carries another, and AKL cargo ships still another. These lists tell you what you are supposed to have on board. But for the *Pueblo*—changed from an AKL to an AGER in June of 1967—there was no such list. Yet, as Operations Officer I was supposed to make sure we had what we needed. But what did we need? I was not cleared to know the details of our operations; nor were the officers on shore in charge of drafting allowance lists for us. So the *Pueblo* was left on her own.

The same bureaucratic situation had our training in irons. We were under the operational control of the Naval Training Command while in San Diego. The command was supposed to establish drills to test our readiness for our mission. But the command's officers were not cleared to know what we were getting ready for. It was just luck that they had an officer formerly attached to our sister ship, the *Banner*. He came through with some meaningful training exercises.

After receiving the training, we came under the control of Commander Service Group One—also located in San Diego. The command was supposed to inspect the *Pueblo* and make sure she was ready in all respects for her mission. Again, however, the command was not cleared to know our mission. The inspecting team who came aboard found that many questions on their list did not apply or could not be answered by *Pueblo* officers for security reasons. Frustrated, they gave up and declared us ready—for something.

My fellow officers had plenty of their own problems. It is always hectic getting ready for a mission, especially a first one, like ours. The secrecy blanket made it particularly difficult. The Captain had to worry about training officers like me to stand watches as officer of the deck, and he lived in constant dread of mechanical failures. The ship's steering broke down regularly. The Executive Officer, as the Captain's administrative officer, was supposed to keep the ship's company working together smoothly and move all of the paperwork along. Steve Harris had his mysterious work to do breaking in the CT's and testing the fancy equipment inside the SOD Hut. Tim Harris, our Supply Officer, was also new on board. He was trying to learn his new job as well as how the ship worked. And Chief Warrant Officer Gene Lacy had his hands full as Engineering Officer in charge of the Rube Goldberg world of engines and pipes below decks.

Meanwhile, having made the rather automatic promotion to lieutenant junior grade, I busied myself as best I could with my own empire of paperwork. The frustrations of getting ready to leave San Diego made the days pass slowly. Dave departed for civilian life after three or four weeks, and with two departments to administer, I had my hands full. As we got ready for our November 6 departure, I knew we still had a lot of untangling to do. I had a pretty good idea by this time that we would be doing electronic intelligence work out of Yokosuka, Japan, but there remained a lot of questions to be answered. I hoped we would learn our job as we went along.

My last weekend ashore held a bad omen. I went to a party in La Jolla. The last thing my date did before we left my buddy's car that evening was slip her address and phone number into his glove compartment. She must have known I was going to be gone a long time.

50

Poets

"Hey, Skip, come on over. We're going to give them our song." It was the Captain calling to me from across the room at the Navy Officers' Club at Yokosuka. The *Pueblo,* after a rough crossing, had arrived there on December 1. It was now December 28. And the Captain had something extra to celebrate: a new stripe, which marked his promotion from lieutenant commander to commander. He was given a party to mark the occasion—a tradition to which he was adding his own colorful touch.

I picked my way across the floor. And it was not easy. The Skipper, to make sure his party was not short on color during this Christmas season, had sown three hundred balloons as thick as grass seed on the floor. I'm sure I looked like a broken-field runner in slow motion as I made my way toward him. The rest of the *Pueblo* officers were doing the same thing, adding to the hilarity of the moment.

We lined up on the Captain's left, put our arms around each other, and boomed out the ship's song to the assembled guests.

"Here's to the *Pueblo,* she sure is a swell ship.
Here's to the *Pueblo,* she sure is a peach.
Boom-yakle-yakle; boom-yakle-yakle; boom-yakle-yakle . . ."

The crowd cheered and clapped so enthusiastically that we gave them the song again—and then again. I could hear the Captain's

51

nasal voice cutting through everyone else's. He was happy. I was happy. We were all happy.

The *Pueblo*, despite breakdowns in its ancient steering system, which had been made for the ship by a defunct elevator company, had gotten us across the Pacific in one piece. We still had lots of administrative problems to solve, and there were personality conflicts on board, but in a few days we were finally going out on our first mission. I felt this would be good for all of us. We would find out who could do what and how well. Then we could change procedures and personnel for the second trip out. We looked upon the first mission as on-the-job training, not as a dangerous Cold War patrol off a hostile coast.

We officers of the *Pueblo* certainly were far from icy-veined James Bonds with cyanide capsules hidden in our teeth. We were hired hands of the American government who happened to wear Navy uniforms on the job. It was accepted quietly by all of us that we might be asked to die in this occupation. But none of our superiors had given us any indication that this mission was going to be dangerous. The married men in the wardroom worried about civilian problems, not the mission ahead: paying the mortgage on the house; putting money away for their children's education; finding ways to keep a marriage together during the long absences caused by sea duty.

The Captain's wetting-down party was a marvelous excuse for putting both on-duty and off-duty concerns aside and enjoying the moment. He was serving rations of Black Velvet punch, which was several wines combined in a potion with lots of spiritual thrust. And the perfumed scent in the room from wives and girl friends was a welcome change from the constant diesel smell of the ship. The Christmasy greens, golds, and reds reminded me of holiday parties I used to attend in St. Louis, and made me wish I were back home.

I chatted with some of the officers, from other ships, the Captain had invited. They included men from all the submarines in port, the wardroom of the *Samuel Gompers*, a destroyer tender, and his old buddies from the staff of Submarine Flotilla Seven. In Yokosuka, the Captain had served as Assistant Operations Officer at SubFlot Seven from July 1964 to December 1966. Then he went to the Puget

Sound Naval Ship Yard, in Bremerton, Washington, to help commission the *Pueblo* for her new role. Before his desk job at SubFlot Seven, the Captain had sailed as executive officer in the U.S.S. *Ronquil,* a diesel submarine. The *Pueblo* was his first command. I'm sure he would have preferred a diesel sub. But he was out to make the most of his command, even though it was a surface ship. And tonight he was making the most of his promotion party.

I couldn't help seeing him, no matter where I stood in the room. He was a walking Christmas tree of color. He had outdone himself sartorially. He had the usual outrageously loud, painted tie, beaming off a colored shirt, and what I felt sure was the only four-button brown-striped sports coat in the U.S. Fleet. And he had somewhere found the brightest-colored trousers I had then seen—a blinding lemon, as I remember.

Clenched in his big, even teeth was one of the thick black cigars he was passing out to his guests. And as the guests approached the Captain, they could read a big round button in his lapel. POETS, it said, in capital letters.

"What does that button mean, Pete?" came the question time after time from the uninitiated.

"Piss on everything; tomorrow's Saturday." The Captain would take the cigar out of his mouth, releasing a chuckle from deep down in his chest. His teeth would flash, and mirth would dance around in his big black eyes. You could not help but feel good in the presence of this man when he was off duty and in a party mood. Many people I had met in the Navy agreed that Pete Bucher—the nickname was that of a football player he admired—was one hell of a guy to be with. He had depth as well as spirit; he was no belly-up-to-the-bar sea dog who could talk only about sex and promotions.

The Captain seemed to have gone through almost everything in life, and had read about the rest. I thought I knew literature pretty well. But I couldn't touch him. He had a complete set of Shakespeare in his cabin, and could quote whole passages from the plays. I think his gray boyhood was why he always liked to have lots of color around him.

The Captain's natural parents had died when he was an infant.

Then his adoptive mother died and the family could not afford to keep him. After that, he ran away from an orphanage whenever he could—trying to get to sea as a cabin boy. He had had to sleep in coal bins and steal food before he was ten. A Catholic nun at one orphanage changed the life of the hard little Bucher boy by arranging for him to go to Boys Town, outside Omaha. The kindly teachers there put Lloyd M. Bucher on his way. He broke through that thick ice of society which often holds down poor boys for a lifetime. From Boys Town, he went into the Navy as an enlisted quartermaster; to the University of Nebraska, where he was an above-average student and a football halfback; then back into the Navy in 1953, this time as an officer.

Life to the Captain was one glorious smorgasbord to be devoured as fully as possible. He never seemed to feel sorry about his rough beginning in life. That was just how it was. He told me how he loaded his plate academically at Nebraska, piling up enough credits to earn a bachelor of science degree in geology, biology, or chemistry. He chose geology.

I knew from watching the ship's company these last two months that there would be no problem between the Captain and the crew. The enlisted men would follow him anywhere. One reason, I think, was that they could identify with him. He had been apprehended, along with others, in a gambling raid in Bremerton while the *Pueblo* was being fitted out. His name made the papers, and this drew a rebuke from his Navy superiors. But the men figured that any skipper who gambled couldn't be all bad.

Besides this social rapport and the crew's respect for his unquestioned skills as a navigator and ship handler, another reason they liked and respected the Captain was that he would back them up if they were in a jam. There was the night in San Diego, for instance, when the Shore Patrol picked up two of his men for wearing part of their uniform with civilian clothes while on liberty. They had on olive or tan Levi's, forbidden by Navy District regulations. The men got word to the Captain, who was in bed, that they were being arrested on unfair charges. He threw on his uniform and went down to the Shore Patrol office where they were being held. He shouted so much about "Gestapo techniques" and "chickenshit regulations" that the SP put him on report, too. The protest went to the Commander of Service Group One in San Diego, and the Captain filed a twelve-page rebuttal of the charges. He even included photographs of how the men were dressed when picked up, arguing that the clothes they wore were being sold by the Navy District's own exchange and that any regulation forbidding their use was pure nonsense. The crew loved him for it. And nothing came of the charges.

I also believe the sailors he had moved around the world with in his own enlisted days gave the Captain a love and understanding that stayed with him as an officer. These sailors were like the brothers he never had as a boy.

I was as doubtful about the relationship between the Captain and the Executive Officer as I was sure of the one between the Captain and the crew. I was afraid that the apparent gulf between them would get wider on our mission under the pressure of operations at sea. They were as different as any two officers running a ship together can be. Bucher was a forty-year-old, cocksure, do-the-job-and-ask-questions-afterward submariner; Murphy, a thirty-year-old, equivocal, don't-do-anything-rash line officer. Bucher was, off duty, a hard-drinking, fast-talking hell raiser who would say an appreciative "mercy" on seeing a well-turned leg; Murphy, off duty, a teetotaler and an introverted man of stuffy decorum and trite speech and mannerisms. Bucher was a product of the Idaho-Nebraska back country who gate-crashed his way from the have-not to the have society; Murphy was tenderly nurtured through his years at the Christian Scientist Principia High School and Principia College, in Elsah, Illinois. Bucher was a muscular blockbuster with a tough look when aroused; Murphy, a spare man who never looked tough.

These differences, and more, in person and personality would not have mattered if the two could have found a way to work together. They had not yet done so at the time of the party. Bucher wanted a take-charge executive officer; Murphy wanted the Captain to tell him exactly what to do. Bucher complained rather openly that when he gave specific instructions, Murphy did not carry them out. Then he would undercut Murphy by going around him, personally assigning chores to other officers, even to petty officers. The Executive Officer was thus isolated on the ship he was supposed to run for the Captain. Not trusted and cut off, Murphy pushed papers around but never really tackled the jobs Bucher wanted done. To make matters worse, the *Pueblo* was too new a ship to have precedents to go by, to hold it together by momentum. Lack of innovation by Murphy meant that some work just didn't get done. The CO-XO relationship was not helped when the Captain found out that Murphy was getting his own laundry done in Japan free by the firm that was doing the *Pueblo*'s wash. Usually the commanding officer is included in this free laundry privilege. Thus both the big things and the little things had the two top officers working at cross-purposes. I felt that during our first mission the problem would either come to a head, which would probably mean a new executive officer for the next trip, or work itself out as both men came to realize they would have to reach an accommodation for the good of the ship.

Relations were also tense at times between Bucher and Steve Harris, the twenty-nine-year-old Naval Security Group Officer. The problem here was jurisdictional. Bucher, as captain, wanted to run the whole ship. Steve had his own budget and on some matters went directly to his superiors in the Naval Security Group at Honolulu, not consulting the Captain. Bucher demanded to be apprised of everything Steve and his boys were doing in the "Black Room" of the *Pueblo*. Steve did not feel he could do this all the time. This split authority gave the ship built-in stresses and strains administratively.

The Captain and Steve were also different kinds of men. Steve was Boston-bred and a Harvard graduate who had enjoyed a quietly intellectual life. Physically, he was awkward-looking. His horn-rimmed glasses stood out from a ruddy boy's face. But he was highly intelligent and chose his words well, though bad puns were part of his droll sense of humor. He made no secret of his admiration for the Captain. The two of them realized they had jurisdictional problems, with few guidelines to rely on, but they wanted to work them out and seemed to be doing so. I felt optimistic about their relationship.

Steve spent most of his duty time in the SOD Hut, out of sight of the rest of us. He took his duties seriously. In off hours, he talked about the lovely girl he had recently married, Esther, and seemed to write a letter to her every night. The Captain worried about Steve spending so much time on the ship. Now, he was obviously glad to see him letting loose at the party by taking some Black Velvet aboard.

I noticed that Steve seemed to be living it up more than was one of the usual stars in that department, Ensign Timothy L. Harris, our twenty-two-year-old Supply Officer. Tim was playing dutiful husband, only sipping at the punch as his dark-haired wife, Linda, stood next to him. Tim had come to the *Pueblo*—after only a brief course in supply administration—from flight school, having decided that airplanes were not for him. He had been thrown on our strange, demanding ship with little preparation and was understandably confused by all the procedures one must master. The Captain liked Tim's willingness to learn on the ship and his free-wheeling high-spiritedness ashore. Something akin to a father-son relationship seemed to be developing between the two. That dynamic duo had pulled off the Great Nude Painting Robbery back in San Diego, somehow stealing the picture of the young lady from behind the bar at the Ballast Tank, the officers' club built by submariners. She had hung in the *Pueblo* wardroom until the "thieves" had been identified and ordered to return her to the club.

Tim was outwardly uncomplicated—a forthright, athletic young officer who wanted to do his job right. Born in Oshkosh, Wisconsin, he had been graduated from Jacksonville University in 1967. He seemed to like the Navy, and planned to make a career of it. The frustrating paperwork of supply officer would sometimes get him down, though, and he would try to shake the feeling off by swinging his head back and forth like a bulldog and swearing.

The sixth in rank on the *Pueblo* but the first in professionalism was Chief Warrant Officer Gene Howard Lacy, our Engineering Officer. The Old Pro—in experience, not age; he was only thirty-six—was playing his usual cool game at the party. He stood erect, looking so dignified that he often was mistaken for the ship's captain.

He was trim, tall, and had clean, chiseled features and disciplined black hair.

Aboard the ship, Gene was all business; he used few words and imposed strict discipline on his men below decks. He had spent so much time in the noisy engine rooms of Navy ships that he was partially deaf. He had entered the Navy in 1948 from Grand Coulee, Washington, High School, and was now the concerned father of three children.

On the beach, the Captain often sought out the taciturn Lacy for a companion. I remember one wild summons. The Captain was gulping a drink in the rather stiff-necked Admiral Kidd Naval Officers' Club in San Diego; Lacy was aboard the *Pueblo,* which was tied up at the pier nearby. With no warning to the higher-ranking brass tippling beside him, the Captain, with characteristic impulsiveness, lunged out of the club. Standing on the terrace in his rumpled uniform, he blew his piercing whistle to catch the attention of the *Pueblo* watch. Then he waved his arms as if trying to take off like a bird. The officers inside the club watched in amazement. But the Captain had merely decided he wanted Lacy to come ashore and was semaphoring that summons to the *Pueblo* watch by using his arms like signal flags. Lacy came in a few minutes later.

I felt that we six officers, backed by our seventy-seven-man crew, could carry out our mission without trouble. I was anxious to get to sea. None of us had any premonition of danger or disaster. We did not see ourselves as men going out to the edges of the Cold War. The officers and crew of the *Pueblo*—men the North Koreans would treat as "war-mongering spies" only a few weeks after the Captain's party—were representative of the nation we were to sail for in a few days.

Steve ended the evening in the same high-spirited way it had begun. He danced a devilish ballet among the balloons scattered on the floor. Then he dipped down and poked his cigar into four or five of them. So Captain Bucher's wetting-down party ended with a bang —in fact, with lots of bangs.

Orders

The cold dawn of Friday, December 29, 1967, broke over a peaceful-looking *Pueblo* tied up at the Yokosuka Navy wharf. She lay in the morning chop beside AGER-1, the U.S.S. *Banner,* and a Coast Guard cutter dirtied from the war of frustration in Vietnam.

The *Banner*, in missions off Russia and China, had picked up information that Navy Intelligence leaders and the National Security Agency considered valuable. Dr. Eugene Fubini's idea of taking a leaf out of the Soviet book of electronic-intelligence-collection platforms had worked. The Soviet Navy used unarmed civilian fishing trawlers. The Navy, starting with the *Banner*, tried light cargo ships. Who would worry about a small unarmed cargo ship drifting around in international waters? Certainly not the Russians, when they were doing the same thing.

Fubini had argued this way in 1965 when he was a deputy secretary of Defense under Robert S. McNamara. Admiral David L. McDonald, Chief of Naval Operations, had agreed. The two discussed the idea often in the early months of that year. McDonald, seeing the scars left on the Navy by the early McNamara years, when George W. Anderson, Chief of Naval Operations, was removed from that post and made ambassador to Portugal for failing to show the requisite enthusiasm for the TFX airplane, was trying to listen to all sides. Fubini, everybody agreed, knew a great deal about electronic intelligence. He thought the Navy was missing a bet by letting the

59

Russians listen to American military radio messages and radar, tag after the fleet to see how it operated, and hang off strategic bases like Guam, where much sensitive information flew out over the air waves. The Navy listened to Fubini. It did not fight his idea.

The only question in McDonald's mind was where to get the money for his special ferret ships; he was already hard pressed for funds to keep combat ships on the line. Yet putting electronic-intelligence units on destroyers and other fighting ships interfered with their regular missions. Moreover, warships looked too provocative. To order them to stations off remote Communist coasts could trigger battle alerts and, perhaps, international incidents. It would be better to use harmless-looking ships, which, he thought, would be perfectly safe in international waters. And if they were not, the country that interfered with a U.S. ship would regret the day. The American government would not tolerate piracy. McDonald felt sure of that, and said so.

After rejecting such bargain-basement suggestions as using tuna boats, the Navy refurbished three ships for ferret duty: the *Banner* and the *Pueblo*, to work out of Japan, and the *Palm Beach*, out of Norfolk. The listening targets for the *Banner* and the *Pueblo* were to be Russia and China, considered the chief strategic threats to the United States. The old land-based listening posts had been disappearing fast. The United States was being forced to take its electronic eyes and ears from places like Turkey and Pakistan and put them on ships. And Fubini hoped for a fleet of thirty ferret ships.

Everybody assumed that the *Pueblo* would prove even more valuable than the *Banner*, because she had been designed more carefully. The question was where to send her on her first mission. The Navy considered the Soviet Union its prime target for ELINT (electronic intelligence). And the officer in charge of the ship's intelligence detachment, Steve Harris, was Russia-oriented and spoke the language fluently. But the National Security Agency—the President's own intelligence arm, headquartered behind the high wire fences of Fort Meade, in Maryland—had told Navy commanders in Honolulu that it would be helpful to take a look and listen off North Korea.

It fell to a balding, friendly Navy Reserve lieutenant named Edward Brookes to reduce NSA wishes to orders for the *Pueblo*. He was Fleet Maintenance Officer for Rear Admiral Frank L. Johnson, Commander of U.S. Naval Forces in Japan, or COMNAVFOR-JAPAN. Though the only ships Johnson had to maintain were the *Banner* and the *Pueblo,* Brookes had both the personality and the know-how needed to exploit the power that lay in being in charge of an admiral's fleet. So, cigar clenched tight in his teeth, he pushed and pushed to make the system work for him personally and the operation he ran. He wanted to be designated a career intelligence officer. To achieve that, he knew he had to make the AGER program work. He used the Admiral's name freely to achieve that end. But, more important, he worked hard.

For tactical purposes he assumed that within the Navy bureaucracy everybody above him was incompetent or lazy, and probably both. To push through a paper proposal, then, he must take care not to stimulate any exertion by higher-ups. The *Banner* had sailed before under orders directing her to stay at least thirteen miles from foreign shores. She also had sailed on missions rated "minimal risk." Brookes knew that such missions had been approved all the way up, by the Joint Chiefs of Staff in the Pentagon and by the civilian 303 Committee, which reviewed intelligence operations for the President. This information was his starting point. He could direct the *Pueblo* to stay at least thirteen miles out from shore and rate the risk minimal. Nobody at the top would exert himself over such a proposal. They would approve it, and thus be responsible. Brookes and his staff would have a mission going with minimum delay. The system would work for him, for the Admiral, and for the AGER program.

Thus, within the limits of his starting point, Brookes could send the *Pueblo* out on her first mission to snoop around the Soviet ships plying the Tsushima Strait, between Korea and Japan. But would that be interesting enough? What about the national tasking requirement—the euphuism for the National Security Agency's request for information on North Korea? The *Banner* had stayed off Wonsan for one and a half days in March of 1967. But a longer stay was desired. Nothing had happened to the *Banner* off Wonsan except for a North Korean SO-1 sub chaser flashing a light at her. So sending the *Pueblo* to North Korea would, as Brookes saw it, be a routine but essential mission from the standpoint of building up "your electronic base," as he put it. The North Koreans were suspected of having strengthened their coastal defenses with surface-to-air missiles for knocking down aircraft and with cruise missiles for sinking surface ships. The *Pueblo,* by being able to hang around longer than either a reconnaissance plane or a satellite, could outwait the North Korean radar operators. They would have to turn on their military radar sometime during the course of three weeks. The *Pueblo* would stand a good chance of intercepting the signals and pinpointing the missile sites. The *Pueblo* might also be able to pick up information about the modernized North Korean air force and the Whiskey-class submarines believed to be steaming along the east coast and perhaps based at the island of Mayang Do. Even if nothing was learned, it would be good training for the green *Pueblo* crew.

Brookes, in consultation with Captain Thomas L. Dwyer, Admiral Johnson's Assistant Chief of Staff for Intelligence, wrote the *Pueblo*'s first "training" mission. He figured it would help satisfy intelligence requests that had gone unfulfilled for more than two years. Also, the *Banner* needed a rest, which only the *Pueblo* could give her. She had been sailing through rough seas off Russia, China, and North Korea for almost three years without an overhaul. She looked beat; her crew felt beat.

The *Pueblo*, compared with the *Banner*, was a comfortable ship. The Navy was in such a hurry to put the *Banner* to work that it had welded a twelve-by-seven-foot box on the aft deck to house some of the extra men needed for ferreting. The men had to go out into the open to reach the head in the other part of the ship. But there was no time to worry about habitability. With the *Pueblo*, there was. Berthing for both officers and crew was more commodious. In addition, the *Pueblo*'s electronic eyes and ears were better, an integrated system compared with the box of intelligence equipment installed on the *Banner*.

The draft Brookes wrote of the *Pueblo*'s orders called for her to leave Japan on January 8, 1968 and return to Yokosuka almost a month later, on February 4. She was to go northward, almost to the North Korean–Russian border, and then work her way back down North Korea's east coast, listening at likely spots of military activity. There should not be much risk in this dead-of-winter mission, Brookes thought. He passed his draft to Admiral Johnson. The *Pueblo* would be the Admiral's responsibility from the moment she put to sea on her mission until she returned to Yokosuka.

"I was very closely associated with all aspects of the planning for a specific mission," Johnson said when asked later how much authority he had had over this first mission of the *Pueblo*.

"I had never found it necessary to disapprove any proposal message on any of the sixteen missions with which I was involved. The security and safety of the AGERs on the high seas was a matter about which I was not too concerned. The reason for this is that the feasibility of this type of an operation is dependent to a large degree upon the safety provided to such a ship by the time-honored international recognition of freedom of the seas.

"Now this freedom of the seas had gone on for over 150 years. No United States vessel had ever been illegally seized on the high seas during this period of time. I would suggest that this is a very excellent precedence on which to base a decision in regard to safety of any individual ship.

"There were no forces assigned to me as Commander of Naval Forces in Japan for the protection of AGERs from illegal procedure in international waters. My concern was not the illegal procedure, but it was a possibility of inadvertently having problems in drifting into territorial water where the country concerned might try to board or take over the ship."

Admiral Johnson approved the *Pueblo*'s draft orders written by Brookes and sent them on up the chain of command, to the Commander in Chief of Pacific Forces, then on to the Joint Chiefs of Staff and the 303 Committee. The 303 Committee was also called the Senior Interdepartmental Group, or SIG, and included civilian representatives of the secretaries of State and Defense.

The Joint Chiefs of Staff—or their representatives, because the

Christmas season found some away from the Pentagon—and the 303 Committee approved the *Pueblo* mission on December 29. There was apparently no feeling of anxiety, so the approvals were routine. Yet in one place in the sprawling, disjointed federal establishment there was a premonition of danger to the *Pueblo*. That was in the National Security Agency, where an unheralded staff member was worried about the increasing belligerence of the North Koreans. His concern prompted Lieutenant General Marshall Carter, Director of the National Security Agency, to send a secret warning message to the Joint Chiefs of Staff the same day, December 29. In this, he set forth facts that challenged the "minimal risk" assessment of the *Pueblo* mission, noting the following:

. . . the North Korean Air Force has been extremely sensitive to peripheral reconnaissance flights in this area since early 1965. . . .

The North Korean Navy reacts to any Republic of Korea Navy vessel or Republic of Korea fishing vessel near the North Korean coast line. (This was emphasized on January 19, 1967, when a Republic of Korea Naval vessel was sunk by coast artillery.)

Internationally recognized boundaries as they relate to airborne activities are generally not honored by North Korea on the East Coast of Korea. But there is no [security deletion] evidence of provocative harassing activities by North Korean vessels beyond 12 nautical miles from the coast.

The above is provided to aid in evaluating the requirement for ship protective measures and is not intended to reflect adversely on CINCPACFLT deployment proposal.

However, it was indeed unusual for the NSA to send such a message to the Joint Chiefs of Staff. As it turned out, the warning never reached the right place for action. The staff of the Joint Chiefs received the message on December 29, let it sit until January 2, then transmitted it to the Commander in Chief for the Pacific, with an information copy to the Chief of Naval Operations, who never saw it. A House Armed Services subcommittee said, after looking into this situation:

"The handling of the NSA warning message by the Joint Reconnaissance Center, the Joint Chiefs of Staff, the Office of the Defense Intelligence Agency, the Office of the Commander in Chief Pacific,

64

and the Office of the Chief of Naval Operations is hardly reassuring. At best, it suggests an unfortunate coincidence of omission, at worst, it suggests the highest order of incompetence."

Therefore the *Pueblo* mission orders came back to Admiral Johnson's office in Yokosuka with all the required approvals. He decided against putting on alert any rescue ships or planes, which could go to the aid of the *Pueblo* if anything went wrong. He did not regard the signs of North Korean belligerence as storm flags for the *Pueblo*. Yet those danger signs included:

A sharp upsurge in North Korean probing across the demilitarized zone separating North and South Korea—thirty-seven incidents in 1966 and 445 in 1967, more than a tenfold increase;

Intensified North Korean naval activity, including the capture of twenty-five South Korean naval ships in the three months before the *Pueblo* mission was approved;

Shrill radio announcements warning that ships intruding into North Korean waters would be severely punished.

Admiral Johnson regarded the hostility of North Korea as a fact of the Cold War. He made no effort to plot its intensity with an eye to drawing conclusions about AGER operations. "I did not receive any specific information," he later said. "I was aware of the increase in the incidents in connection with the DMZ, and I was aware over the past year [1967] of certain actions that had been taken by the North Koreans." Shortly after the sinking of a South Korean ship in January 1967, he had sent the *Banner* to stay off Wonsan for a day and a half. "There was," he said, "no reaction whatsoever by the North. . . . I was aware a North Korean vessel fired at one of our reconnaissance planes. . . . But in view of our experience at sea [with the *Banner*] this did not indicate to me any necessitative change in the risk evaluation."

With the paperwork approved for the mission, Admiral Johnson inspected the *Pueblo* on January 4. Because of the Israeli attack on the unarmed U.S.S. *Liberty* in 1967, the Chief of Naval Operations had ordered two fifty-caliber guns installed on the *Pueblo*— an installation done at the last minute in Yokosuka. The Israelis had changed the rules of the game for ferret ships. The American

Navy reacted quickly concerning guns, but did not rethink the whole concept of the AGER program to the point of changing orders for ferret skippers to follow. Admiral Johnson, certainly, made it clear to Commander Bucher that it should be business as usual out there at sea. The guns were to be ignored; they could even be stored below. The Admiral later explained his concern about the guns on the *Pueblo* this way:

"I was particularly desirous that the ships keep their guns covered or stowed near the location of the stands in order not to elicit too much interest or to disclose their presence unnecessarily. . . . I was not in favor of arming the AGERs. . . . I was concerned about the provocative nature of the weapons. . . . On several missions the *Banner* had been closed by unfriendly forces. They had pointed their guns at the *Banner*. I was not particularly happy about the thought of my captains having armament of their own; having them manned—pointing back in return—and thereby creating the exact opposite of the situation I wanted, which was to have the ships operate safely on the high seas. . . . I mentioned to Commander Bucher my desire that these guns be kept covered until it was necessary that he use them. . . . My over-all impression of the ship was favorable. I formed an excellent opinion of Commander Bucher."

Favorably impressed with the Skipper and the ship, Johnson cleared us for our first mission. The *Pueblo* left Yokosuka for Sasebo, Japan, on January 5, with a temporary set of sailing orders to authorize her to leave port. The sailing orders for the mission were radioed to us on January 6—after some communications problems. Here are the mission's sailing orders, with abbreviations spelled out and explanatory matter in brackets:

ICHTHYIC ONE SAILING ORDER
A. Commander, Task Force 96 [Rear Admiral Frank L. Johnson] Operation Order 301-68 NOTAL [not to all]. [This was the umbrella set of orders—still classified—which set forth the reporting instructions, methods of communications to be used, and some specific instructions about the mission off North Korea. The ICHTHYIC ONE sailing order was designed to provide a set of special instructions for this particular mission, as distinguished from the more general guidance in 301-68].

B. Pacific Command Electronics Intelligence Center 210734 Z [time] December 1967 PASEP NOTAL.

C. Commander in Chief Pacific Fleet Instructions 003120.24A. [These classified instructions—which the North Koreans captured—detailed, country by country, how close to Communist shores American ships could go. One part states that "patrols to the three mile limit off North Korea are authorized." The North Koreans later used the phrase "three mile limit" to prove that the *Pueblo* had been ordered to violate their territorial waters, ignoring the specific orders to stay at least thirteen miles from North Korean land. The same instructions said the skipper of an American ship being harassed should brazen it out, even if this meant steaming toward the harasser's land. The lightly armed *Pueblo,* under these instructions, was supposed to act brave if harassed but not be provocative.]

D. Commander in Chief Pacific Fleet Instructions 03100.3D. [This was part of the same set of instructions. They were not declassified either.]

1. ICHTHYIC ONE formerly Pinkroot One. [These were the present and former code names of the *Pueblo*'s eavesdropping operations. The letters A through D above told the *Pueblo* that those instructions were to be followed as well as the ones coming next.]

2. Depart Sasebo Japan when ready for sea about 8 January 1968. Check out of movement report system and proceed via Tsushima Straits to arrive operating area Mars about 10 January.

3. Attempt to avoid detection by Soviet naval units while proceeding operating area Mars.

4. Upon arrival Mars, conduct Ichthyic operations in accordance with provisions Reference A [Operation Order 301-68].

A. Operate operating areas Mars, Venus and Pluto, concentrating efforts area (or areas) which appear most lucrative.

B. Depart operating areas 27 January and if not under surveillance, maintain strict emission control condition. [This condition consists of avoiding the use of radio and radar, in this case so their signals could not be intercepted by Communist forces—an interception that would give away the *Pueblo*'s presence and pinpoint its position; and enable North Korea to control its own emissions, which the *Pueblo* wanted to record in the cat-and-mouse game of electronic intelligence.] Proceed south along Korean coast to vicinity Tsushima Straits.

C. Intercept and conduct surveillance of Soviet naval units operating Tsushima Straits. [This was a leaf out of the Soviet book. The Russians had been monitoring American fleet movements for years with their fishing "trawlers."]

D. Terminate surveillance to arrive Sasebo 4 February 1968. Earlier departure authorized to ensure ten percent on-board fuel upon arrival Sasebo.

5. Operating areas defined as follows:

A. East/west boundaries all areas are contiguous to Korean Communist coast extending from thirteen nautical miles closest point of approach to land mass/off-shore islands seaward to sixty nautical miles. [In other words, go no closer than thirteen nautical miles to any North Korean land—island or coastal.]

B. North/south boundaries [expressed in latitude] are:

Mars, 40-00N4 to 39-00N2;

Venus, 41-00N5 to 40-00N4;

Pluto, 42-00N6 to 41-00N5.

6. Special instructions:

A. Collect electronic intelligence in accordance with provisions Reference B, on not to interfere basis with basic mission. [Reference B provided guidance for collecting electronic intelligence that would be most useful to the Pacific Command's Electronic Center, the clearing-house for electronic information in the Pacific. This command supplied the *Pueblo* with charts of known North Korean radio and radar centers, airfields, and naval bases. The *Pueblo* was to check these locations by determining if the signals she picked up matched the type and source locations indicated on the material prepared on the basis of other ELINT missions, by both ships and aircraft.]

B. Closest point of approach to Korean Communist/Soviet land mass/off-shore islands will be thirteen nautical miles.

C. Upon establishing firm contact with Soviet naval units, break emission control and transmit daily situation report. [In other words, if the Russians discover you are there, transmit lots of information, so they will know from their intercepts that the U.S. is doing the same kind of electronic fishing with this species of "trawler."]

D. Operate at least five hundred yards [from Soviet units] as necessary for visual/photo coverage. [This is close quarters on the open ocean. My guess is that the United States wanted the Russians to get a good look at the *Pueblo* before her mission was over and conclude that the Americans were serious about surveying the Soviet fleet. The Soviets, of course, would take their own pictures of the *Pueblo,* as they had of the *Banner.* The Kremlin would know the United States had at least two ferret ships in the western Pacific; that the *Banner* was not one of a kind. The concept of "parity"—each side capable of doing the same thing as the other—would thus be established firmly by the *Pueblo.*]

E. Do not interfere with Soviet exercises but maintain a position on the periphery for observation purposes. [The *Pueblo* would thus help to write the book of etiquette for seagoing snoopers. The Navy hoped the Russians would learn from it and do likewise, discontinuing the game of chicken they had been playing too often for either nation's safety. Who wanted to go to war over scraped fenders?]

F. If unable to establish or gain contact with Soviet units within twenty-four hours arrival Tsushima Straits area, advise originator immediate precedence. [This was another expression of eagerness to have the Soviets spot the *Pueblo*.]

G. Provisions Reference C apply regarding rules of engagement. [This meant that the dictums in 003120.24A, about brazening it out if harassed, applied.] Reference D applies regarding conduct in event of harassment or intimidation by foreign units.

H. Installed defense armament [the two fifty-caliber machine guns, one on the bow and the second on the stern] should be stowed or covered in such a manner as to not elicit unusual interest from surveying/surveyed unit(s). Employ only in cases where threat to survival is obvious. [Bucher elected to cover the mounted guns.]

With these orders in hand and with two Marine translators who had come aboard at the last minute, protesting they could not speak Korean fluently, the ship plied its way from Yokosuka to Sasebo—the last stop before going on her first Cold War mission.

Sasebo is one of those gray port towns dotted with cheap, neon-lit bars and listless bar girls who speed the flow of money out of sailors' pockets. The *Pueblo* officers spent the last night ashore in a graceless Japanese club. We were dressed in civilian clothes and did a lot of shouting and drinking. I left the bar early and went back to the ship to sleep. Captain Bucher stayed out all night.

"Jesus Christ," he said as he shook me awake upon returning to the ship at 5:45 A.M., "get up. We're all ready to go, Skip?"

I went through the checklist up on the bridge and decided we were. The *Pueblo*'s lines were slipped off the chocks at six o'clock. Her bow took the swells in the channel easily and then swung northeast, toward the Tsushima Strait. At 9:00 that morning of January 11, 1968, the order came from the bridge to start keeping the log of this, the first and only, patrol of the U.S.S. *Pueblo*, AGER-2.

That same day, North Korea sent out a broadcast in English

from Pyongyang stating: "The U.S. imperialist aggressor troops again dispatched from early this morning hundreds of fishing and spy boats disguised as fishing boats into the coastal waters of our side off the eastern coast to perpetrate hostile acts. This noon our naval ships on patrol duty on the spot detained the vessels involved in the hostile acts. As long as the U.S. imperialist aggressor troops conduct reconnaissance by sending spy boats, our naval ships will continue to take determined countermeasures."

The *Pueblo* sailed on toward North Korea.

My Longest Day

"It's 0315, Mr. Schumacher. Hey, Mr. Schumacher." I could foggily hear a voice in the dark. "Time to get up, sir."

I looked into the red-lensed flashlight Quartermaster Third Class Alvin H. Plucker was shining in my eyes.

"You awake, sir?"

"Yeah. Okay, Plucker. Thank you." I lay back against the warm, comfortable pillow as Plucker left to rouse the rest of the next watch.

Time to get up. It always seemed to be time to get up on this ship. In disgust, I closed my eyes. But then, realizing the futility of even this momentary escape, I forced them open and contemplated my next few hours of January 23, 1968. My roommate, Tim Harris, who slept in the berth above me, would be just finishing his watch in the black cold of the bridge. At least my stint, the 0400 to 0800 morning watch, wouldn't be as bad as his. But none of the watches out here had been very exciting.

In fact, I reflected, this whole trip had been pretty unproductive. We had been twelve days out of Sasebo now, and had picked up nothing new or interesting for the intelligence boys back in Japan and Honolulu. Well, maybe they could learn something from the inactivity; at least they would know that the Koreans were smart enough not to chase around in the Northern Japanese Sea in the dead of winter.

I had to agree with what the Captain had put down in the space reserved for "Commanding Officer's Comments" in one of our daily narrative reports. He stated categorically that the mission had been a worthless exercise. He referred to it, in Navy language, as "unproductive" and a "poor utilization of the platform," which could be translated as "stupid" and a "waste of the taxpayers' money." I wondered how the staffs who had put together this mission would like reading that. One thing about the Skipper, though, was that if he had a place on a Navy form to put down his opinion, he put it down straight. 'Well, they asked me, damn it, didn't they?" he would say.

Keeping the narrative report was one of the things I had been doing for the past twelve days. It, like everything else about this mission, was dull. The first night of lying to, dead in the water, was off Chongjin. I put down in the narrative that we saw, but were unable to identify, a couple of merchant ships. The CT's were not doing any better. They would intercept and record radar signals, dutifully log them in, report them, and then the ship would drift to another spot. They would intercept the same signal and go through the whole process again. Intercepting the same radar signal from two different points theoretically located the sending radar station. It was merely a matter of drawing the lines on a chart from the ship back to the source. The lines would cross where the radar station was located. Most of the time, though, the equipment had not been accurate, and the lines would not cross. When they did, they inevitably fell on a site the Navy had long known about anyway. It had already been accurately plotted on the charts provided for our mission. Sailboat skippers do the same kind of plotting, subject to the same limitations, when they are trying to fix their positions off a visible coast. We just had fancier equipment and worked with radar antennas and radio direction finders instead of the peloruses or trusty thumbs weekend sailors used.

The Captain told our two oceanographers, for lack of anything better to do, to go ahead and conduct as much oceanographic research as their time permitted. Dunnie Richard Tuck, Jr., thirty, a lanky Virginia charm boy, who claimed many feminine conquests, was our chief oceanographer. Friar Tuck, as we called him, was a civilian, with a warm sense of humor, which dissolved us all when he was in form. His assistant aboard and liberty companion ashore was Harry Iredale III, also a civilian. Harry, small but gutsy, was a good counterpart to Friar; he was younger—twenty-four—and more serious. Sent out by the Naval Oceanographic Center, in Washington, they had joined the *Pueblo* about five days before we left Yokosuka.

Friar and Harry had mapped out some forty different locations along our route where they would like to take water samples. They also wanted to record water temperatures by dragging a fancy thermometer behind the ship. However, these oceanographic stations, our briefers had informed us, did not have to be covered by the *Pueblo*. They were to be included only if we had time. As things were turning out, we had time, plenty of time.

The Captain at sea was a much quieter man than the Captain ashore. He spent a lot of time reading and studying in his cabin while we were looking and listening. After he had plowed through the professional literature—publications, directives, related operations orders, and so on—he spent time with his favorite authors—Robert Service, Shakespeare, and William F. Buckley, Jr. He read voraciously, not in any particular area, but here and there, in history, biography, literature, political science. He'd try anything. He once told me he had read Durrell's *Alexandria Quartet* in just two days, because his skipper at that time had recommended it. A favorite on the trip to Japan had been Mark Twain's *Letters from the Earth,* good ribald finger-poking at some of the mores and morals of the human animal.

But, though submerged most of the time, the Captain's old fun-loving, keep-em-off-guard, do-what-you-can-get-away-with spirit was still there. When we first started accumulating ice, about four or five days out of Sasebo—and too much ice on the already top-heavy *Pueblo* could cause her to capsize—he called out all crew members who were not on watch to help remove it. Of course he went out there himself, wooden mallet in hand, to knock off ice. As the work came to a close, he egged the men into a snowball fight. He saw it as a chance to re-establish rapport with his crew and to break the monotony of the rough winter voyage. It was a lot of fun.

That was the Captain at his best—get the job done, then have

73

some fun, with everybody welcome. He loved his ship and his crew. He lived his job to the fullest, acutely aware of both the onerous responsibilities and the capricious freedom of his position. Yet he also demanded excellence from his crew.

One cold, gray morning I was on watch on the bridge as we were lying to, taking more water samples and looking and listening with our electronic eyes and ears. The Captain, in his shirt sleeves and shower slippers, came bounding up the ladder. Something was up, something bad. All the danger signs were there: teeth grinding, fists clenched, eyes full of fire.

Surprised by his sudden appearance on the bridge, I saluted and asked: "What's up, Captain?"

"Aw, that damn ship's office," he replied in a voice filled with fury and frustration. "I'm so damn mad I need to cool off. If I saw him now, I'd probably break his neck."

The him, I knew, was the Executive Officer. He was responsible for the ship's paperwork, and the system for it hadn't improved any since San Diego. All the officers knew that. Just how bad it was we weren't sure.

"Go on down and eat, Skip," he said. "If I'm going to be up here, I might as well drive."

I had never seen the Captain this angry before, and it seemed clear to me that whatever it was he had found out had destroyed any chance of a reconciliation between him and Murphy. Scuttlebutt later was that the XO was down in his cabin writing out his letter of resignation.

But the Captain wasn't through. He unburdened himself to me in hot bursts. "Jesus, I've never seen such a mess. Hell, Canales never even sent off the security forms. None of these guys are cleared for anything. They could have our necks on that. Christ, I just don't know what he's been doing down there. I found Gene's fitness report in one of the drawers—signed and everything. It had never been mailed. And reports, letters . . . Christ, maybe I ought to scrub the whole thing and head back to Sasebo. I've never seen anything so screwed up in my life."

I left the bridge and headed below. There wasn't much a junior

74

officer could say to his captain in a situation like this. There wasn't much anyone could say. He had to be left alone.

He finally worked out an accommodation, letting Murphy know just how he felt and telling Yeoman First Class Armando M. Canales just where he stood. He avoided the XO as much as possible, dealt with him on a strictly professional basis, kept his plans to himself.

One indication that the worst of the Captain's temper storm had passed came a couple of days later when he bolted out of the wardroom right after lunch and started speaking, in a rush, over the 1 MC, the loud-speaker reserved for alarms, all-hands orders, and other serious matters. He announced that Seaman Edward S. Russell was hereby appointed the ship's "carpetbagger"; that he would make the rounds selling candy bars. Nobody—not even Russell or Murphy—knew the announcement was coming. Why the Captain felt compelled to charge up the bridge to announce this scheme, I'll never know. It was a good idea, as it turned out, but the way he did it was peculiarly Bucher. Any money made was to be used to build up the ship's recreation fund. From that afternoon on, we would hear periodically over the 1 MC: "Now the Carpetbagger is making his rounds."

Such had been the mission so far. Today—January 23—would be our thirteenth day out. I gave in to the inevitable and readied myself for the morning watch. I reached up to flick on the tube of fluorescent light mounted on the bulkhead above my head and took a quick look at my watch. It was 0325. I'd better get moving. My day-in, day-out routine had settled down to a familiar pattern: stand the morning watch from 0400 to 0800; have breakfast in the wardroom; from 0900 to 1130 type the report of the previous day's patrol and go over it with the Skipper; eat lunch; take an afternoon nap or watch a movie in the wardroom or read in my cabin; go back on watch from 1600 to 2000; eat late dinner in the wardroom; sleep until Plucker or another came at 0315 to start the cycle all over again.

It was a routine life of watch, eat, sleep, and watch. The *Pueblo* was a loner. We had no admiral giving us speeches on the fantail as flags snapped in the breeze. We dressed for the loner role. And to fit in with it, the Captain had long ago selected the ship's nickname: The Lonely Bull. He chose it because he knew we were going to do a lonely job. But he looked upon the ship and himself as tough enough for it. He also liked Herb Alpert's record "The Lonely Bull."

Gingerly I swung my legs out and onto the cold tile floor. The light illuminated this "home away from home" for Tim and me: an eight-by-ten-foot L-shaped cranny painted standard Navy gray, with a gray metal desk, wardrobe built into one wall, lockers along the other wall, storage cabinets and more lockers skillfully tucked into various nooks, a medium-brown leatherette-covered desk chair. It was utilitarian and dull—fitting decor for the mission. But the room also had one very comfortable double-decker berth, a washbasin, head, and shower—really all we needed to feel civilized.

I smiled as I thought about how this room had come apart when we were in rough water. A lot of things you think are secure aren't when a ship is thirty-five or forty degrees off center. This was always the bane of the OOD's. Sometimes rolling couldn't be avoided, but if it could, God help you for letting it happen.

In fairness, I suppose, I must say that I performed the most devastating and unexpected roll of the trip. It happened about the fourth day out. The watch had started off calmly enough, with moderate seas but a freshening breeze. The CT's were up on the forward mast working on some of their gear. I kept the ship heading into the seas at slow speed to make it as smooth for them as possible. Their jobs took nearly all of my 0800 to 1200 watch. As they scurried below, into the warmth, the Captain, fearing we were too close to North Korea, ordered me to reverse course. Lunch was being served. The cooks had set out large bins of spaghetti just as I ordered left full rudder. I immediately realized that the ocean was rougher than I had calculated. I yelled down the voice tube to pass the word "Stand by for heavy rolls." The rudder had already been swung over. It was too late to get back on course.

The ship went halfway through the turn, then stopped. She wouldn't go any farther. She stood broadside to the heavy seas, rolling back and forth a good forty degrees. The spaghetti flew all over. Tim Harris sailed—chair, plate, and all—into the wardroom passageway on his side. The Captain's brand-new commander's hat shot out of his stateroom, followed by his personal library of thirty to forty books, seven years' worth of *Playboy* magazines, and his coin collection of some hundred pieces. His hat crumpled. It was too ruined to look salty.

I knew I was doing something wrong. I told the helmsman to reverse his course and head us into the seas.

"What the hell's going on up there, Skip?" the CO screamed at me over the intercom.

"Trying to come around, Captain. It's a little worse up here than I thought. I'm getting it straightened out now."

"You realize you just cost us our lunch?"

"Yes, sir."

"Well, let me know before you try that maneuver again, huh?"

"Yes, sir, will do."

About ten minutes later the Captain came to the bridge. He explained clearly how the maneuver should have been done. Then, in about twenty seconds, he did it, mentioning, rather casually, that, in addition to the normal "scrambled eggs" (the gold braid on his hat) from the Navy, he now had a couple of strands of spaghetti from me.

The crew and the officers ate cold cuts and crushed potato chips. I, properly chagrined, ate a bag of peanuts in my room.

Getting dressed for the morning watch had become a ritual for me. Honeycomb-weave long underwear went over Navy skivvies; then came khaki trousers, white turtleneck sweater (in deference, I felt, to my German ancestry), and khaki shirt. Finally, I would put on the riding boots I had bought on a quick vacation trip to Arizona the previous spring. They had heavy heels of hard leather, and made me sound like a guy with two peg legs when I clumped over the steel decks of the *Pueblo*. In this cold weather I would have donned a pair of arctic thermal boots, except that I planned to spend the better part of this watch in the heated pilothouse. Last, I slung on my jacket of green nylon and adjusted my dark-blue baseball cap on my head. A Japanese tailor had sewn my name, my job, and a fierce-looking eagle (which looked more like a buzzard) on the cap in gold braid. Thus suited up for the cold, and fortified with a thermos bottle of hot but rotten coffee, I headed up to the pilothouse.

"I'm ready to relieve you, sir," I said with a salute to Tim. The Captain—in trying to make the *Pueblo* as much like a submarine as possible—wanted us to run the ship from the flying bridge on the open deck. We nearly froze driving the ship from there on the trip from San Diego to Yokosuka. At Yokosuka, the Captain had had the navy yard add a windscreen. The screen helped, but it was still cold standing out in the open. So he relented off North Korea to the point of letting us run the ship from the pilothouse, where the wheel and the navigation and communications controls were located —plus heat. The Captain liked to stay out there in the cold, the old submariner on his own little conning tower; the rest of us preferred the closed-in pilothouse.

Tim filled me in on his watch. There had been nothing extraordinary except for an orange flare he had seen go off in the black night several hundred yards from the ship. He had also seen some running lights, but had not been able to make out the ships that went with them. He had notified the Captain of the sightings. We knew the North Koreans had spotted us. The previous day, two of their fishing trawlers, *Rice Paddy* and *Rice Paddy I*, had circled us slowly and then sailed off toward Wonsan. We had been drifting off Wonsan all night as well as during the previous day.

The *Rice Paddy* twins had circled us at about 3:30 that Monday afternoon, January 22. The Captain had directed me to prepare the radio situation report advising COMNAVFORJAPAN in Yokosuka that we had been detected. We were going to break our radio silence for the first time since sailing from Sasebo. The Captain, Steve, Murphy, and I had gone over the report in great detail. We studied the ship photographer's pictures of *Rice Paddy* and *Rice Paddy I* to make sure our description would be precise. Finally, about 10:00 P.M. that Monday night, we were all satisfied with the description. But we had not been able to get it to Japan. The radio-

78

man had been trying to establish secure communications since 6:00 P.M. I found out from Tim when I took over the watch Tuesday morning that we still had not gotten through to Japan.

Communications had been a problem on the *Pueblo* ever since she had been commissioned. Because of the uniqueness of our operations, we used special code lists and different procedures. The *Banner* had also experienced great difficulty in this area. We had held a conference in Japan with our shore commanders before we left to try to establish co-ordinated procedures.

First, we had decided to maintain communications silence until we had something important to report. We could receive messages, however. We listened on two or three circuits for incoming messages. When we had a message to transmit, we would first call Japan on an insecure—or open—CW (continuous wave, or Morse code) frequency and ask them to "open circuit 21P." The Navy radioman in Japan would know, by this unique signal, that it was the *Pueblo* calling. He would radio us on one of the circuits to which we were listening that he was ready to receive and would suggest a frequency. We could then transmit by teletypewriter, which was much faster and, through an electronic coding system, absolutely secure.

Second, we had agreed to keep a complete log of our communications difficulties at sea. Since we all considered this first mission a shakedown cruise, we felt we would have time to correct communications problems before subsequent missions.

Third, it had been agreed that, in an extreme emergency, we could transmit on the Pacific Fleet High Command net (HICOM). Our HICOM radio signals, as insecure as a radio-telephone, could be heard by anybody in range. This was the fastest method.

And, finally, it had been decided to assign to the *Pueblo* one extra man, who understood both the ship and the shore end of communications. This was CT1 Don E. Bailey, a happy-go-lucky country boy, who had suggested the extra billet, then volunteered to fill it.

I reviewed these communications options in my mind as I organized myself on the bridge for the morning watch. Looking over the chart kept of the ship's movements before I took over, I

79

saw that the *Pueblo* was drifting south and east. That was good. I didn't want to be drifting in toward the North Korean shore in the dark. I plotted a couple of loran fixes. We were a good eighteen to twenty miles from the nearest land. That meant the biggest worry was still the lack of communication with Japan.

Radioman Second Class Lee R. Hayes, who had been transferred to the *Pueblo* the day before we left Yokosuka, was standing by in the radio shack at the rear of the pilothouse setting up the transmitters. He also manned the CW circuit with Japan. "No luck," he reported when I asked about his success. "We can read Japan, but they can't read us."

That made sense. Japan had much more powerful transmitters than we had. But we had to find a way to get through. Anxious, I phoned down to the SOD Hut and spoke to Bailey. He said the CT's down there had tried six or seven frequencies that Japan recommended, but, so far, they had had no luck. He said there was a lot of static on the recommended frequencies. He thought he could get through once the sun was up, which would reduce the atmospheric oddities. The early-morning hours, from about 0400 to 0600, when the sun is just coming up over the horizon, are always difficult times to try to communicate. Bailey said he would stay with it. I asked him to keep me informed.

I turned my attention to the logs spread out on the pilothouse chart desk. The previous day's activity had created a couple of pages of entries. They would have to be collated and put into a logical format for the Captain's narrative report. That meant no time for my afternoon nap.

My morning watch wore on uneventfully, the communications a gnawing worry, but no activity on the black sea outside to be concerned about.

The day dawned slowly in the Sea of Japan. It was cold. As the sky slowly lightened in the east, I could see light fog filtering the morning light. The sea was relatively calm, with slow gentle swells untouched by wind. I had not been able to see the shore by 7:00 A.M., the hour for calling the Captain in his cabin.

"Good morning, Captain," I said over the pilothouse phone connected with his cabin. "It's 0700, and everything is secure."

"All right," Bucher replied sleepily. "Very well. Thank you."

Fifteen minutes later, Lacy reported to the pilothouse to relieve me. He was not due until 0745.

"Hey," I said, "you're early, Gene. Go get yourself some coffee."

"No, I'm ready to go."

That was Gene—always ready to go. I suspect he thought that taking this troublesome old ship, with all its problems, out into the winter cold off North Korea and going nowhere was stupid. But if it was his watch, he figured he might as well let the poor guy up there get off a little early. All the OOD's naturally admired and liked Gene for this.

Briefly I filled him in on what had happened during my watch—in a word, nothing. I told him about the communications difficulties, and then went over the chart with him.

"You're not sure where you are, are you?" Gene said good-humoredly.

"Of course, dummy," I answered. "In the Sea of Japan. Anyway, don't sweat it. We've been drifting in the right direction, and Law's on his way up to take the morning posit."

"All right," Gene replied. "I guess there's nothing else I can nail you with. I relieve you."

With that I left the bridge to Lacy. The final watch chore, insisted upon by the Captain, was to make a walking tour of the ship, inspecting for leaks or loose gear or anything else that looked hazardous. That completed, I went to the wardroom for breakfast.

I had just sat down when the Captain, dressed in a T shirt, khaki trousers, and shower slippers, shuffled in, poured himself a cup of coffee, yelled for the steward, and mumbled a good morning. He ordered eggs and chipped beef. I filled him in on the night's inactivities. *Rice Paddy* and *Rice Paddy I* had not returned. No one seemed much interested in us.

The Captain thought my report over while chewing on a piece of toast. "Draft up a message, Skip, saying we consider the incident closed and that we're returning to EMCON [Emission Control]. Also, while you're at it, check on the communications. Christ, I can't figure out what the hell the trouble is, but I don't trust those goddamn electronic machines. Tell 'em to go off-line if they can't get through in an hour." This meant to encrypt the messages separately and send them by CW.

Just before I left the wardroom, word came down from the bridge that we had drifted a good twenty-five miles from the nearest land, somewhere south of Wonsan.

"Jesus Christ, how the hell did we manage to get so far out?" the Captain asked the wardroom at large. Then, in one of those quick decisions that can change the course of history, he told the bridge, over the wardroom phone, "Let's get back in there!"

I could hear the twin diesel engines start up as I walked toward the SOD Hut. I punched the panel of black buttons on the door to gain entrance. CT2 Donald R. McClarren was on watch inside, up to his neck in work. I riffled through the messages we had received during the night from Japan while we attempted to establish communications. Then I sat down in front of one of the receivers and listened. The only frequency that sounded clear was 9881 kilocycles. All the others were still blocked with static.

I phoned to Hayes up in the radio shack and told him to signal Japan by Morse code that we would be sending on 9881. This was not in line with the established procedures. But we had tried some six or seven frequencies over the past twelve hours or so with no success, which was not exactly the instant communication we should have had. The plan worked out on shore was not getting us through at sea. I figured: What the hell! Here's a good frequency. Let them sweat tuning it in.

"Open channel 21P on 9881," Hayes tapped out like a nineteenth-century railroad man on this ship pregnant with twentieth-century communications equipment. He called me back on the phone linked to the crypto room, where I was sitting by a teletype. "They rogered for it, sir," he reported, "and told me to stand by."

I punched out the *Pueblo*'s call sign, NGVE, on the teletype paper tape, along with a few other requests in a communications shorthand: how were they reading us, signal strength, et cetera. I fed the tape into the machine and waited for a response to type itself out in front of me on the teletype machine. Nothing came.

82

I tried a few more times. Still nothing. It was nearing 0900, and I had other work to do. I turned the teletype machine back over to the radioman and told him to keep trying. My big chance to be a supercommunicator had gone.

I went to my room, drafted the Captain's latest message, sent it out for release, and then, after gathering up the various logbooks from the previous day's activities, spent the rest of the morning working on the ship's narrative report. About 10:50 A.M., Steve Harris stopped by to tell me that his operators had finally broken through to Japan. It had taken fourteen hours. Both Steve and I were at a loss to explain why. We had anticipated lousy communications; now we had documented proof. We would come down hard on this problem in our patrol report, in the hope that the situation would be resolved before our next patrol.

I resumed typing the narrative report of the previous twenty-four hours. While I was doing this, an order I had never heard before came over the 1 MC speaker mounted in the passageway outside my door.

"Now, Mr. Schumacher," the monotone voice said, "lay up to the bridge on the double."

I swung out of the chair and grabbed my cowboy boots. My watch said 11:54. As I grabbed my jacket on the way out, the speaker buzzed again.

"Now, Photographer's Mate First Mack, lay up to the bridge on the double. Photographer's Mate First Mack, lay up to the bridge on the double."

Whatever was happening on the bridge, the Captain wanted help with identification and photography—right away.

"Skip," the Captain asked me as I scrambled up the ladder to the flying bridge, "what do you make of this?" Still in his shower slippers and thin khaki shirt, he was looking through the Big Eyes, the high-powered binoculars mounted on the deck. He stepped aside and motioned for me to take a look.

"Looks like a patrol craft," I said. "Let me check the pub."

The Captain turned to me. "I've got the one you're looking for down in my cabin. It's on my rack. You'd better get it."

I dashed below, found the book, and returned to the flying bridge with it. I was pretty familiar with the contents of this special manual on the North Korean Navy and quickly located the section on patrol craft. Putting the book on the small hooded desk provided for the signalman on the flying bridge, I thumbed through the photographs. The Captain and Quartermaster First Class Charles B. Law, who had the watch, crowded around. The three of us were looking for the picture of the ship speeding toward us. We were approximately sixteen miles from the nearest land, south of Wonsan. We were lying dead in the water, with engines off, in our listening mode.

"What's that?" Bucher said, pointing to one of the pictures. "I think it's this one."

"SO-1 submarine chaser," I replied. "Yeah, that's it. What do you think, Law?"

"I agree, sir. That's definitely it."

The three of us studied the port side of the subchaser as it bore down on us. It was a trim craft, about 130 feet long, armed with a fifty-seven-millimeter cannon forward of the bridge, another cannon aft, and several machine guns around the bridge. It had a short mast, with a domed radar on top. The North Korean ensign snapped smartly as she sped on. She bore the number 35 on her bow. CT 1 Michael T. Barrett and CT 3 Steven J. Robin joined us on the bridge. Photographer's Mate First Class Lawrence W. Mack snapped pictures of the SO-1 with the ship's Leicas; I shot pictures of it in color. The Captain sent below for his jacket and boots. He was dictating a minute-by-minute account of the activity into a tape recorder slung over his shoulder by a strap.

We were most intent on recording the presence of this ship in detail—our first encounter with anything military since leaving Sasebo. We were not worried. We had been told in our briefings to expect harassment. Our specific sailing orders had instructed us to play it cool. We were supposed to stand fast in any seagoing game of chicken. We had international law on our side as long as we stayed in international waters. The sense of our orders was that we should stay put, brazen it out, find out as much as we could. I figured that the *Pueblo* was about to make a name for itself in the intelligence community. Detailed color photographs of a usually elusive North Korean ship would be welcomed. And hard evidence—our pictures—of North Korean harassment in international waters would be exploitable by our government.

"Skip," the Captain said as he watched the subchaser start to circle us a second time, "start working up a harassment message."

Harassment had become of such interest to the Navy that a standard format had been devised to systemize the collection of information. I went into the pilothouse to get the forms and started filling them out back up on the bridge.

The Captain, meanwhile, ordered our oceanographers, Tuck and Iredale, to begin a Nansen cast, an oceanographic job. He also ordered international day shapes for hydrographic work—red ball, white diamond, red ball—hoisted to the yardarm. We thought the North Koreans were checking up on the report from the *Rice Paddy* boats about an oceanographic ship off the coast.

The subchaser, while circling us a second time, asked our nationality by signal flags. The Captain ordered the American flag raised in response. Down in the pilothouse, the Executive Officer requested and received permission to light off our radar, thus fixing our position as exactly 15.8 miles from the nearest land. The Captain then ordered Lacy to relieve Law as OOD, so that our best navigator could go to the pilothouse to double-check the ship's position. When Tim came up to the bridge, the Captain told him to write a running narrative of the events unfolding, including a plot of the subchaser's movements. I left the bridge to phone down to the crypto center to make sure the radioman stayed in communication with Japan; then I began typing the harassment message. Hayes, who had been up and on duty for the last twenty-four hours, raised his head from his desk to set up the transmitter on the HICOM circuit in case we needed it to back up messages sent out from the SOD Hut.

The subchaser started its third circle of our ship, this time hoisting signal flags of "Heave to or I will open fire." The Captain yelled down the voice tube to the pilothouse, "XO, what the hell does 'Heave to' mean?"

"It means to stop, sir," Murphy yelled back.

"But we are stopped, goddamn it. XO, look it up in the dictionary."

Murphy rushed below. He returned with a dictionary of nautical terms and read the definition into the voice tube. "Heave to," the book confirmed, did mean "stop."

The Captain signaled the North Koreans that he was in international waters.

The skipper of the subchaser did not seem to care. His ship, with helmeted, armed men, stood at general quarters. He trained his guns on our bridge. Unknown to us at the time, he, too, was radioing his headquarters. I learned afterward that a friendly party—not our own interpreters, who were not fluent enough to translate instantly the Korean radio chatter we heard—intercepted these communications. "The name of the target is GER-1-2. I judge it to be a reconnaissance ship. It is American guys. It does not appear that there are weapons, and it is a hydrographic mapping ship." The same friendly party also heard the subchaser commander give his position as nineteen miles off the coast. At the time, we were, as our double check showed, 15.8 miles from the nearest land, which was Ung Do Island, in Wonsan Harbor. This was well beyond the twelve-mile limit supposedly claimed by North Korea.

The Captain himself checked our position again by radar, and then checked my harassment message against the ship's position he had written down. He told me to inform Japan that our intentions were to stay in the area if feasible, otherwise to withdraw slowly to the northeast. He hoisted a new signal to the subchaser, stating that he intended to remain in the area now and depart the following day. He initialed the harassment message and sent me below to get it transmitted to Japan.

I took the message down to the SOD Hut at 12:50 P.M. and watched the CT on duty there, McClarren, quickly pound it out on the teletype. It took him two minutes to punch a paper tape and feed it into the teletype machine for mechanical transmission to Japan. So it was 12:52 when the machine started transmitting. Two minutes after that, Japan rogered for it. Our commanders on shore knew from that moment on that we were in a tight situation.

This first message was called Pinnacle I/JOPREP (Joint Operational Report) 3. "Pinnacle" identifies a dispatch as one of special interest to the Joint Chiefs of Staff, the National Military Command Center at the Pentagon, and the White House. We assigned a message transmission priority of Flash to this first harassment report. "Flash" meant that the message should be transmitted by the worldwide Navy communications system ahead of any other message. There was only one designation higher than Flash. Steve Harris reminded me of it in the SOD Hut. "We have a Critic tape already cut, Skip, if the Captain wants to wake up the President."

"All right, Steve, I'll tell him about it."

The "Critic" designation is supposed to assure speedier handling by opening a clear channel direct to the White House, the National Security Agency, and the Pentagon. It is a designation reserved for the most urgent crises.

When I returned to the bridge, I found the situation worse. Three torpedo boats were speeding toward us from Wonsan. We could see their rooster tails and then their profiles. We decided from the pub that they were Soviet-designed P-4's, which were eighty-two feet long and had a top speed of over fifty knots. The *Pueblo*'s pitiful top speed was 13.1 knots.

The subchaser kept circling as the PT boats closed in. The PT's trained forty-millimeter machine guns on us. They also had loaded torpedo tubes and carried helmeted troops armed with AK-47 automatic rifles.

Two MIG fighters screamed overhead, banking into wide circles off our starboard bow. One of them, the Captain told me, had fired a rocket way beyond us while I was below. A fourth torpedo boat came out from Wonsan to join the others. We could just make out a second subchaser on the horizon.

Against these four torpedo boats and two subchasers, the *Pueblo* had its two covered fifty-caliber machine guns, mounted on the open deck, with no protection for the gunners, and an issue of small arms consisting of ten forty-five-caliber Thompson machine guns, one thirty-caliber carbine, seven forty-five-caliber pistols, and fifty anti-swimmer grenades, which were too weak to do much good above water. We also had the military backing of the United States, we thought, and the protection afforded by the internationally recognized right to sail on the high seas.

We sat tight. The torpedo boats surrounded us as we lay dead in the water, swinging as close as fifty yards, like sharks getting ready to rip. I asked the Captain if he wanted the guns manned. He shook his head no. I felt when I asked the question that any men sent to the guns would be shot long before they reached them. The Captain evidently felt the same way. And, as he was to tell a highly critical board of admirals afterward, "Attempting to man my fifty-caliber guns and breaking out my forty-fives would only give them the excuse perhaps to turn what might be glossed over into a full-blown incident."

The Captain weighed his narrowing options. His orders said not to give way to Communist harassment. But he was responsible for the safety and security of his ship and crew, even if that might mean running away. He had to decide on his own when the Communist bluffing stopped and the real danger to his ship began.

The Captain told Lacy to start the main engines and to have the word passed to prepare for emergency destruction. I drafted a follow-up harassment message while Lacy and the Captain discussed the possibility of scuttling the ship. Gene said it would take too long—two and a half to three hours—and that we would lose all propulsive and electrical power in the process. He reminded the Captain that the depth was only thirty-five fathoms, shallow enough for divers to recover the ship and its contents. He said the water temperature was around thirty-six degrees, cold enough to kill a man within fifteen minutes. Scuttling did not look too inviting.

The subchaser raised a new flag signal. "Follow in my wake; I have pilot aboard." The Captain did not respond.

The subchaser halted about three hundred yards off our starboard bow. One of the four torpedo boats joined her, another took station three hundred yards off our starboard beam, and the third positioned itself three hundred yards off our starboard quarter. And then, to our surprise, seven or eight troopers jumped off the subchaser onto the torpedo boat pulled up alongside. They were dressed in blue quilted coats, and were armed with AK-47's. With these men standing on her bow, the torpedo boat threw over some rubber tires and woven ropes as bumpers, and started to back down toward our stern. The obvious intention was to have the men jump aboard us aft, where the two ships were the same height above water.

"I'll be damned if they're going to get away with that," the Captain shouted. "All ahead one-third." He asked Murphy for the best course to put maximum distance between the *Pueblo* and land. We sailed on that course, 080, the Captain trying to leave with as much dignity as possible by increasing the speed only gradually to full. He ordered up a new set of signal flags as we left our position: "Thank you for your consideration. I am departing the area." He hoped to confuse the Koreans, to buy time.

Flying that message was the only thing I would have done differently that day. I felt it was a bit flippant. I favored—but did not suggest—a more threatening signal, such as "My government has been notified; help is on the way." Maybe this would have given the North Koreans pause. I did not know at that time that the subchaser had already chosen his course of action, and at 1306 had radioed his superiors, saying, ". . . according to present instructions we will close down the radio, tie up the personnel, tow it and enter port at Wonsan. At present, we are on our way to boarding. We are coming in."

I added the boarding attempt to my next message, scribbling while the Captain pounded me on the back and shouted, "Get it going, get it going. Hurry up, goddamn it." I raced down to the SOD Hut. For the first time, I felt fearful about what would happen. I believed, and wanted to believe, that we were in for some rough harassment only. But a cold dread was building up inside me.

In the crypto room, where the men were sealed off and unable to see what was going on outside, my arrival caused great excitement. Steve rushed to me, grabbed my message, handed it to McClarren. The SOD Hut also seemed full of dread. Steve's face was drawn; his usual jovialness had disappeared.

"How's it look, Skip?" he asked.

"I don't know, Steve," I replied. "I think it looks pretty bad. I think we're into some pretty serious trouble."

"Well," Steve said, "we've got good communications with Japan. And we've prepared a Critic message. It's all ready to send."

"Okay, Steve. I'll keep you informed."

McClarren handed me a copy of the message as it was being transmitted to Japan. This was Pinnacle II, bringing everyone up to date, and it was quickly receipted for by Japan. It was 1:15 P.M.

When I returned to the bridge, it looked as if the Captain's withdrawal stratagem would work. We got up to full speed without the subchaser following us. It stayed astern. The torpedo boats, however, stayed with us, surrounding us in a diamond formation. The two lead boats crisscrossed back and forth about twenty yards in front of our bow. It was still the tense game of chicken, but still according to the rules. The torpedo boats could be just showing off, rubbing it in that they were forcing us to move farther out.

I looked back at the subchaser, now some 3,000 yards astern. A familiar signal was flying from the mast: "Heave to or I will open fire." The hell with that, I thought; we're getting out of here. I decided I'd better draft another message, and went down into the pilothouse to start typing it.

Shortly, I stepped out onto the wing of the pilothouse to bring myself, and the message, up to date. The four torpedo boats had now dispersed themselves into a wide diamond formation, and the subchaser had moved up to our port beam, his "heave to" signal flags still flying.

Hayes, sensing disaster, confronted me as I came back into the radio shack. In his arms was a load of secret message files. "Request permission to commence emergency destruction, sir," he said rather stiffly.

I had taken only two more steps toward Hayes when it happened: the whole foundation of the AGER program collapsed as the first salvo of fifty-seven-millimeter shells whammed into the *Pueblo* at 1:30 P.M. on January 23, 1968. Relying on international law had not worked. In that moment off Wonsan the *Pueblo* suddenly became as helpless as a turtle stripped of its shell. All the assumptions made about the safety of unarmed ships looking through the keyhole at a hostile nation blew up in that first salvo. The order makers back on

90

shore never expected a fight as long as we stayed in international waters. They were wrong. So we were alone. Nobody back at headquarters, with whom we had been in communication, told us to do anything different from what we had done. They never did. They were leaving it all up to Captain Bucher. Only much later would he be second-guessed, and recommended for trial by court-martial.

A shell from the first salvo, or the next one—I couldn't tell which —shattered the windows in the pilothouse. I hit the deck, along with the others, as glass zinged around like shrapnel. Boatswain's Mate Second Class Ronald L. Berens had been at the wheel when the shell hit. A veteran of the Navy's Market Time operation in Vietnam, he now reached up and continued to steer the ship from his position on the deck. "Jesus Christ, I'll take Vietnam over this," he said to me and Hayes.

Almost immediately, the word came down through the voice tube from the bridge, to be passed over the 1 MC: "Commence emergency destruction." I called the CT's in crypto and told them to send off their Critic message. They said it had already gone. Then I unlocked all the small safes we had on the bridge containing classified publications. Grabbing an armload of them, I headed for the ship's small incinerator on the starboard deck.

The Captain, who had been standing on the exposed flying bridge, was slightly wounded by that first salvo. He quickly left the bridge and came down into the pilothouse, as did Law, Robin, and Signalman Second Class Wendell G. Leach.

Robin and Barrett were at the incinerator, tearing pages out of secret publications, when I arrived there. They had not yet got a fire going. We felt naked out there on the starboard deck, trying to set fire to a bunch of papers.

"Jesus Christ," Barrett said. "They're shooting at us."

The three of us hit the deck, diving for what precious cover there was under the whaleboat. We could hear machine-gun bullets pinging into the *Pueblo*'s sides as the torpedo boats, following the sub-chaser's lead, opened up on us. With almost complete detachment, we watched the bullets work their way aft from the pilothouse, past the stack, and then over our heads and into the whaleboat.

91

Barrett looked over at me and said, "If this doesn't make a Christian out of you, nothing will."

Well, I thought, he's right. It's time for some quick prayers. It's also time to get moving. I pulled my cigarette lighter from my pocket and handed it to Robin. "Okay, Robin. Here, use my lighter." We were struggling for matter-of-factness, pretending those bullets were all for somebody else. "Yes, sir," Robin answered, and soon had the first fire going.

Maybe it was our smoke that caught the eye of the Korean machine gunners. A burst came at us, denting the stack just above where our heads had been before we hit the deck. Barrett caught a ricocheting bullet in the arm. "Hell of a way to get a Purple Heart," he muttered.

I got up and ran back inside the ship for another load of secret papers. I could hear the big fifty-seven-millimeter shells thudding into us with a ba-wham, ba-wham sound. But they were hitting above my level. The subchaser was concentrating on knocking out the command-and-control section of the ship—the open bridge. We were still racing—for the *Pueblo*—for the open sea. It looked more and more to me like we weren't going to make it.

The once orderly pilothouse was a shambles. The windows on the port side had been shattered, and broken glass lay over the decks. Some of the men had received small cuts from the glass. Everyone had picked himself up off the deck, though, and was moving to get our classified gear destroyed. Mack came up to me and asked for permission to throw his cameras and several thousand dollars' worth of other photography equipment into the sea. Resignedly, I gave my permission. He asked if I wanted my own Nikon camera equipment heaved overboard, too. "Yeah," I replied, "pitch it."

Tim—despite the shattered glass on the floor and the possibility of more to come—was back in the captain's chair on the port side of the pilothouse, by the window. He was still recording the movements of the North Korean ships. Hayes and Radioman Third Class Charles H. Crandell were clearing out the radio-shack files. Hayes also kept trying to get one of the transmitters set up on the HICOM circuit. He told me it would not load up with power, and his antenna could not be tuned to the proper frequency. He asked if he should set up another transmitter—we had three—on the HICOM circuit. I told him to set up the spare transmitter on the same frequency we were using to communicate with Japan. That way, I figured, if one transmitter went, the other would be immediately available.

Berens was back on his feet at the wheel. The Captain was standing over on the port side behind Tim, eying the subchaser. I told the Captain I was going to my stateroom to destroy classified papers. He agreed. We didn't discuss what was happening, or what was going to happen. We tried to think only of what had to be done. There was nothing much I could tell the Captain. He was on his own now. He had no one to turn to.

I found a smoky and confused scene below. Men were busy removing and burning in the incinerator the contents of the ship's safe. The door to the SOD Hut was open—highly irregular for that secret place. Papers were being burned on the deck of the passageway outside the door, and CT 2 Peter M. Langenberg was standing over the fire with a fire extinguisher. Other papers were being burned in wastebaskets in the main passageway. Smoke from these fires made it difficult to see and to breathe.

The main passageway was a poor place to have a fire. I grabbed one of the waste cans and carried it back to the starboard passageway, where it would be out of the way. Someone else grabbed another wastebasket to set it in a better place. Other crewmen threw fresh armloads of paper on the fire on the deck.

I headed for my room, where I unlocked my publications stowage lockers. I had quite a few operational files set up, all of the ship's secret instructions and publications, and a lot of other classified information. Systematically I started pulling these notebooks apart, one by one, and carrying their contents back to the fire.

While I was hunched over the fire, the 1 MC hummed on again. "Now hear this," came the order. "Set modified general quarters. All men who have stations topside are to remain inside the ship. All hands are cautioned to remain inside the ship."

General quarters, I thought, would affect engineering more than any other department. The men would man the damage-control system and be prepared to find, report, and fight small local fires touched off by the shelling. It was obvious from the order that the Captain did not want the guns manned. He had told the topside crew to stay below—away from the guns on the open deck. This meant our job was to burn and destroy as quickly as possible. It was 1:45 P.M.

On my second or third trip to the fire with secret papers, I ran into Steve coming out of his office. He looked distraught and shaken. For the first time, I realized the enormity of the destruction task facing him and his CT's.

"I don't know, Skip. The book says we can't throw this stuff over the side; it's too shallow. We'll just have to burn it."

I didn't have any real answer for that problem. Steve left me, saying he was going to ask the Captain if he could jettison the secret material in the SOD Hut. I continued with the burning of my own papers.

The fire had grown large from so many people feeding it. Burning the thick publications was not easy. They had to be crumpled page by page. That took time. I did not think we had much time.

I had got rid of the most sensitive material in my room and I was working on lower-classified stuff when I remembered the filing cabinet full of secret papers up forward. I remembered one whole drawer of top-secret intelligence objectives for the Pacific. What I had in my room was nowhere near as sensitive. I also remembered that, apart from an envelope in the Captain's stateroom safe which had the combinations inside, I was the only one who knew how to open the forward file cabinet. Shaken by my own forgetfulness, I headed for it.

I poked my head into the SOD Hut on the way. The scene was frantic. It had been transformed from the orderly laboratory of coolly professional workers tending humming machinery into a wild scene from Dante's *Inferno*. Two or three men were swinging sledge hammers at the equipment. Others were running back and forth to the fire in the passageway with stacks of instructions and manuals, clearing out desks and book racks. Back in the crypto section, Chief Ralph D. Bouden was systematically taking apart the encoding machines—a hard job to hurry. I asked him how it was going. He just shook his head negatively. Not even looking up, but with needle-

94

nose wire snippers working, he mumbled that he needed Ayling. He had already put some of the pieces out on the deck. In disgust, I smashed the delicate electronic wiring with the heel of my boot.

McClarren and Bailey were still on the circuit to Japan. They said they had received no new information. I left the SOD Hut to the CT's and headed for the files up forward. Seeing the equipment in the SOD Hut being so completely demolished upset me. Here was two or three million dollars' and countless man-hours' worth of equipment being smashed. If we ever do get back, I thought, there will be hell to pay for our hasty action.

Crandell and Seaman Robert W. Hill were already working up forward when I arrived. They were busy destroying and burning the communications files. I opened the safe over in the corner, pulled out an armload of files, and headed for the fire. Crandell and Hill followed.

While we worked down below, the Captain, up in the pilothouse, was faced with a dilemma. The subchaser kept pumping shells into the *Pueblo* as she ran for the open sea. One shell had gone through a window of the pilothouse and then out the opposite side. If its explosive, armor-piercing head had detonated from impact with the first window, everybody in the pilothouse would have been killed. Yet if he stopped the run, the North Koreans would come aboard before the crew had destroyed all the secret material on board. Would it be better to keep running and risk getting everybody killed and losing the ship? Or should he stop the ship in the hope that the Koreans would cease firing? He explained his command decision afterward to five admirals sitting in judgment on his actions that day.

"I was giving as much thought as I could to possibly aiding in the destruction of classified material or thinking if there were something else we could do—hoping that we could get the material destroyed before the ship was either sunk or we were all killed. I was giving thought to this matter when one of the fifty-seven-millimeter shells passed in the window just behind the chair that Ensign Harris was sitting in. . . . [The shell] came directly past Ensign Harris' head and out the windows just in front of him. . . . Other explosions were going on all around the ship from this particular salvo. . . . I ordered Leach, my signalman, to go to the bridge at approximately this time and raise the international signal for protest. . . . I still had the conn, and Mr. Lacy was still OOD. . . . Mr. Lacy asked if we should stop the ship—I presume in order to have the firing stopped in order that we might more successfully continue with our destruction. I nodded to Mr. Lacy, and Mr. Lacy rang up all stop. As the ship stopped, the firing stopped.

"We continued to destroy classified material. And I decided at that time that if the destruction of classified material was progressing successfully, and depending upon what their next action would be, I would surrender the ship.

"I felt that any further resistance on our part would only end up in a complete slaughter of the crew. I felt there was no point in showing any further resistance at this time. Both messages that I had sent out with respect to the situation had been receipted for, and I had been informed that they had been receipted for.

"I went below to my cabin at this time, gave Mr. Lacy the conn and told him to lay to and keep me informed, that I would be gone for only a couple of minutes. I went below to my cabin to see whether I had any classified material in my cabin and to see that it got destroyed." [His papers had been cleaned out, but, not wanting the Koreans to have them, he took his gift side arms from his cabin and threw them over the side.]

"I returned immediately to the bridge, and the SO-1 had closed to a range of approximately eight hundred yards, but had not closed any closer. He himself was lying to and had hoisted a signal which said, 'Follow me; I have a pilot aboard.'

"I ordered the ship ahead one-third and I put the rudder over to about five degrees in order to make a slow turn and in order to follow him in. I had decided at this time, providing that the destruction of classified material would be complete, that I would offer no further resistance and that I would surrender the ship. I felt that the situation had been accurately reported. . . . I felt that all the information that I needed to give, or was necessary for command decision to be made by higher authority—that I had given them as much information as I could.

"I turned the ship very slowly. No attempt was being made at this time to come close to the ship by any of the North Korean ships.

The firing had ceased. There had been approximately ten to fifteen salvos of 1,000 to 2,000 rounds of light-machine-gun fire from the four torpedo boats.

"The torpedo boat immediately on the port side of the ship was motioning for me to go faster. . . . I stepped out on the bridge indicating by raising my hands and shrugging my shoulders that it was not possible for me to go any faster. I intended to follow, to carry out the orders from the SO-1 as slowly as possible in order to effect completely the destruction of classified material. I was prepared at any time that it looked like we were not getting the job done to turn around and ring up full speed and risk whatever fire would have been encountered in order to insure the destruction of the material remaining.

"The water we were steaming in was still less than one hundred fathoms [the depth thought to be necessary for throwing secret material over the side]. This presented a problem to Lieutenant Harris, who felt he could not throw his classified material over the side and therefore had to burn it. . . .

"By the time we had turned around and headed back and followed the SO-1, we had opened the coast to perhaps as much as twenty to twenty-five miles. . . . Lieutenant Harris said he would like to send a message to COMNAVFORJAPAN and our radio contact in Japan explaining that he would not be able to complete the destruction of all the pubs due to their volume; that the cryptographic material for the most part had already been destroyed and this was material of his own which was of a technical nature. I had second thoughts about the destruction of classified pubs that was going on. I decided that I would stop the ship and make an inspection. . . ."

The Captain stopped the ship again. The torpedo boats, which were herding the *Pueblo* toward Wonsan, radioed the stop to the subchaser. Once more, fifty-seven-millimeter shells from the subchaser slammed into the *Pueblo*. One of the shells caught Fireman Duane D. Hodges as he was carrying a bag of secret papers to the makeshift wastebasket incinerator on the starboard deck. It went into his right hip, blowing off his leg and ripping open his stomach. Other crewmen were wounded by the same shell, though not as seriously.

"It became apparent to me at this time, and it was my considered opinion," the Captain later told the Naval Court of Inquiry, "that to remain stopped as I was would only invite additional firing and would in all probability give us less of an opportunity to complete the destruction which was going on at the time. So I ordered the ship to go ahead one-third and made a large sweeping circle. . . . We continued to follow the SO-1 in. I turned the deck and the conn over to Mr. Lacy at this time and went below to make an inspection of the research spaces to see exactly for myself how the destruction of classified material was coming along."

In the SOD Hut the Captain found a confused scene: two men swinging sledge hammers, smoke filling the compartment, and three big white bags stuffed with secret papers lying on the floor, still undestroyed. He was shocked to see the quantity of secret papers still there. He told Steve to get rid of it fast—burn it, toss it over the side, but get it out of the ship. He then stood over the teletype operator and had him send this message, at 2:05 P.M., to Japan:

"Have O keylist [that is, none left] and this only one have [except this one], have been requested to follow into Wonsan, have three wounded and one man with leg blown off, have not used any weapons or uncovered fifty-cal. mac. Destroying all keylists and as much elec equipt as possible. How about some help, these guys mean business. Have sustained small wound in rectum, do not intend to offer any resistance. Interrogative QSL [please receipt for this message]. Interrogative QSL. Do not know how long will be able to hold up circuit and do not know if comm [communications] spaces will be entered."

The Captain watched this reply come back two minutes later from Kamiseya over the teletype in the crypto center:

"Roger, roger. We doing all we can. Capt here and CNFJ [Commander Naval Forces, Japan] on hotline. Last I got was Air Force going help you with some aircraft but can't really say as CNFJ coordinating with I presume Korea for some F-105. This unofficial but I think that what will happen."

The Captain left the SOD Hut and returned to the pilothouse. I stayed below, to try to finish the job of burning our secret papers.

The shell that had hit Hodges had momentarily ceased all activity at the wastebasket fire on the starboard deck. Everyone below figured that the Koreans had fired at the smoke. In a crouch, I looked fearfully at the holes the shell had made in the new steel that formed the outside wall of the passageway connecting the rest of the ship with the SOD Hut. I could see dust hanging in the shafts of sunlight streaming through the gaping holes. I knew for sure, then, that there was no safe place in the ship. I somehow had thought that the *Pueblo*'s skin was thick enough to protect us. It was not. I thought that the next shell could be in the breech right now, and it might be for me. It seemed such a dumb way to die.

I pushed myself out of the crouch. Unable to think of anything better to do, I picked up the secret papers Hodges had been trying to burn in the wastebasket. They were soaked with his blood. They burned so slowly. I looked up the short passageway to where Hodges was lying, attended now by Hospital Corpsman First Class Herman P. Baldridge and Commissaryman Third Class Ralph E. Reed. Pieces of Hodges' flesh were splattered against the bulkhead. The deck was slippery with fresh blood. Nauseated, I turned my head and angrily took up the job of burning.

I watched with admiration as Langenberg picked his way along the cluttered deck with a weighted sack of papers over his shoulder. He stepped over me and walked to the exposed outside railing, where he tossed the bag over the side. Then, though blood was streaming from behind his right ear, where a piece of the shell that got Hodges had hit him, he went back for more.

I couldn't believe what I was experiencing. My anger rose as I worked, and I thought: Where are the planes to help us? Where is anybody? We can't just let those little bastards shoot us up and take our ship in broad daylight. Oh, please, dear Jesus, see us through this safely.

The Captain ran past and into his stateroom. When I followed, I found him sitting on his bed grinding his teeth in anger and frustration. He reached for his arctic boots, put them on, and rose. He put his new commander's hat on his head. My captain—the rough-and-tough guy who had won over so much in his turbulent life—was dressing for surrender. He looked pathetically alone. We didn't speak. I couldn't have spoken anyhow. I would have burst into tears. What was there for me to say to him? What was there for him to say to me? He left me standing in his room as he hurried back to the bridge.

I found Law in Murphy's room, where he had a fire going. Marine Sergeant Robert J. Chicca lay on the floor, with a small wound in his neck and a much more serious wound in his leg. Since Law had this area under control, I turned to leave.

Law grabbed me. "We're on course 220, Mr. Schumacher. What does that mean?"

"I think we're going in to Wonsan."

"I sure hope you're wrong, sir," he said.

I moved swiftly along the passageway to my own room. What could I do? Dejectedly, I looked around the room, a shambles of empty lockers. How did one dress to be captured? Deciding to follow the Captain's lead, I chucked my baseball cap and put on my regular gold-braided Navy hat. I briefly considered putting on my long underwear, but I decided there wasn't time. Nothing else came to my mind. I grabbed my wallet, pushed a pack of Lucky Strikes into my jacket pocket, and headed for the bridge.

The Captain could see his humiliation opening before him. The North Koreans escorting the *Pueblo* toward Wonsan ordered him to stop the ship. He did, then ran out on the deck above the SOD Hut, his hands shoved deep in his pockets. He walked over to the rail, looked down at the sea for a moment, and kicked the deck hard as he charged back aft.

One of the four torpedo boats backed down along our port side. About ten armed soldiers and two officers stood on the deck of the boat, obviously intent on stepping across the foot or so that would soon be all there was separating these ships of the United States and North Korea.

Tim came alongside me on the wing of the bridge before the Koreans jumped aboard. He also had put on his Navy hat. "Looks pretty bad," he said. My profound answer was "Yeah, it does."

Lacy, in the pilothouse, stepped to the 1 MC and passed the word for the Deck Department to prepare to receive boarders. He reminded the crew at the same time to give the Koreans only name, rank, service number, and date of birth, as required by the Code of

Conduct. I didn't hear any of the last part. I seemed to be deafened by my bewilderment over what I was watching but not believing.

The Captain was standing still as a stack—and smoking as much inside—near the ladder that led from the deck below, where the Koreans would board. Tim and I watched with disbelief as, after missing the first time, they threw a line from their small boat onto our deck. Mechanically, a sailor slipped the hated line over a bit. The *Pueblo* was deathly quiet. Stillness also enveloped the boat alongside. No orders came from it, no yells. The feeling was one of hearing a last breath followed by the silence of death. The *Pueblo* died at 2:32 P.M. on January 23, 1968, on the high seas off Wonsan.

Rigor mortis set in in my spirit. My ship, my Navy, my captain, my crew, my life—all gone. We had followed our orders. But the Koreans hadn't. They were on board my ship. Would anybody ever be able to understand how it could have happened? We had taken a step at a time. But the last step was right off the cliff. We had no way to go back up the path away from the cliff. We had gone too far. Our orders had left us no other path. "Keep the guns covered. Don't start a war out there." That's what our Navy superiors had told us in pre-mission briefings. Okay, we followed your orders. Now where are *you?* We have walked off the cliff; we're falling. Only somebody on shore can save us before we hit Wonsan and death. Don't you know what's happening out here? You've received our messages. Where are you?

I was to learn much later that no one who was not with us that day could understand how we came to give up our ship without firing a shot. Our orders contained no provision for what the rest of the Navy would think about our following them. The Captain tried to explain to the Naval Court of Inquiry why he gave up the ship. The admirals could not accept it. They heard his explanation; they recommended him for court-martial.

"There was no hope in my outrunning these people," the Captain told the Court of Inquiry a year later. "I did not feel at that time, nor at any time thereafter, that there was any point of attempting to go to war with this group of ships that were surrounding me. I was completely and hopelessly outgunned. And in order for me to man

101

my fifty-caliber machine guns, which would have been the only effective weapon that we had at a range of fifty yards, I knew to send a man up to that gun would have meant certain death for him, because he would have been walking to within thirty yards of a mount of machine guns. At that time we would have had to remove the covers to these guns—which were in fact frozen and could not be easily removed. I felt that the minute that I sent people in that general direction, they would be immediately shot. And I saw no point in senselessly sending people to their death."

To Captain Bucher, his crewmen were "people"—not "gunners" who die easily. The Navy found this a fatal flaw in his ability for command. The fact that his humanity might have saved the world a war did not enter into the Navy's judgment.

The North Koreans moved about our ship as if they knew exactly what they wanted to do, as if they had rehearsed this hijacking. The first on board was an officer carrying a forty-five-caliber revolver in his hand. The Captain went up to him and presented himself as the commanding officer of the U.S.S. *Pueblo*. With the revolver pressed against the Captain's head, the Korean waved him into the pilothouse, with the rest of the boarding party following. Berens was still at the wheel. The Koreans directed him, Tim, and me, along with the others in sight, to the fantail. With bayonet-tipped AK-47's, they herded us back and motioned to us to sit on the deck.

The officer, with his cocked pistol still leveled at the Captain's head, went into the radio shack at the rear of the pilothouse. Though he could speak only a little English, he ordered the Captain to disconnect the transmitters. The Captain refused. Angrily, the Korean yanked out what looked to him like the correct parts. The transmitters went dead. Down in the SOD Hut, the crewmen had smashed the last of the vital parts of their coding equipment. Our communications with the rest of the world were cut. The Captain could, however, still give orders to us over the ship's internal 1 MC amplifier if planes should arrive to rescue us.

The North Korean officer, helped by a guard armed with an AK-47, next pushed the Captain back to the machine-gun mount on

102

the aft deck, where he ordered him to remove the tarp. The Skipper said he could not. We, down below, under this mount, could hear the officer whack the Skipper with his pistol before he and the guard took the Captain back into the pilothouse, leaving two guards to chip away at the ice on the gun's canvas covers.

I learned later that the Koreans rang up two-thirds speed on the engine-order telegraph. The Captain reached over and rang it back down to one-third speed. It was one of the *Pueblo*'s last acts of defiance.

With about fifteen members of the crew, I was squatting down on the cold steel of the fantail. The Koreans had fired a burst of rifle fire over our heads to make sure we got down and stayed there. After about fifteen minutes, they came out on the deck with strips torn from our sheets and blindfolded us. Nobody tried to speak. The eerie silence among us went unbroken. Seaman Ramon Rosales was squatting in front of me, shaking badly. I leaned over and whispered some false encouragement in his ear: "Don't worry, Rosales, we'll get out of this somehow."

"I'm not scared, Mr. Schumacher," came his cheerful reply, "just goddamn cold."

I wondered, now that they had the crew under guard and the ship in their hands, whether they were going to shoot us and kick us into the ocean. I kept telling myself it was all a bad dream, that it could not really be happening. I was so cold that I figured their plan might simply be to let us freeze to death.

"Take your blindfolds off." It was our Captain speaking. He tried to sound reassuring, as if this were still his ship. This was the last show of authority the Koreans let him have aboard it. We removed our blindfolds so that we could see to walk to the forward berthing compartment, where the crew normally slept. It was slightly warmer there. I was blindfolded again as I reached the bottom of the ladder into the windowless hold, with its three-tier bunks. I had to feel my way to a space on a lower bunk where I could sit. The other men were doing the same thing. The awesome silence gave a clear field to my wild thoughts about what would happen next. Tortures I had read about galloped through my mind. How would

I hold up to fingernail-pulling, to ball-beating, to hot irons, to being maimed? Scared, bewildered, depressed, frustrated, angered—I was all of those things in that dark world. Only the desperate cry of *"Benjo"* from a shipmate reminded me I was not alone. *Benjo* was the Japanese word, which the Koreans understood, for the need to go to the head. I reined in my wild thoughts and tried to use reason. What was the logical explanation for all this? I had always prided myself on the ability to attack any problem logically, but I could see no logic in this situation. Did the North Koreans want to provoke a war with the United States? That wasn't logical. Did they want to hold us for government ransom? They must know that the United States would not so humble itself. What *was* their game? And was there anything I could do to keep them from winning it? My mind produced no answers, no answers at all. I was like flotsam caught in an unfriendly tide. I would just have to wait and see where I washed up.

I learned from the Captain afterward that he had not had an easy time of it either while we were in the forward berthing compartment. The first boarding party was followed by a second. Accompanied by an interpreter, a colonel with a scar from the top of his head to the back of his neck jumped off the second torpedo boat to tie up to the *Pueblo*. These two later were known to the *Pueblo* crew as Colonel Scar and Max. They had brought a civilian pilot with them to take the wheel and get us in to Wonsan. Guards in the engine room made certain the pilot's commands for speed were obeyed. Colonel Scar, through Max, ordered the Captain to take him and some of his men on a tour of the ship. The first stop was the passageway where Hodges lay dying. The Koreans ignored the Captain's pleas for medical help, and walked on. The door to the SOD Hut was open. The Captain's heart stood still. There on the floor were those same bags full of secret papers he had told Steve to throw over the side. The teletype was still buzzing, and Max ordered the Captain to turn it off. He refused. The guards, who had already kicked him in the back on the way down, punched him. Luckily, the Koreans shut the SOD Hut door behind them when they left. Now they would have to cut it open to get inside.

Hodges died on the way in to Wonsan. Wounds inflicted by the

104

same shell on Steve Woelk went unattended. Also still bleeding from wounds were Chicca and Crandell.

In the crew's compartment I heard a few hisses of whispers as the men tried to communicate. Each time I heard a whisper, I also heard the boots of a guard moving toward the noise. The guards hit anybody who made a sound. I could hear the engines still throbbing, even though they were in strange hands. My ears strained for the roar of American planes. After what seemed hours of sitting in the blackness, I felt a jolt and heard a crunch-bang noise, which I judged to be the *Pueblo* hitting a wharf. Our engines stopped. Nobody had come to save our ship. We were in Wonsan, North Korea.

Hard-soled officer's boots clattered on the ladder to the crew's compartment. A sharp command—in English, so I knew it was Max —was shrieked at us blind men. I stood up with the others and felt my way among the bunks toward the ladder. An occasional rough shove from a guard guided me.

"Give me your gun and your knife," Max barked in my ear.

"I don't have any." Hands walked over my body, probing for a hidden weapon. My gloves were yanked off my hands and stuffed into my jacket pocket. Then they not only tied my hands, but also immobilized my arms by running a line around my neck from the ropes around my wrists. The blindfold stayed on.

A guard, by pushing on my elbow, guided me to what felt to my feet like a gangplank. The last words I heard on our dead ship before walking off filled me with dread. Max declared with a sneer, "Now they are in our land. They will be tried by the laws of our country."

I could tell by the smell and the sounds that we were indeed in a port town, and I felt sure it was Wonsan. My blindfold was too tight to see anything but the planks on the pier under my cowboy boots. A guard gave me a shove once in a while to steer me. My feet came to what felt like the metal steps of a bus, and after a couple of hard shoves I found myself in a seat. I felt for another body. There was none. I was alone on a double seat. But I could hear others breathing. I figured—and hoped I was right—that it was the breathing of my shipmates.

I could hear and feel the bus straining its way up a hill. After about ten minutes, it stopped, and the engine was turned off. A guard yanked me out of the seat and shoved me down the aisle toward the front door. I walked out into the open air again and was immediately assaulted by shouts of hate. I could not understand what the crowd was saying, but there was hysteria and hate in the voices. I braced myself, waiting to be torn up by the mob. The only hard hand on me was that of the guard. He shoved me forward and then held my elbow as I walked up some new steps. This time they were train steps. The crowd was still yelling. I was a dumb, blind animal to my mind and apparently a hated Yankee imperialist in the mind of the mob. I was led to a seat. The guard gave my head a fierce punch, then held it down on my chest to let me know that this was the required position for me to assume in his country. I had no rights; they had been lost on the ship.

I felt that my mind had left my body and was looking at my flesh in disbelief. How could Lieutenant (j.g.) Frederick Carl Schumacher, Jr., of the strongest Navy in the world be sitting head down in the middle of the night on this foreign train? The bad dream would not die. I raised my head to test the reality of the situation. Smash! The guard's fist came down on top of my head again. It was a caricature of a Punch and Judy show. Only I was in it—not watching. The disbelief of those first moments on the train crowded out the fear.

We started to roll through the night at what I judged to be about 9:00 P.M. Where were we going? What would happen to me when we got there? Where was the Captain? Where was the crew? Did Max really mean it when he said that we would be tried under North Korean laws? Were the Communists going to stage a kangaroo court for their world? Would they drug and torture us? Would they accuse us of being war criminals? Or would they just shoot us once this train got out in the countryside?

Questions, questions. No answers. Just more questions. Why the hell hadn't the planes come? We were in good communication with Japan. The planes had had time to reach us. What happened? Didn't anybody get the word? "You're in one hell of a fix," I said to myself. "Now that you're off the ship, nobody knows where you are.

But you can see a little more down there by working your blindfold up with your forehead. Try. The work of your hands down there may be over. They're dying on you. See, they're getting dark from the tight ropes. They're puffing up. What the hell do the Koreans care now? They've got the ship, your ship. Remember those hands just this morning? They held a coffee mug, guided a thin pencil over a chart, held a cigarette, but now they can't do a damn thing. I'll try to look around. Oh, God, help me."

I chanced turning my head ever so slightly to see more down there in the yellow light. There were somebody else's boots, black with rubber soles and cracked leather tops. They had to be a North Korean soldier's boots. "He is my guard," I said to myself. "His feet are smaller than mine, but I'm his prisoner. Size doesn't make any difference right now. He's got the AK-47; you've got the tied hands and the blindfold. And you're on his train going somewhere inside his country. I wonder if he knows what a junky train the Democratic People's Republic of Korea has put him on. Look at the bare wooden floor with the dirty, uneven boards. Why, in the States . . . But you're not in the States. Remember? Old Black Boots up there above your bowed head is Number One. You're Number Ten. And he's not going to let you forget it."

Black Boots moved. I felt a hard, ungentle hand on my bound wrists, the first bare touch of the enemy. The hand was red, calloused, puffy, and hairless. The skin of the fingers was cracked and filled with dirt. I did not move. Black Boots sent his other hand into my crack of vision under the blindfold. The hand held a lump of white bread, not a slice. It looked like it was made by throwing a handful of dough in an oven.

"Eat," Black Boots commanded.

Where did he learn English? I thought. Who is he? Does he want to kill me? Or is he swept up in this thing, too? I wondered if he thought the whole business was crazy. I raised the bread to my mouth with my bound hands. The bread felt warm. I bit into it, and found that it was tasteless. I saw Black Boots' feet moving toward me again and felt a cup of something hot on my lips. I drank. It was either plain hot water or weak tea. It was the first sustenance I had had since lunch on the ship. Why was this man feeding me at all? Did it mean they were not going to shoot us? Maybe, I thought, now that this strange communion on the swaying train is over, I can raise my head a little. I tried it. Whack! No go. Black Boots must have had his orders; the head must be down on the chest in the proper attitude of subjection. He also tightened my blindfold, and my crack of vision was closed.

An American voice shouted out painfully that "these things are too tight." It sounded like Ayling. I heard some guttural conversation. Then Black Boots untied my hands and retied them more loosely. I was grateful. But I had other, bigger, worries. The state of my hands, though painful, seemed inconsequential alongside the hard facts of losing our ship and facing trial in North Korea.

The scenes from the afternoon attack floated back into my mind and demanded to be looked at. As if the battle had come to life again, I felt the old fear. I saw the gaping hole made by the fifty-seven-millimeter shell in the newest and thickest steel on the *Pueblo*. The sun lighted the dark passageway on my side of the hole. Sunlight had never been there before. Dust hung in the new light. I felt again the belly-clutching realization that there was no place to hide. No place on the ship was safe from those shells.

Poor Hodges, he never had a chance. A shell buried itself in his hip and then exploded. Those bastards, I thought, those little bastards with the big Russian guns. And all I could do was burn papers, papers made wet with Hodges' blood. What kind of war was this, anyhow?

I forced myself to think of Black Boots. I stared at his feet through a new crack my forehead-wrinkling made. His feet did not move. I looked at my khaki trousers. They were spattered with Hodges' dried blood. He was that close. He never even cried out. I hoped I would be that brave when my turn came.

"Your turn," my mind told me, "may be as soon as this train stops. No American is going to greet you when it stops. And you may never get off this train. Black Boots may get orders to shoot you right here. Why not? Oh, why the hell didn't somebody get to us in time? Where were those planes? They heard us. They knew what a fix we were in. Where were they? They had time, plenty of time."

I fell into a fitful sleep as the train swayed through the night. I had no way of knowing that the North Koreans were speeding us to Pyongyang, the capital. It was a trip of about a hundred miles, directly west of Wonsan across the waist of a tortured land of stripped hills.

Neither had I any way of knowing just how hostile our captors were toward Americans, the imperialists they claimed were holding South Korea in bondage. Navy commanders in Japan had not bothered to radio Captain Bucher that a North Korean suicide squad had tried to take over the Blue House, the South Korean White House, in Seoul. Such a desperate raid, on January 22, the day before the *Pueblo* was captured, would seem enough cause for the shore commanders to recommend caution. No such recommendation came. Nor had any of the intelligence officers in Japan who helped plan the *Pueblo*'s mission off North Korea paid much attention to those shrill warnings issued by Pyongyang. Indeed, on January 11, the day we sailed out of Sasebo, the North Koreans had broadcast that warning about taking "determined countermeasures" against "spy boats."

Thus, with no warning, we had sailed into an international maelstrom. From the open sea to Wonsan to Pyongyang to the Barn— all in twenty-four hours. It was too much, too fast. It couldn't be happening. But it was.

The Confession

While the afternoon of Friday, January 26, wore into premature darkness, I could feel my bodily processes and my mind slow down as I sat stupidly in that chair in my room. My suicide attempt at noontime seemed in the distant past. I was sinking into remoteness. I wanted to go all the way down—out of sight. But total blackness would not come. A light kept burning in me. It was like lying on your back on a summer night staring at a dark space between two stars. Soon you can see a fainter star in that dark space. And the longer you stare at that faint star, the brighter it becomes.

My life came back to me brighter as I stared at myself. And I did not like what I saw. I winced as I remembered snide comments I had made to nice guys. The jibes had seemed so witty at the time. Now I saw them as hurtful remarks. I wanted to apologize to everybody, all at once. I wanted to apologize to my parents for never really telling them how much I loved them, how much I appreciated all they had done for me. I had never told any of my friends how much I thought of them. It was too late now. How casual I had been with those who meant much to me. Failure after failure showed up. I wanted to reach out and touch some of those people I had slighted. But I could not even write to them.

A guard came to get me at about 4:00 P.M. Still seated, I stared at him, not giving a damn if he lowered his AK-47 and pulled the trigger. At least I would be out of it. But for some reason I obeyed his motions to follow him. I did not know where I was going. I did not care where I was going. I moved slower than I had ever moved before.

I was motioned into another room on the same floor. The guard had gotten pretty good at giving directions with his rifle. Inside, sitting improbably on a big pile of blue clothes, was Max.

"Now," he began, without moving off the blue pile of clothing, "is time for you to change clothes." He said the words through a white gauze mask, which made his eyes look even blacker. Two guards were standing with him. Their AK-47's did not look menacing in that setting. I noticed about eight bales of blue trousers, piles of red anklets, stacks of those boots with black rubber soles and green canvas tops, white muslin boxer shorts, white muslin bloomers that went all the way down to the ankle, long-sleeved undershirts, and padded outer jackets and trousers.

"Write your name," said Max, pointing to a stack of white slips on a table. I wrote my name laboriously, in big letters, as though I were signing the Constitution. Max deigned to make a motion—that of taking off my clothes. I stripped off my soiled American clothes, dropped them in the center of my spread-out jacket, put the name slip on top and tied the pile with the jacket sleeves. A guard put it in the corner, as if he were taking in a bundle of laundry. I redressed and was now ready for my part in this Gilbert and Sullivan production, feeling quite ridiculous in the new clothes. I noticed there were quite a lot of clothes. This made me hope that most of the crew was still alive. I did not dare do any more than hope, though. The guard took me back to my room, the same stark prison. I hated the chair and everything else in the room.

About 9:30 P.M. that same long Friday the guard ordered me into a different room, across the hall. It had the same white walls and cracked, blue-painted woodwork. But its radiator was ice cold. There was no heat in the room at all, and it was below freezing outside. They apparently were going to try freezing me and starving me to death at the same time. I got into bed. It was the only way to keep warm; the clothes helped. Sleep came fast.

. . .

Saturday morning arrived. So another night had passed without my being tortured or shot. No food at breakfast time. No heat. But no bullet. I knew the guard, who could look in on me through the vertical cracks in the wooden door, would pound me with his rifle if I lay in bed. I decided to get into the chair before his morning duty began. I was shivering from the cold, though, so I paced back and forth. When I heard the guard pass by, I pounded on my door. He opened it and escorted me down the hall to the head and back. I tried to see a fellow crewman through the door cracks as he hurried me down the hall, but we moved too fast.

I spent the morning puzzling again. Why had they given me clothes? How come they were so organized, even to white name slips for the clothes turned in? I realized that some kind of decision about what to do with the Americans had been made. Would they have given us new clothes to be shot in? Of course not. Would they have bothered to label our bundles of clothes? No. Something has happened, I thought. I dared hope that our fortunes were improving. I even entertained the idea that the State Department had found a way to get us out of the Barn.

I felt I was flickering into a brighter light as they burst into my room at noon. "Now we will see how strong you are," an interpreter I had never seen before said with a sneer. He was leading a line of five officers. I knew I was in for it. These were no dull-witted Deputy Dawg or Snot Nose.

"Get down on your knees."

I pretended I did not understand. The interpreter knew his English was perfectly plain.

"Get down on your knees!" he shouted.

I did as I was ordered. Two of four guards standing in the hallway came into my room. I could hear them cock their guns, which were tipped with ugly blunt-looking bayonets. Each guard aimed at one of my temples, shoving the bayonet to within inches. My head would hit a bayonet point if I moved it to either side.

"What oceanographic measurements did you take?" the interpreter said with precision.

It was too late to turn back now. I continued the line I had used the day before on Snot Nose. "Why did you shoot at our ship?" I stared at the interpreter as I said it and kept my eyes riveted on his.

"Are you going to force us to make you talk?"

I did not reply. I continued staring at him. He did not look away. I saw his coal eyes burning. As I kept fighting his stare, I expected the bayonets to jab me to make me blink. I hoped they would shoot soon, because I was having trouble trying not to tremble from kneeling so rigidly in the cold room. I could not keep it up much longer. "Hurry up," I said to myself.

One of the officers stepped toward me and swung a fist at my head. I instinctively ducked, somehow missing the bayonet and escaping the fist.

"Hands up!"

I raised my arms. The old routine Deputy Dawg had tried on me was being escalated. A guard on one side of me kicked my elbow every time my arm started to falter; the other one kicked my chest. I struggled to keep my balance, desperately trying not to fall over backward into the iron radiator. The kicking continued for at least fifteen minutes. Now I was struggling for breath as well as balance. The pain shot into me from my elbow, and the chest-kicking made me feel I was suffocating.

The guards paused on the interpreter's command. Then he said to me again in English: "What oceanographic measurements did you take?"

"Why did you shoot at our ship?"

The guards started again. The kicks felt harder. Afraid I would pass out or become incoherent, I fought for control of my mind. What would I tell them if I grayed out? "You can't hold on much longer," I told myself. "You can't take much more pain. They have all day. You're being stupid. Lie your way out of it. Stop the kicking before you lose control. You can do more good sane than semiconscious. You're not doing anybody any good letting this happen. Tell them something—anything. Do it now. You can't hold out. Get back in control."

"I don't know."

"You lie, you lie!"

The kicking resumed. I could not hold my arms up straight any more. I didn't even try hard. I fought for my mind. I knew I had to do that. But I was jiggling inside. My thoughts were breaking up. The kicking seemed to be going on inside my head. The pain blazed in there. I had to stop that pain, so I could think again.

"All right. Stop kicking me and I'll tell you." The kicking stopped. I let my burning arms sink. The guard kicked my elbow again.

"Stop kicking me and I'll tell you." The interpreter gave the guards a command. They stopped.

"Get up. All right, you may sit. Now what oceanographic information did you get?"

"The temperature of the water. The depth." The interpreter shoved a piece of paper into my hand.

"Write it down," he commanded.

I did. My hand was shaky, and I was breathing hard. My chest felt crushed; my elbows shot pain into me, like a heavy drumming on my funny bone. But I was thinking straight again. The pain was no longer burning up my thoughts, though remembering how close I had come to losing control, I felt scared. I wrote the idiotic sentence "We were taking the temperature of the water and its depth." All that beating for those silly words. Yet I realized that the Koreans had kicked me open. I had violated the Code of Conduct by stating more than name, rank, service number, and date of birth. They would want more. How long could I keep whatever I told them as innocuous as this sentence? I handed the paper to the fierce-eyed interpreter who had ordered the answers kicked out of me. I I hoped my own eyes showed the defiance I still felt. I wished he were a stupid son a bitch like Snot Nose. But he was cruelly efficient. How many times had he done this? How many men had he ordered kicked to death? Plenty, probably.

He did not even look at the paper I handed him, but started right in on me again. "What about the radars? You could intercept radar signals? You know about this. Couldn't you?"

"Yes." I could feel that question picking right into the lock on the part of my mind I was determined to keep sealed off from them. I prayed to God that they would settle for my matter-of-fact yes, and

114

leave the radar discussion. I was trying to indicate with that flat yes that of course everybody intercepts radar signals, and everybody else knows it.

But my yes did not do the trick. This bastard had prepared an interrogation, step by step. He read off from a pad in his hand the names of the different pieces of equipment in the SOD Hut. My mind was back working full power. I could tell from the order of the names that someone had walked around inside the SOD Hut, moved from one piece to the other, and copied off the names from the metal labels that survived the sledge-hammering. They had given the SOD Hut careful study. They had the key to that lock in my mind. I would have to take the pain. "Let them kick you until you pass out," I told myself. "Just don't say anything, Schumacher. They're too close. Oh, God, make it quick. Let me pass out fast. I can't lose this one. Oh, God, please help."

I gave the interpreter my answer: "I don't know. I don't know."

I tensed, waiting for the first kick. The interpreter stared at me. He said something to the four officers, who had been sitting around me like doctors watching an intern conduct an operation. The officers rose. I sat there dreading the order to get down on my knees again. My thoughts were racing, too fast. I tried to rein them in, to fight for control, to turn them to the problem at hand. But they would not be braked. They were running away from my situation in that tense room, that room so cold that the breaths of the officers showed. I felt that my thoughts were pulling me off a cliff. Yet I could not let this happen. The Koreans were too close to something I could not break on, no matter how hard they kicked.

The standing officers threw me a look of contempt, as if getting ready to spit. Then—inexplicably—they left. The interpreter and the two guards followed them out. The guards were breathing hard from all the kicking they had done. But they seemed to have enjoyed it. One had drawn blood with a vicious kick under my ear. The last guard out closed the door behind him without looking back at me.

I was left alone again in that cold room, sitting in the chair, drained. It had been too close. They were escalating the terror. No food. No heat. Isolation. Beating. They had lots of combinations.

115

And I knew the really tough stuff could come any time. The kickings had given all those other, worse, tortures terrifying credibility. The Koreans probably knew that. They were experts at terrorizing. The known made the unknown searing to think about. Today was horrible; tomorrow looked worse. The objective was achieved that way, by the prisoner sinking into a state of hopelessness. Any thread of hope was cut off. The sinking of the captive into the quicksand of hopelessness must be started early. I watched it happening to me. I tried hard to regard it as an interrogation exercise; to pull my mind out of the pit. It was becoming more difficult to do this. Since each interrogation was tougher and more terrifying than the last, control was harder and harder to keep. I consoled myself with the thought that I had figured out their game plan: steady escalation of terror. They were in no hurry. They knew that thinking about beatings was more terrifying than enduring them. The unknown was worse than the known.

But this consolation was to be denied me. That night the turnips —food—returned at the supper hour. The terror campaign was abating. What did it mean? Not humaneness, certainly. It means they think they have broken you, I thought. You don't think you told them anything. They obviously do.

More evidence came a few hours after the turnips. The duty officer came into my room with a mimeographed form. He put it on the table with a pencil, motioning me to fill it out. I let it sit there. They've broken you, as far as they're concerned, I thought. They've just started. They'll want more and more information, until you spill everything. Suicide is still the only answer. You were right the first time.

I waited until about nine o'clock that Saturday night to look at the form lying on the table. It was written in English. The information requested was all innocuous: name, rank, home town, dates of naval service, schooling. The Code of Conduct said I should not give out all the information requested on the form. Yet if I didn't, I would be in for another kicking session. The Koreans already knew more about me from the records they had captured on the ship than they were asking on the form. I decided that filling it out was the lesser of

116

two evils. Why give them an excuse to go back to the really sensitive questions? I rationalized that it made more sense to buy time by filling out the form. I did so. The act depressed me. Telling myself that it was the logical choice did not help. My sense of duty hammered me deeper into the pit of depression. I crawled into the cold bed feeling like an ugly slug retreating under a rock. The naked light bulb burned over me. I prayed that the sleep coming to me would be permanent.

It was not, of course. I woke on Sunday to the pounding on my door by the guards coming on duty. I was in the cursed chair again when the wordless waitress came into my room with the bowl of turnips and pitcher of hot water. She poured the hot water into my cup and left. I found a lump of white bread on top of the turnips. As I chewed away on the breakfast, my jaws painful from the kicking of the day before, I delivered myself a stern lecture.

"You've got to do it this time, Schumacher. No more fooling around. They're too close. They're going to kick off that lock in your head. A few minutes in that bucket can't be as bad as the torture you'll get if you try to hold out. The last time, you weren't really sure. Now you are. No more Deputy Dawg and Snot Nose. The real pros are going to give you their full attention. Maybe the Captain and Steve won't crack, so they've decided to crack you. You can't let the ship down, your country, your Navy. They're not asking all that much of you. Look at what Hodges went through. Think how upset they'll be when they find your limp body. You'll beat the bastards. Going into the bucket is the only clean way out of this room. You know it. You've kept control so far. Just one more thing to do and then you can rest."

I knelt by the bucket for the second time. I was more determined than I had been on Friday—the first time I tried it. I felt it was fitting to go out of life for a noble cause on a Sunday morning, about church time. Everything seemed right this time. I had no doubt to pull me back from the edge of death.

This time I dove in, letting my head hit the bottom hard—perhaps subconsciously trying to jam it irretrievably under the water. I breathed the water in. I felt the stinging cold down inside me. I waited, more relaxed this time. I felt that it was working. I was drowning. I could not breathe in or out. Death was coming this time. The explosion was building up. Then it would be over. I felt the water pressing in on my life. . . . But I waited a long time. Then something took over again. My head jerked out of the bucket, and I was back on the floor, retching out water, still very much alive. I was fighting for life's breath again. My body was doing everything without my telling it to. It was putting up one hell of a fight. My mind had to admire my body for that, and as it gradually took over again, it told me I was going to live. With every second, I was backing away from the edge of the cliff I had been close to going off. Now, the edge of the cliff was nowhere near.

I lay on the floor completely defeated. I had kidded myself that I would really do it the second time. But I knew after this attempt that I would never be able to do it. The Koreans had won. Schumacher had lost. I could not take my own life even though I wanted to. If I had a gun, I thought, I could do it. But I didn't have a gun. I couldn't just squeeze a trigger and let the piece of metal do the rest. I had to kill myself with will power, not a weapon. And I didn't have enough will power. I was face to face with myself again, and my mind lashed me for my failure.

My depression was absolute. I was at the bottom of the black abyss. I crawled along the floor to the hated chair, like a beaten dog, and sat there, lonely, cold, scared, hungry, defeated. I actually moaned. I wondered where God was. I shivered through the morning and into the afternoon in that chair, trying to make my mind black out. It would not.

Around 4:00 P.M., I forced myself from the chair and the pit of depression. I paced the room with painful strides, rubbed my hands in a vain attempt to keep warm. My mind—thank God for my mind —started talking to me again. "If things are this bad," it told me, "you know damn well they can't get any worse. You have hit bottom. Remember Job? That's you now. If you can get this low and still not succumb, there is a greater power than yourself keeping you going. You know there is. You didn't want to keep going. You tried to cop out. God didn't let you. He has been pushing you along after you yourself quit. How else can you explain it? You've got God with you. He is the one who carried you through."

I was never to reach such a low point again. My mind had showed me where God was. I knew the Koreans could kill me, but I also knew that God was working for me, not against me. I knew for the first time what the expression "God sustained me" really meant. He had sustained me. I decided that He was going to see me through. With Him, I would be able to keep my mind in control somehow.

About 9:30 that night, Guinny, as I nicknamed one of the duty officers, came into my room to tell me not to go to bed; I was going to get a bath. I didn't believe him and went to bed right after he left. I was awakened about midnight by the shouts and poundings of Guinny. He was upset. I had gone to bed against his orders. He told me to get dressed in a hurry. A guard then escorted me down the hall and out of the Barn. I was put on a bus, where the guard slammed my head down on my chest in the old abject position. I was not blindfolded, but I could not see much in my head-down position. The ride lasted about six minutes. I was led out of the bus to the entrance of what must have been the bathhouse for the nearest village. The midnight hour was probably selected so that the villagers might not see the hated Americans and organize some violence. The bathhouse was a low, one-story building of grayish concrete containing several little cubicles with sunken cement baths in them.

There, thank God, I saw Gene and Tim, and knew that at least two other officers were alive. I figured that the Captain had been shot. Steve, I thought, must have committed suicide. Where was Murphy? Because he was second in command, the Koreans might have shot him, along with the Captain.

I was allowed to bathe myself, and this first real washing in almost a week felt good. But I did it mechanically, concentrating my thoughts on what the presence of only Gene and Tim could mean. Then the three of us rode back to the Barn on the same bus. We were not allowed to speak, of course, but it was comforting to see that neither Gene nor Tim looked maimed in any way. I was led back to my cold room on the third floor and told to stay dressed.

119

Somebody wanted to talk to me, Guinny said. I waited in the chair for over an hour. Finally I gave up and crawled into bed, hoping to recapture the warmth I had felt briefly in the bathhouse.

"Get up! Get up!" It was Guinny shouting in my ear. I looked at him, then at my watch. It was three in the morning. What a way to start a Monday! Something ominous must be up. Guinny was frantic. The guard with him kept motioning me toward the door with his rifle. I slipped my boots on, pushed my hair out of my eyes, and followed them down the hall. Through the open door of one of the rooms on the way I saw Harry Iredale, kneeling with his arms above his head. The Koreans were torturing him, too, then. I sensed that another round of torture lay ahead for me.

My escorts took me to the Big Room, the one at the end of the hall where the General had told us on that first night in the Barn that we would be shot before sunrise. The Big Room was in the same semidarkness it was at that first confrontation. Seated where the General had been was Colonel Scar. He was stout, muscular, and had a thick white scar on the back of his neck. He looked like a heavyweight wrestler. He had the stern face, cut off square at the bottom of a big jaw, to go with his build. He smiled as I approached. An interpreter sat on his left. Scar spoke to the interpreter, who relayed a warmly spoken invitation: "Come in and sit down."

I did so, thinking to myself these were the same bastards who had ordered my chest, head, and elbows kicked. "Stay loose," I told myself. "Keep ahead of this guy."

"We have heard that your father is very worried about you," Scar said. "Worried about your safety and well-being," the interpreter added. He spoke softly, as if he wanted to ease my depression. "We think it is not right that you should be in such unfortunate circumstances, and we want very much for you to go home. We Koreans do not like pain and suffering." Scar, evidently understanding the interpreter's English words, nodded his head up and down in affirmation. "We know all about your ship and its mission," the interpreter continued softly. "We know that it was a spy ship; that you were to spy against our country. We have your documents."

120

Which documents did they really have? They were bluffing, I decided. They were trying to soften me up. But where was this line of questioning leading? Where were they trying to take me?

"And we know who ordered your mission," he went on. "We know their policy. We know that you were only a military man carrying out your orders; that you had no choice in the decision. And we do not like to see you suffer for what others have done to you."

He punctuated that with a long silence. Then he resumed, in the same sympathetic tone. "We Koreans do not want you to suffer. We think that those who are truly sorry for what they have done should be forgiven. If you will confess your part in the crimes of your ship, and apologize for them, then we will let you go home— to return once again to your father, who is very worried about you."

It was quite a pitch. Colonel Scar made no move. The silence was complete. I could hear my breathing. As I reviewed all that had happened since Saturday afternoon, I could see what they were doing to me. One cycle had run its course. I was sure they had others, plenty of others. Every man had his breaking point. They knew that. Super C most likely had masterminded my breaking from the first day, working through officers like Scar. I both hated and admired him for his skill. The only piece that did not fit was the reference to my father. I learned much later that the Koreans—who somehow seemed to read every word printed anywhere in the United States—had obtained an Associated Press story quoting my father's hope that the American government could find a way to get the *Pueblo* crew home.

Colonel Scar was letting the silence in the darkened room build. Neither he nor his interpreter had asked me a single question. I was just the errant boy getting the fatherly treatment from two sympathetic elders who happened to be running a reform school outside Pyongyang. Guessing that the suspense had gone on long enough to deliver his punch line, Scar sat up abruptly and nodded to his interpreter, who said, "We want you to write a confession of your crimes completely; to confess fully the crimes of you and your ship."

I played dumb. "I don't know what you're talking about."

Colonel Scar ignored my answer, as if he had not even heard it.

He continued to explain his request as if it were the least I could do for them. "We know that you are not responsible; that you only executed the orders of your superiors. We only want you to confess to your part in the crimes." Looking at me in mock disbelief, he asked rhetorically: "Could you confess to the policy makers' crimes?"

The main part of the lecture was over. I was supposed to appreciate the unassailable logic of it and accept the generous terms for repatriation. Just in case I had missed the point, Scar leaned over near enough to my face so I could smell his breath, and intoned solemnly: "If you confess honestly, we will allow you to go home."

I could not bring myself to acknowledge the deal they were trying to make with me. I came back with the same stupid line: "I don't understand. What is it you want?"

Briskly, in the old machine-gun delivery of the colonel in charge, Scar dropped the fatherly pretense and snapped: "We want you to confess honestly, to include the following points—" The interpreter walked over to my chair and handed me pencil and paper so I could copy down the points. "A little bit of your background, mission of the ship, who gave you orders, when you left, what you did, who you were supposed to report to, and how you were caught spying red-handed. Then you should explain how sorry you are. Apologize to the Democratic People's Republic of Korea. Ask to be forgiven and be allowed to go home."

The session was over. Colonel Scar motioned to the guard standing behind my chair. I got up. Scar nodded at me as if we had just made a deal. The whole show had taken an hour. The studied silences gave Scar's performance real impact. I was dealing with a pro.

When I got back to my cold room, the duty officer on the floor handed me a pile of white paper and a yellow pencil with no eraser. I was told to stay up and write the confession Scar had asked for. I had copied down the points to be covered, as ordered. The challenge for me was to write down the information covering the points without telling the Koreans anything they did not already know from the papers captured with the ship. Exactly how much did they know? That was the big question.

I organized myself for the writing chore by blocking out those areas I knew positively the Koreans had information on already.

122

Several times during the previous nights in the Barn I had been shaken awake to help the interpreters in their reading of documents captured on the *Pueblo*. "What means PACCOMELINT?" "What means NSA?" "What means NAVSECGRUPAC?" The stomach-churning question came one night from Specs, the most intelligent and humane of the duty officers. He asked me, through an interpreter: "What means CPA TO KORCOM/SOVIET LAND MASS/OFF SHORE ISLANDS WILL BE 13NM?" I realized from that question that the Koreans were translating our secret sailing orders. They would know, if they did not know already, what the true mission of the *Pueblo* was. The cover story of conducting oceanography—the one the Navy had told us to give if anything went wrong—was clearly untenable. Specs asked the question so politely, almost apologetically. But he knew what he had. I did not tell him. He did not ask anything but what the acronyms stood for. I figured that telling him what CPA was would kick a hole in their attempt to portray us as spies who had violated North Korea's territorial waters.

"CPA," I said, "means closest point of approach. In other words, 'Don't go any closer than thirteen miles to North Korea at any time.'" Specs looked surprised. But he did not argue. With an affirmative nod, he wrote my answer down.

I knew, therefore, that they had our secret sailing orders. I could restate some of that information without telling them anything additional. The fact that Scar had not pressed me for details of the mission was a fantastically lucky break. The orders gave him a hard outline for penetrating questions of the most sensitive nature. While I did not know all the answers, I knew the communications technicians who did. In pondering what to write in my confession, I came to the conclusion that the Koreans were playing us for propaganda, not hard military information. That was certainly the lesser of two evils for us. Could this mean that we were pawns in a diplomatic struggle, rather than war criminals to be given a kangaroo-court trial before the world and then shot? I hoped, but was afraid to believe, that the emphasis on propaganda meant a diplomatic battle, though I still felt that the odds were against any of us leaving Korea alive. But I wrote from 4:00 A.M. to 10:00 A.M. that Monday. I weighed each word before putting it down, as though I were a tombstone carver writing on marble. But I became bolder as I went along. "Now that I have seen how much we can expect from a peace-loving people," I wrote, for the benefit of the head-kickers, "I am ashamed of what we have done." I went on like that for ten pages, using clear but small handwriting.

Max came into my room at noon to pick up my masterpiece. I had dropped the bomb and now waited to hear the explosion when it hit. It came at 9:00 P.M. A guard motioned me out of my room fiercely and gave me a hard shove down the hall toward the Big Room. I found myself back in the same chair, but with the big boss of the compound, Super C, sitting at the table where Scar had been earlier.

"What do you take me for—a fool?" he screamed at me. He looked mad enough to order me shot on the spot. Wearing a long gray coat, whose red shoulder boards had two glistening gold stripes and four silver stars on them, and with a shining shock of black hair shooting straight back from his forehead, and burning black eyes, he looked like a cruel dictator. He stood up and slammed his fist hard on the papers piled high on the table—a huge pile. I could see that they were secret papers from the *Pueblo,* many top secret. My heart sank. National security had really been compromised. How did so many papers get from the SOD Hut to that table? I was shocked.

"Stand up!" Super C ordered. His eyes roved over me. He twisted his head with an air of revulsion, managing to make me feel awkward and uncomfortable. I tried to act relaxed.

"What are you," he asked icily. "A military man or a civilian?"

"A military man."

"Then you must stand like one before a senior officer!" he screamed.

"Yes, sir," I snapped, in spite of myself, straightening my loose posture. I had never called any of my captors "sir" before. Super C's commanding manner had penetrated to my reflexes.

"Now sit down. From a military man we expect military answers. Your confession is not complete. What do you take me for," he repeated, "a fool?"

Without pausing for an answer—he knew he was in complete

124

command of the situation—he held up the top-secret narrative of the *Pueblo* mission that I had typed myself, day by day. I had destroyed my copy. Two other copies had been sent to the SOD Hut, where they must have been found. The narrative had every detail of our mission: radio and radar signals intercepted and their characteristics; ships sighted; our positions each day. This narrative, right there in Super C's hand, made all the previous painful questioning of me and everybody else superfluous. It contained more information than I could have remembered even if I had tried. The whole purpose of beating me and the others must have been for terror, not information—to soften us up for the confession-writing.

He put the narrative down. I wanted to grab and swallow it. Then he picked up other papers. "How about this?" he would ask, confronting me with one sensitive paper after another, until I felt I would vomit. "How about this?" I felt lightheaded as well as sick as I watched him hold up document after document. They had got so much. I felt I would fall out of my chair and off into space.

Super C was riffling through the papers we had all felt duty-bound to die for when he hit me again with that same question: "What do you take me for—a fool?" There was a long silence. He stopped picking up documents and waving them in my face and asked, with fierceness and finality: "Do you admit you were spying?"

"Yes, sir," I said in a drained voice.

"Why didn't you say so here?" he asked, holding up my wise-guy confession.

I had no answer. He had won. I felt dead inside. My great writing tricks were for nothing. He knew more about the mission than I did if he had read all those documents. Yet he asked me no questions about them. He showed not the slightest interest in the technical gold mine spread out on his table. He just wanted abjectness and a confession that reflected it. He had all the weapons he needed to break me: terror, psychological shock treatment, and hard information, which made the Code of Conduct a mockery of the true situation in the Barn.

"Are you a military man or a civilian?" he asked again.

"I'm a military man."

"A military man," he shouted, pounding the table, "should answer more forthrightly." Then he added, with a hiss: "You bastard." His interpreter, Wheezy, repeated the "you bastard" in the same hiss.

"Yes, sir," I heard myself answering.

"I am empowered by my government to have you shot right now."

I believed him. I did not respond. The suspenseful silence lengthened, Super C no doubt enjoying my guessing whether I was indeed to be shot in this ugly room.

"Is this the best you can do?" he asked, again holding up my confession.

"No, sir."

He paused, as if weighing my answer as a request from a prisoner in the death house. "Well," he said at last, "I'm going to give you one more chance. We will test your sincerity."

"Yes, sir."

"This time you must write more honestly."

"Yes, sir."

"Do you have any questions?"

"No, sir."

"We're going to give you one hour. Go back to your room."

I was not sure I could get out of the chair. I felt rubber-legged, dizzy, and my stomach was whirling. Sweat dripped from my armpits. My hands, too, were hot. Super C had done this to me in one ferocious confrontation. I felt as if I were walking away from the open grave he had dug for me in that room. I was glad to get away from it.

I tried to regroup my thoughts as, still shaking, I sat alone in my cold room. I noticed a rim of ice on the water left in my cup on the window sill. It was that cold. I gave myself another lecture as I prepared to write a second confession for Super C.

"He had a hell of a lot of stuff on that table. No doubt about it. The Navy could hang us all for losing so much sensitive material. Does he know what he has? He could not have read it all yet. He is trying to fake you out, Schumacher. He is trying to make you feel he has the whole iceberg. Maybe he has just the tip. Limit yourself to what you are sure he has in hand. And for God's sake, don't mention the CT's. He doesn't know how much real meat he has on the hook in them. Don't let him bowl you over with theatrics. Play it cool on paper. He doesn't know as much as you think he knows. Be conservative in what you tell him."

I was exhausted as I picked up the pencil again. I added a bit more about radar-signal interception. I did not go beyond the *Pueblo* narrative. But where it was "safe," from an American security standpoint, I put down some information in straightforward military language to show my sincerity. I was too tired to weigh each word. I had been under the gun since three in the morning. My fingers were stiff from the cold. I wrote a confession of about half the size of the original one, still not putting down anything the Koreans did not already know. I finished about midnight—making it twenty-one hours since I had last been to bed. I crawled in the sack. If they wanted the confession, they would come on in and pick it up. I was too tired to worry about whether it was good enough or not. Let them shoot me.

The game of truth-or-consequences resumed at 10:00 A.M. on Tuesday. It was like going to the end of the line and starting all over again. The guard led me down to the little room where Deputy Dawg and Snot Nose had started questioning me. This time the questioners were Max, the interpreter, and an officer who had on bright-blue socks. I was seated in a chair facing Blue Socks, who was also sitting. Max, who was standing, shouted down at me: "We must have more detail!"

Blue Socks had a chart in his hand. They obviously had been doing considerable homework on our mission, apparently trying to make it fit their propaganda. Yet the *Pueblo*'s own chart did not bear out their charge that we had intruded into their territorial waters. They were going to make it fit, no matter what they had to do to us. Blue Socks had our chart on which we had marked our three operational areas off the North Korean coast: Mars, Venus, and Pluto. The North Koreans had written on this chart a description of where we had been and what we had seen: locations of ships sighted, places where the SOD Hut CT's had tuned in radio and radar signals and where we had practice-fired the guns.

I did not feel like co-operating that morning. Super C had burned me out the day before. So I stared back at Max listlessly, refusing to respond to his sense of desperation.

Blue Socks, a senior captain wearing four gold stars, spit out a line for Max to give me: "You will be shot."

I had heard that so many times that I was beyond flinching. They had flicked out that card too often.

Max must have sensed my reaction, because they got down to the object of the interrogation. "When you were off Mayang Do, did you see two lights at night that you thought were a freighter?"

Of course we did. It was right there on the *Pueblo* chart in Blue Socks' hand. But I was not in the mood to play. Let them kick away again. I felt only semiconscious anyway.

"I don't remember."

"On the nineteenth of January," Max persisted, "did you not fire your guns?"

"I can't remember."

"Did you not come close in to shore to spy on the Democratic People's Republic of Korea?"

I gave my answer to that one loud and clear. "No. We were always thirteen miles out."

"No, no, no, no, no," Max said in a machine-gun burst of guttural English. "You lie!" he screamed. "You lie. You will be shot. Do you want us to make you talk?"

Blue Socks and Max discussed in Korean what to do with this insolent American lieutenant sitting before them. I figured that the next command would be to get down on my knees for the kicking game. Max stared at me for a moment, then said: "We will give you one more chance. We must have more detail."

The guard, denied his morning workout on me, shoved his AK-47 rifle sideways against my back to launch me down the hall toward my heatless room. The duty officer had brought in another stack of confession paper and a pencil. The Koreans wanted more

128

detail. Yet they had more in hand than I could possibly give them. The secret documents I had seen in their hands must have been studied. Yet they wanted me to write more detail. I was up against the mystical Oriental mind. What was this charade, this pretending that they needed my help? If the interrogations were just an excuse to terrorize me, why the chart? They could beat me in more terrifying ways than they had up to now. My Western logic failed to show me the way out of this Korean labyrinth I was in. I was baffled. Every time I figured what their wave length was, they would do something to make me feel I was not tuning them in correctly at all.

I decided to gamble once again in this weird game. I added to my previously written confession only those details Max had mentioned—loose phrases, such as spotting lights that might have been those of ships, and that somebody had fired the guns for some reason at some point in the journey. I did not accommodate him on his spy question, making no admission about going into North Korean territorial waters.

Max himself came into my room at 6:00 P.M. to pick up my revised confession. I was through for the day—the end of my first full week in the Democratic People's Republic of Korea.

At 10:00 A.M. on Wednesday, Max screamed at me, "Getting information out of you is like pulling teeth." It was my eighth day in North Korea. God, it had been such a long, continual nightmare. My seven days in the Barn seemed an eternity, not just a week. I was back in Deputy Dawg's little interrogation room, being harangued yet again by Max. Blue Socks was with him, sitting, as usual.

"You are a fox," Max yelled. He never seemed to be able to speak normally. "Getting information out of you is like pulling teeth. You want to be beat? You want to die? You want us to make you talk?"

Then Blue Socks and Max discussed some notes they had on the *Pueblo*'s course and speed. Max turned to me and said: "You saw smoke. Doesn't that mean you were very close to shore?" His question, I realized, was prompted by a notation on the chart. We had seen smoke while off Orang Dan and had noted it.

129

"No," I told Max. "We always stayed thirteen miles out."

"You lie! Why do you lie?"

I did not answer. Max continued with other information taken from the chart, such as the notation about our spotting the navigational light above Songjin Harbor. Max told me we could never have seen the light if we had been thirteen miles from the North Korean coast, as I claimed. The ensuing argument, my knowledge of navigation versus Max's ideology unhindered by scientific facts, would have been funny in other circumstances. I told him how the curvature of the earth limited our vision across the surface of the ocean to six and a half miles. But the light also could go six and a half miles out from shore without bumping into that hump of the earth. Besides, I told him, the light was elevated. This meant its beams could travel more than six and a half miles before running into the curve of the earth. Max was not buying this.

"No, no, no, no," he shouted again. "Why do you lie? You lie!"

I sensed a desperation in their insistence that the *Pueblo* had intruded into North Korea's territorial waters. I wondered if they felt they had to have my sworn statement of intrusion to keep the United States from blowing North Korea off the map in retaliation for hijacking the *Pueblo*. I had no idea what the other crewmen had said. These North Koreans knew the truth. They would not accept it. They insisted that I tell them our own documents were a lie. If I did admit to spying in their waters, I would be shot. If I refused to admit it, I would be shot. The Koreans indicated that the odds for survival lay on the side of lying, so they would have the "truth" they needed.

Back at the table in my room, with yet "one more chance" from Max, I pondered what additional information I could safely write down for them. I decided to play back only their words in my words. I wrote down a lot of garbage about the smoke at Orang Dan. I delivered a circumlocutious treatise on the range of navigation lights, admitting to having seen one at Songjin. I was getting pretty facile at throwing their questions back to them in the form of wordy statements. I finished my latest revision of the confession at about noontime. The duty officer picked it up. Nobody bothered me for the rest of the day. Not knowing what was coming kept me on edge.

But I had made my decision: I would play it out, keep writing nonsense. I had not admitted to intruding into North Korean territorial waters.

About 2:00 P.M. on Thursday, a guard walked through the door, motioned me out into the hall, and pointed to the Big Room at the end. I was walking the last mile, I figured. Super C would be in there to explain with military precision why I was being shot. He had asked for straight answers, and had not received them. "Therefore," he would explain, "the Democratic People's Republic of Korea has ordered you shot. Take him away."

I looked up at the long table as I entered the darkened Big Room, dreading the confrontation with Super C. With vast relief, I saw my adversaries were Colonel Scar, who had tried to soft-soap me about my father's worries, and his interpreter, Wheezy, who, whenever he was stuck for an English word, would cough to mask his ignorance. I was motioned into a chair facing them, and there was no softness this time.

"Read this over," Scar said. Wheezy took a paper out of Scar's hand, walked from behind the table, and handed it to me. It was typewritten. To my horror, I saw that it was a confession I had never written. It began:

I am Lieutenant Junior Grade Frederick Carl Schumacher, Jr., of the U.S. Navy. I am the Operations Officer on the armed espionage ship *Pueblo* which was captured by the Navy of the Korean People's Army at a point 39 degrees, 17.4 minutes north, 127 degrees, 46.9 minutes east off Wonsan while carrying out military espionage activities, having intruded deep into the coastal waters of the Democratic People's Republic of Korea.

There is no excuse for my criminal act as the facts have already been made clear. Now I shall frankly confess the criminal acts of aggression committed by the U.S.S. *Pueblo* and my own crimes. The *Pueblo* is originally an armed espionage ship. The ship has carried out purely military espionage missions up to now since she was commissioned. In the past the *Pueblo* carried out the military espionage missions intruding into the coastal waters of socialist countries.

Anyone in the U.S. Navy could see that such a confession was phony. Even without checking the position, which was stated falsely,

131

the Navy knew the *Pueblo* was on her first mission when captured. Also, she was not an armed ship originally—the guns having been added in Japan. I had not written a single line of the typed confession handed to me. Why had the Koreans gone to all the trouble to make me write a confession and forced me to revise it time after time? As I read on down the typed confession by the faint light from the naked bulb hanging over me, I had no answer. The confession continued:

It was in December of 1967 that I was assigned Operations Officer of the *Pueblo*. After graduation from naval officers candidate school and communications school, I had served as communications officer on a ship for some time, obtaining the knowledge of military espionage activities. Later I came to learn that all the crew of the *Pueblo*, like myself, were espionage specialists who had been engaged in the field of coast espionage.

According to the mission stipulated in the U.S. Army, Navy and Air Force Joint Chiefs of Staff, the Defense Department, Washington, D.C., we arrived at the naval base at Yokosuka, Japan, on 1 December 1967. There we received a specific mission from Frank A. Johnson, commander, U.S. Naval Forces Japan. He personally came on board and gave us the mission. Our mission was to detect various military installations around the coastal waters of the Democratic People's Republic of Korea, the radar sites, accommodation capacities of the ports, the number of incoming and outgoing vessels and their capacities, and the maneuverability of the naval forces, and especially various electronic waves from military sources of the Korean People's Army. We had a mission again to conduct military espionage deep into the far eastern coastal waters of the Soviet Union after spying on the important state secrets, including the distribution of industry of the Democratic People's Republic of Korea. The espionage mission was set down in stages involving three operational waters. The concept of operations was to conduct intelligence activities against socialist countries.

Phase one of the program was to prove the feasibility of using a trawler-type ship as an intelligence-gathering platform. Phase one was completed. Phase two, in which we participated, was to expand this program of espionage activity to the other countries, including the Soviet Union and China. We were to gauge the reaction of these countries to a trawler-type espionage ship intruding into their coastal waters. We also had on board a set of specific intelligence collection requirements given us by the commander, U.S. Naval Forces Japan. These originated in Washington and were desired to fill specific gaps in our intelligence.

132

These were turned over to Lieutenant Harris and he used these requirements. We were also directed to verify suspected radar sites along the coast of the Democratic People's Republic of Korea.

We carried two Marine sergeants with us who spoke the Korean language. Our plan of action after receiving the order to commence the mission against the Democratic People's Republic of Korea was to proceed undetected to the first of our three operation areas. In order to avoid being detected we did not radiate any electronic waves. We secured our radars, transmitters, and the depth finder and proceeded north in as much secrecy as possible. Our plan was to stay out of known radar ranges until we reached the third operation area, when we would come closer to shore and try and listen to military radio transmissions of the Democratic People's Republic of Korea.

What was the most important in our mission was to reconnoiter off of four ports known to be the naval bases of the Democratic People's Republic of Korea. These were Chongjin, Songjin, Mayang Do, and Wonsan. We had to penetrate deep into the coastal waters of the mentioned areas and use various electromagnetic equipment to intercept radio waves in these areas to see if we could gather any communications intelligence.

For this espionage mission the naval security group at Kamiseya, Japan, provided us with a list of frequencies known to be used by the Korean People's Army. In this espionage mission my job as an operations officer was very important. I had many things to do with the operations aboard and especially had to stand eight hours of watch and keep the narrative of the search for the captain. I also had to pay attention to any change of course and speed while conducting visual and electronic search and putting the results in my narration. Performing the mission after we departed Sasebo, we were supported by the intelligence section of Commander, U.S. Naval Forces, Japan; U.S. Pacific Command Electronic Intelligence Center; and our U.S. Naval Security Group located eight miles from Yokohama. We operated under the operations orders of the CTF 96 of the U.S. Navy. Daily at 0900 hours throughout the mission the research operations gave me a list of the radars they had intercepted the day before. I made this list part of my daily narrative I wrote for the captain.

The details of our espionage activities in the three operations areas were as follows: At the first op area I conducted electronic detection to identify the activity of the naval vessels and aircraft of the Korean People's Army. We reached the vicinity of Songjin, where we detected electronic waves from MIG's for many minutes and marked them on the charts and recorded the information in my radar log. We sailed by night deep into the area off Songjin to get more accurate information.

At that time I saw a navigational light from Songjin harbor, so we put out the lights at the mast so as not to be detected and, while lying there for two hours, intercepted various radar signals. As there was a danger of our being detected we sped off into the sea for two hours and again came up to the preplanned area to continue the espionage. It was at this point that I detected two ships steaming two one five and several naval vessels of the Korean People's Army circling nearby. Together with Lawrence Mack I took, in a clandestine manner, photographs of the ships that came in sight. In this area I detected the land-based early warning radars on a number of occasions. Although I reported the electronic waves I had detected I did not know what sort of radars they were. I just tape-recorded those electronic waves.

I conducted espionage activities in the second op area roughly as follows. While our ship was conducting espionage activities in the second op area, I continued visual and electronic surveillance and entered the intercepted electronic waves in my log. That time I caught on more than 30 occasions radars, including ground-based early warning radars, and recorded the data obtained. We made our way deep into the coastal waters to confirm more intelligence information. When our ship reached the Orang Dan area, keeping close to the shore, we could see with the naked eye smoke rising in the vicinity. I checked the area on the map. It was Orang Dan area no doubt.

To be exact, we approached waters 41 degrees, 25 minutes north, 130 degrees, 3 minutes east, 11.2 miles from Orang Dan. Here I sighted several vessels and took photographs of their movements. After recording the results in the narration, I informed the captain and Lieutenant Harris of the material.

Further, we changed the course to Mayang Do, the main point of our detection. We got underway for a while and I sighted two ships heading north. One was about 400 feet long and the other was about 300 feet. We also took photographs of the movements of these ships. Here we intercepted navigational radars and various others and put them on record. That night we hurriedly headed for Mayang Do for the purpose of detecting submarines in the vicinity of the island. That night we approached waters 39 degrees, 48.9 minutes north, 128 degrees, 1.9 minutes east, about 8.2 miles from Mayang Do when I saw lights from the island. We lay there for a long time in order to detect military installations on Mayang Do and whenever there arose a danger of being detected we got out of the waters at full speed and then again approached the waters to go on with our search. Meanwhile, around 1700, 0200 Korean time, a submarine chaser was sighted when my ship was lying less than 1,000 yards from her. There we made every effort to spot submarines of the Korean People's Army, but in vain.

134

The day before our capture we proceeded for the port of Wonsan. Under the screen of night we approached close to the port, where we watched shipping to identify the movements of the naval vessels of the Korean People's Army and gather data on the number of incoming and outgoing ships and their conditions to ascertain the capacity of the port. We also detected electronic signals transmitted in the area of Wonsan and intercepted various electronic waves. I photographed the movements of scores of naval vessels and fishing boats while pinpointing them on the charts.

In the third operation area I intercepted various special radars, including early warning radars ground based in the Soviet Union. During my mission in the third operation area I intercepted various radars on 135 occasions, and photographed the movements of military ships and fishing boats on scores of occasions. The obtained intelligence information on radar networks was to be reported directly by Lieutenant Harris to the chief of the U.S. Naval Security Station, Washington, D.C.; all the other military intelligence information was to be reported by myself to the U.S. Chief of Naval Operations through the Commander Naval Forces, Japan, the Commander Seventh Fleet, the Commander U.S. Pacific Fleet, and the Commander in Chief U.S. Pacific Command.

We further proceeded into coastal waters off Wonsan. It was at this moment that the naval patrol boats of the Korean People's Army appeared suddenly and signaled for our nationality. To hide our identity we signaled hydrographer and hurriedly made ourselves away from there, while firing immediately on the naval patrol boats of the Korean People's Army. However, our ship had gone so close to the coast of the Democratic People's Republic of Korea that it was no use for us to try to escape and we were arrested at last by the naval patrol craft of the Korean People's Army.

Since I was arrested I have thought again and again about my criminal acts. What I have done against the government of the Democratic People's Republic of Korea and the Korean people is a criminal act that can never be tolerated. I humbly beg of you to forgive me my crime. The crime was committed by myself and our ship on the personal direction of the Commander U.S. Naval Forces, Japan, with the approval of the U.S. Army, Navy, and Air Force Joint Chiefs of Staff, Washington, D.C. The intelligence material collected by me was to be used for the attack against the Democratic People's Republic of Korea. This is a most serious crime and an act of aggression. I am a criminal who has committed a capital crime against the government of the Democratic People's Republic of Korea and the Korean people.

Frankly speaking, I concealed the truth only a few days ago because I feared it would make my crime greater to confess my crime as it was.

135

But that was not the attitude I could take any further. I am deeply moved by the humanitarian treatment accorded us guilty persons by the government of the Democratic People's Republic of Korea. I am grateful for this opportunity of confession offered to such a criminal as I. As such a serious criminal, I admit that I should be punished by the laws of the Democratic People's Republic of Korea. I beg of the government of the Democratic People's Republic of Korea to forgive me my crimes leniently. Please forgive me and let me go home. Then I will never repeat such a crime as long as I live. I swear before God. I say this sincerely. This is my honest confession. I cannot yet say that I have confessed all my crimes. I will go on with my confession in earnest.

I wondered after I had read this typed confession whether Super C or Scar had ever bothered to look at my handwritten confessions, or had simply been told by their translators that I had nothing new in them. When did they write my confession for me? The third day? The fifth? Was it all a sick game, those interrogations? Or were Snot Nose and Deputy Dawg victims, in their own right, kept ignorant of all the *Pueblo* documents that contained the information they were trying to get out of me? I did not understand.

Finally Scar delivered the ultimatum I had been expecting. "Will you sign it?"

I looked at him, hating him, hating the events that had put me in his hands, hating myself for not being able to kill myself, hating the whole Democratic People's Republic of Korea and everyone in it. Would I sign it? I said to myself: "You knew on Sunday as you faced the bucket that it was either die there or confess to something against your will here. This is your moment. Just thank God there is nothing really sensitive in that confession. What choice do you have? You cannot kill yourself. We have had that course, Schumacher."

I was filled with despair as I answered Scar. "Yes."

"Take it back in your room," he ordered.

The guard and I walked out of the death house again. I carried the typed pages of my "confession" with me. I put them on the table where I had tried to outmaneuver the Koreans on paper. But they had all the guns, once again. Max came into the room. He told me to copy it down in my own handwriting. I block-printed it.

At 6:00 P.M. that same black Thursday, Scar called me back to the Big Room. A camera crew—we called them the Warner Brothers —wheeled lights into the dim room. I found myself stung by the same glare I had felt upon arriving at the Pyongyang station eight days earlier. I could see an Arriflex camera, despite the lights, and hear it whir.

"Sign it," Max commanded as he pointed to the offending confession in front of me—written with my own hand. Sign it, he said. Just like that—sign it. Look, world! See? We yank the string; the puppet's hand moves across the paper. The pen writes his name. Sign it! Max was asking me to sign the death warrant of my spirit. I knew it. My mind searched one last time for an escape. It could not find any. I took the pen and signed the paper.

I had lost. That act of signing a phony confession was my surrender. I had lost my own cold war. The realization depressed me. I had let myself and everybody else down. I sank deep down again, though not as deep as on Sunday.

I was not only ordered to sign the confession again, while sitting at the long table under a floodlight, but I was also directed to read every word of the typed confession into a Sony 500 tape recorder. The camera whirred all the while. Then the guard took me back to my room.

I was alone again with my thoughts. Self-incrimination took over. I lay there on the bed, facing the white wall. I felt violated, unclean. The only good I could see that might come from what I had just done was that it would let my family know I was alive—physically, at least. My spirit had died the moment I struck the paper with the pen at the end of the typed "confession." I had let down myself, my country, my Navy, my family. The fact that I had had no choice failed to lighten the cold darkness inside me.

Rewards for Pawns

It did not make me feel any better when, after that awful day of confession, the North Koreans expressed their thanks. They sent their no-nonsense waitress into my room the next day with a small dish of candy, some cookies, and a cup filled with a warm milky substance.

I had been hungry ever since the capture of the ship—ravenously hungry at times. I had lost, I figured, close to twenty pounds. Yet I eyed the goodies as though they were forbidden fruit. I knew only too well why there was something more than the usual bowl of turnips and a cup of plain hot water.

But the treats had been introduced with no fanfare, no lengthy speech about how I was to be rewarded, no statement that I was being treated better than the others, assuming that there were still others. I sat and looked at the dishes on my table. Were they crazy enough to think that I signed that confession for this? Or were they simply playing on the guilt they knew I must feel?

Imprisonment is made up of all kinds of minute decisions like this one before me: to eat or not to eat the rewards. The loneliness of being locked up in a room by yourself makes normally small decisions into outsize ones. The mind wants to win something, anything. To let go of everything is to lose everything. The man locked up alone and tormented by his conscience and his captors must hold something back. His self-confidence and his pride must be protected inside him.

So I tried to search for perspective. I was well aware, by now, of the psychological game of dependence the North Koreans were playing. They knew too well how sanity is preserved by the little comforts and regularities, by a daily routine, by some sort of system and order. The cookies represented a threat only if I became dependent on them, only if, by their denial, the Koreans could inflict further suffering. By presenting these overt rewards, they were assuming an attitude of guilt on my part. My best response, therefore, would not be defiant rejection, but melancholy indifference. They were playing by their rules; I decided to play by mine.

As I had done before in the Barn, I compromised. I decided there was not much point in letting these little things have a large effect. I ate a couple of the cookies and left the milky stuff untouched. The Koreans considered the hot milk a big treat and asked why I had not drunk it. I said I didn't like hot milk.

The rewards extended beyond these few bright spots in my gray diet. Clean Floors, our name for the officer who was the Barn's custodian, showed sudden interest in the icy temperature of my room. He felt the heatless radiator one morning and shook his head disapprovingly. The wind, which was blowing against him from the loose-fitting window at the time, made the sheet between the double windows billow out. He held up his hand, as if to test the wind's strength. Then, like an unfeeling landlord in a slum tenement, he left my room. That was the end of his participation. But he must have said something to Snot Nose, who came in the next night after the supper hour to appraise the frigid room. There seemed to be nothing he could do about the faulty radiator, but he had a definite idea for the leaky window. "I get weather stripping," he said, leaving me to wonder what that was going to mean.

He returned a half hour later with strips of tissue paper in one hand and a bowl of rice paste in the other. Since it was after 10:00 P.M., I was in bed. He ordered me up and instructed me in the Democratic People's Republic of Korea art of weather stripping. The idea, as his sawing of the air and instructions indicated, was to paste the paper not only over the cracks between the window frame and the window, but over most of the glass as well. I was tired, cold, disgusted, depressed, and irritated with everything and everybody—most of all myself. The last thing I wanted to do was this. But Snot Nose was insistent: "Tonight you fix window."

He left me with the paper strips and the rice paste. The paste was fast turning lumpy from the cold. I smeared around—not being any kind of skilled handyman—with the paste and paper until 1:30 in the morning. I did a lousy job, but I didn't care if they shot me for it.

The next morning I expected Snot Nose to conduct a pompous inspection, bringing along a guard whose kicks and punches would show me the error of my ways. But hardly anything ever worked out as I expected. The guard did come into my room, but only to tell me to grab my bed, table, chair, and cup, and to move out. I was getting the empty room in which I had spent so much time with Blue Socks and Snot Nose. This room was heated and on the sunny side of the building.

Another bit of amelioration then showed up in my old, still-heatless room: a barber for the *Pueblo* penitents. The guards carried in a barber chair with padded arms and tilting headrest, a table for a bar of soap and a crude-looking straight-edged razor, a large cracked mirror, and, finally, a barber. He was short, unsmiling, and wore a Western-style white coat. Stranger still, by Western standards, he never said a word as he hacked away at the whiskers of the hated Americans. His shaves, administered with a dull blade, cold water, and gross indifference, felt to me more like eyebrow-plucking, but I must admit that he never once drew blood. His haircuts were quickie jobs. He got so cold, however, that he was moved out after one week to warmer quarters. Four unfortunate crew members got the cold room.

For once in my life, I would have welcomed a talkative barber. I was still in solitary confinement. When you have no one to speak to day after day, your thoughts are like a poison gas filling up a room. No matter how trivial the thought, or no matter how hard you try to stay thoughtless, whatever is in your mind escapes all through your being. You lose the ability to compartmentalize, to put troubled thoughts to one side and go about doing something else. There is nothing else.

140

Like the prisoner I was, I scratched out a calendar in a patch of soft plaster in my new room. I was trying to put some confines on this ordeal, to retrieve a sense of dimensions. Marking the changeless hours into days again would help, I thought. I tried to marshal my thoughts on points outside myself. I focused on the crew, on the Koreans' strategy, hour after hour. It seemed certain to me now that they were not going to kill us. We obviously were hostages. Just how we would be used by Kim Il Sung was the big question. A public trial seemed a real possibility.

There was no one in those dreary days of February to try my ideas on. This made it difficult to keep things in proportion. Did the blackout curtains recently put up over the Barn's windows and doors mean the U.S. was massing carriers for a bombing raid against Pyongyang? Did that smirk on the duty officer's face mean there was a new turn of events? Was the apparent absence of Super C proof that meaningful negotiations for our release were about to begin? I could ask the questions day after day, then toy with the answers. But all by myself.

Although he probably never realized it, and I had no way as his prisoner to put it into words, I appreciated, as much as anything in that low period, the visit from the Korean officer called Specs. He wore glasses—hence his nickname—and had a gentleness about him. He had the more distracted eyes of the intellectual, not the crafty, cruel look I had steeled myself against in those first terrible days. He came into my room one evening after supper and talked to me as though I was a human. In response to my questions, he said that I could not see the other crew members, but I could take his word for it they were alive. The wounded were being treated, and the one man who had been seriously wounded had been taken to the hospital for an operation. The other officers were all getting along well.

Specs spoke no English and used as an interpreter an officer I had never seen before and never saw again. Specs was circumspect, and I was baffled in trying to understand the real purpose of his visit. Though he was the number-three officer in seniority, his visit seemed to be prompted by pity. As he was about to leave, he looked me straight in the eye and said, "I hope you will be going home soon." I knew he meant it.

. . .

It became increasingly clear what kind of game the Koreans were playing now that they had my confession and those of other crew members. We were pawns in a tense diplomatic chess game between the United States and North Korean governments.

Evidence of this came late in the evening of February 7 when the "Habitability" colonel paid me a visit and told me that I was "invited"—that is what he said, "You are invited"—to celebrate the twentieth anniversary of the founding of the Korean People's Army the next day. I stared uncomprehendingly at the high forehead of this rather pompous officer. "It will be for you a holiday," he continued. "You must make yourself ready."

I didn't see much that I could do to get ready, but the Koreans did. Clean Floors decided that I needed a shave to make me presentable. Using his own straight-edged razor blade, sharpened on his own wide duty belt, a cup of cold water, and a bar of soap, he proceeded to give me a shave, much to the amusement of the two duty officers accompanying him. Completing the ordeal quickly, he groveled out, eyes down, inspecting the floor boards, as always, for stray dirt. One of the duty officers instructed me, in broken English: "All right, now you sleep. For tomorrow. Holiday is okay, all right?"

As it turned out, the big party consisted of me, all by myself in my room—a joyous party in solitary confinement. A guard escorted into my room that same wooden-faced waitress, who this time was loaded down with Korean delicacies: fried fish, an egg, salt, hot sweet bread, a piece of fried chicken (or was it rabbit?), turnips—always the turnips—butter, mashed potatoes, dried squid, potato soup, and even a slice of sausage. She spread a green plastic cloth on my wooden table and then arranged the food on it. I felt it was too good to be true when a liter of North Korean beer and a glass of the native liquor called "ginseng" were set on the table alongside the food. But I was reassured by the tray full of glasses.

Then I assumed that the meal was just a trick, and that they would whisk the food away just before my first bite. A slender, effete officer flitted into the room to approve the arrangements. When he was satisfied, he urged me to eat and smile at the same time—no mean trick. I dug in, just as the room was invaded by photographers.

142

This was the same wonderful team that was present at the signing of the confession, back again for scene two: "See the confessed American stooge eat. See how nice we treat him. See how the glorious Democratic People's Republic of Korea is so gracious to the hated imperialists." The smile, of course, was to show the world how grateful I was. Grimly, I lowered my head and changed the grip on my cup to show the world the unmistakable "fuck you" extended finger. The photographers' lights eventually went out. And, to my surprise, they let me finish eating.

A few other rewards followed the meal. Max came with a stack of books and handed me a thick volume of the writings of Comrade Kim Il Sung. It consisted entirely of speeches and addresses Kim had made during the course of his life establishing the directions and goals of his Communist party for "the peace-loving 40 million Korean people" (30 million of whom live in South Korea). Max was back in a few moments with another gift, of far more consequence: a set of Chinese playing cards. These, quite naturally, superseded the heavy writings of Kim. I occupied countless hours with solitaire and poker and bridge hands. Later that night still more propaganda was handed out: pamphlets detailing the "gross violations" of the armistice agreement by the United States and the various "atrocities" committed by the U.S. Eighth Army stationed in Korea. I put those aside to study later.

But the Koreans' strategy was beginning to become clear. They certainly had no intention of showing their own people a film of an American eating food they themselves did not have. They must be planning to play to the world audience outside their own country, and I had just finished being an unwitting collaborator in this effort. I figured that there would be more propaganda charades. Yet where was I to hide? How could I prevent it? I was reduced to waiting for and wondering about the next gambit in this new program of humiliation.

I didn't have long to wait. Three days later, on February 11, a Sunday afternoon, Colonel Scar called me once again into that end room. With scarcely a word of introduction, he handed me a stack of typed pages and said that I should read it "to see if there are any errors in it." A quick glance at the twenty-five typed pages told me that this was a copy of a confession prepared for Captain Bucher's signature. At least that buttressed Specs' assurance that the Captain was still alive.

I must have revealed my surprise, for Scar was beaming. With a patronizing tone he handed me a package of cigarettes and said I should smoke. "Take your time," he said, speaking jovially, through that hated interrogator Max. "I want you to study it very carefully."

The typed confession was excruciatingly complete, demonstrating a thorough understanding of the *Pueblo*'s mission. In fact, it was too thorough, and too complete, and reflected the documents from which it came, not the Commanding Officer.

. . . The operation order directed me to sail from Sasebo about 10 January into the East Sea of Korea and operate in three operational areas. . . . While in these three operational areas, I was to determine the electronic environment with emphasis on determining the naval order of battle of the Korean People's Army and the extent of the naval activity in four areas; namely Chongin, Songjin, Mayang Do and Wonsan areas, and on fixing the positions of radars on the coast of the Democratic People's Republic of Korea.

The operation order also directed me to determine the reaction from the Democratic People's Republic of Korea and the Soviet Union, respectively, to an overt intelligence collector operating in the periphery of the Democratic People's Republic of Korea and actively conducting surveillance of the Korean People's Army and U.S.S.R. naval units, and to evaluate USS *Pueblo*'s capabilities as a naval collection ship.

This operational order was transmitted to me by the message from COMNAVFORJAPAN dated 16 December 1967, and our operation was called Pinkroot One. . . .

We were also provided with the "specific intelligence collection requirements" for determining the present strength of the submarine force of the Korean People's Army. . . . We were told that possibly the submarines were kept at Mayang Do area and were instructed to try to confirm this by sighting. . . .

So far it was a complete reconstruction, probably from those same documents I had seen on Super C's desk ten days before. But the next paragraph told me the Captain was alive.

I was personally ordered to check the flights of U.S. satellites if I

144

could spot them and was provided with a chart showing the paths of U.S. satellites.

Well, I thought, that was a complete fabrication, but definitely something the Captain might well have devised. The rest of the statement continued to echo documents captured with the ship.

We were provided with another chart which showed the locations of known radars which were located in the coastal areas of the Democratic People's Republic of Korea. We were told to intercept and reaffirm these radars and to record any new radars accurately when detected. . . .

We were told to record all radar signals so they could later be analyzed by others who specialize in this work. . . .

Our electronic detector measures the frequency of the transmitted pulse of the target radar and identifies it as whichever type it is. . . .

In the Songjin area we intercepted a new radar, not before known. It was a radar designated as crosslot, which I thought was for early air warning. But I was not able to confirm the location of this radar due to its infrequent operation and the fact that my direction finding equipment was unreliable. . . .

After this last operation, *Pueblo* was to operate in the vicinity of Vladivostok of the Soviet Union from about February 20 to March 20 and then to be along the Kamchatka Peninsula. . . .

Scar let the import of the "confession" sink in. I knew I could be beaten for not having revealed the same details. But Scar's motive was different this time. He had shown me the confession so I would realize how much information about our mission was already known to him. Then he stated his proposition: "We are planning a press conference. We would like you to participate. We will send officers to assist you in the preparation. All of the *Pueblo* officers will participate. We have not decided when it will be held."

I leaned back in my chair and studied Scar. Perhaps he could read my thoughts, too. They had found another pressure point, but were parlaying it this time into a greater capitulation. They let me see from the pages I had just finished reading that they had a perfect right—under their rules—to press down on those points and cut off my blood. Scar could have said, thundering, "Schumacher, you bastard! How insincere you are. Do you take us for fools? Do you really think your 'confession' was anywhere near complete?

You have lied to us, and we are going to show you what we do with liars." That was their scenario. Scar had the drop on me and knew it. But he was apparently not interested in going over past ground; he was gearing up for his press conference. So there it was: go along with our little press conference or we will go back to beating a better confession out of you. At least I had the choice, it seemed.

Blue Socks and Captain Nice—so named because he smiled all the while he was translating dire Korean warnings into pleasant-sounding English—came into my room the morning after the session with Scar. "Here," said Captain Nice, "are some questions you might be asked at the press conference." Blue Socks then went over the list, dictating the answers I was to give. The answers, they said, were "for learning." That was Monday, February 12, Lincoln's Birthday, an ironic day to have to memorize enemy propaganda to spew out into the world as my own.

Tuesday was the big day. Blue Socks and Captain Nice came into my room that morning for a rehearsal. They asked me the questions; I spouted out the memorized answers. They left very pleased with themselves. I was ordered to remain in my room until called out for the press conference.

At 2:00 P.M. a guard came in and motioned me with his AK-47 to come out into the hall. There—to my disbelief and transcendent relief—stood all the officers of the *Pueblo*. I knew they were all alive for the first time since the "you will be shot before sunrise" threat of January 24. We nodded grateful greetings to one another, like men resurrected from the dead, searching each other's eyes for a clue or an answer. I wanted to touch each of my fellow officers to make really sure he was alive. But that was impossible. Everybody looked worn and thin. The Captain, with his barrel chest and burning eyes, still looked rugged. But his face was devastated. The horror showed. None of us looked very proud of what we had been through; none of us looked forward to what was coming. We wanted to talk but couldn't because of all the guards. Instead, we were marched into that same grim interrogation room at the end of the hall on the third floor of the Barn.

Inside, about twenty people were jammed, all dressed in civilian

146

clothes. All but four of them were Korean officers, easily recognized despite the mufti. The room looked like a rough approximation of a televised Senate hearing—lots of smoke, lights, cameras, hoselike cords, shuffling technicians, confusion, heat. We sat down at a rectangular table facing a U-shaped one occupied by the "correspondents." Surprisingly, one of those four was a frizzly-haired woman, whose only concern seemed to be how many children we had. The only other distinguishable face belonged to a quietly precise questioner who spoke as if he were wearing a dog collar with a long leash back to Pyongyang.

Our table was laden with cigarettes, apples, candy, and cookies. Gene, who sat on my right, and I proceeded to eat as much as we could. Ed Murphy sat on my left; next to him, the Captain; then Steve, Tim, and, for some reason, Friar Tuck. The questions were asked in Korean first, and then translated into English for us.

"You officers look well and fine," a "correspondent" began. "How is the health of the crew of the *Pueblo?* You, Captain, please."

"The health of the crew of the *Pueblo,*" the Captain began, giving his memorized answer, "now in general is good. . . ."

"Well," the correspondent said, "it's some time since you came here. I would like to hear your impressions of your life here."

"Yes, sir," said the Captain. "My impression, as Commanding Officer, has been that the Democratic People's Republic of Korea is very progressive and has a gentlemanly and understanding people."

After a few questions like that, the press conference got into the technicalities of the mission. This was the exchange between a "correspondent" and Steve Harris:

CORRESPONDENT: Research Officer, I have a question to ask you. You said that you had a special detachment under your command, and I want to know how the detachment performed its mission.

HARRIS: Yes, I, as Research Officer, am in charge of a special detachment of thirty people including myself whose primary purpose is to assist the Commanding Officer in his intelligence collection efforts by providing him any information which may be intercepted through listening to radio signals or intercepting radar waves. The second function of the special research detachment is to intercept, collect, and record all radio or radar signals of interest to us, submit the recordings and copied transmissions for analysis to the National Security Agency near Washington, D.C. It is also to collect radar signals, make recordings of these, and submit them to the Pacific Command Electronic Intelligence Center for analysis. On technical matters concerning the collection of electronic signals, I receive my orders directly from the Director of the U.S. Naval Security Group Pacific located in Hawaii.

I winced as I heard those details go out to the world. It became more obvious to me what a large bundle of detailed documents the Koreans must have captured from Steve's spaces. My turn to gag was coming, as the Communist catechism about our intruding North Korean territorial waters was recited by the Captain. Then I cut in with the following, as directed beforehand: "As all of us put forward in our confessions and as the documents about the position log were obtained from the *Pueblo* and other papers and documents, charts, and so forth on board the ship, there was absolutely no basis by which anyone can say that we did not violate the territorial waters of the Democratic People's Republic of Korea. . . ."

The press conference served two purposes for the Koreans. It buoyed up their claim that we had invaded their territorial waters and it projected us as repentant criminals in case the Korean government wanted an excuse to spare our lives at the end of the chess game with the American government.

None of us at this time felt sure how the game would come out. I asked Gene, in a whisper, what he thought our chances were. "I don't see how they can ever let us go," he said. Murphy just shook his head, equally baffled. We had no further opportunity to discuss the prospects at this first reunion. But the Captain did make a point of asking each of us if we had suffered any "permanent damage." And he also passed the word that Hodges had died shortly after our seizure, but, he emphasized, in American, not Korean, hands.

The press conference did not depress me too much. It was merely so much window dressing. And there was a certain humorous irony to the proceedings, because the correspondents probably had to spend just as much time memorizing their lines as we did. Moreover, seeing the press corps stacked with Korean officers was a clear example of what they meant by a "free and open" press conference.

Evidently believing that lies gain credibility with repeating, the North Koreans decided that individual confessions and a filmed press conference were not enough. Their propaganda offensive gained momentum during the rest of February, with round three opening the day after the press conference.

"Well," Super C said as he opened the first of many sessions with the *Pueblo*'s officers, "we think that the press conference was very successful. And we think that your individual confessions are very *sincere*"—the interpreter emphasized that word—"are very sincere and complete. Individually each of you has asked for mercy, but we think the collective, the whole crew together should apologize to the Korean people for your crimes. You see, under the Korean correct system of justice, leniency is shown to those who are truly repentant and earnestly seek forgiveness. Therefore, we would suggest that you write a joint letter of apology to the Korean people." He urged us to proceed immediately. Then, in typical Communist-party fashion, he formed a committee, consisting of us and his trusted Lieutenant Colonel Scar, to write the document. The result of this forty-eight-hour "joint" effort was a document, immediately broadcast to the world, establishing the North Korean position on the *Pueblo* incident. It said:

We, the whole crew of the USS *Pueblo,* captured by the naval forces of the Korean People's Army while conducting espionage activities after having intruded deep into the territorial waters of the Democratic People's Republic of Korea, frankly admit and truly repent our serious crimes. We hereby submit a joint letter of apology in order to request the government of the Democratic People's Republic of Korea to deal with us leniently.

That line—written by the Koreans for our signature—seemed to commit Kim Il Sung to treating us humanely. Otherwise, why talk about leniency with the whole world listening? But the next paragraph contained the escape clause in case the United States made an unfavorable move.

We deserve any punishment by the Korean people regardless of its

149

severity for the crime we have committed by making overt intrusions into the territorial waters of a sovereign state; namely, the Democratic People's Republic of Korea, and perpetrating grave hostile acts.

In the next sentence we had to sign away our right to be treated as prisoners of war—not that our signatures would really make any difference.

Since we are not mere prisoners of war but criminals caught in the very act of espionage, we cannot have any complaint even should the worst come.

The Koreans' concern for their world image showed in the next lines.

The government of the Democratic People's Republic of Korea, however, has treated us in such a humanitarian way that there is little difference between our present life and our life before our detention except for our guilty consciences as criminals. We are deeply moved by such leniency as accorded us by the government of the Democratic People's Republic of Korea, for which we would like first of all to express our heartfelt gratitude.

In case another government might try to undercut this confession by claiming that it was beaten out of us when we had no idea that it would be beamed to the world—otherwise we would have held out longer—the confession next stated:

We are all well aware, in connection with the incident of the *Pueblo*'s intrusion into the territorial waters of the Democratic People's Republic of Korea, that the attention of the Korean people and the world is focused on us, the party to the crime, and especially on our attitude.

The shrewd North Koreans next played their real trump card, emphasizing again that as long as we were in their hands we were playing their game.

Since we know better of what we did than anybody else, we alone, the men of the *Pueblo,* are witnesses who can give the surest evidence of these crimes and, therefore, we are bound to honestly confess our grave criminal acts.

Already on a number of occasions we have stated in our confessions the true nature of our crime and our true sentiment. However, we do not think that that is sufficient. Therefore, we would like to take this

150

opportunity to disclose once again the real facts of our crime and thereby make our sincere deep apologies to the government of the Democratic People's Republic of Korea and the Korean people. We humbly request them to show generosity in dealing with us and have mercy on us if possible, so that we may return home as soon as possible.

Should a skeptic ask why, if the facts were as stated, we did not come right out weeks ago and admit our "crimes," the North Koreans had an answer.

We were reluctant to make honest confessions of our crimes at the initial stage of our detention for we thought so great a crime might reflect on the honor of the United States of America and our own fate. But this foolish idea could not last long and was shattered before the stern truth evidenced by various espionage papers, documents, and corroborative data of our crimes which have been thoroughly reviewed and analyzed by the Korean People's Army.

We think that the Democratic People's Republic of Korea has ample evidence to convince the world. . . .

There followed a restatement of the *Pueblo* mission, parts of our previously signed confessions, and false data claiming that we had intruded into Korean territorial waters. "We have to say," read the apology, concerning the last, "that the intrusions were not caused by any inadvertent technical error on our part but were pre-arranged and pre-meditated acts of espionage." That statement, we quickly realized, would make it difficult for the United States government to pave the way for our release by stating that we had erred navigationally.

Through "our" apology, the North Koreans were giving themselves all sorts of options, while trying to close any for the United States. We were eighty-two pawns. I recognized this; yet, like every other member of the crew, I could see no way out of the dilemma. The harsh reality of this kind of captivity, we learned, is that pain can make you do anything. Once you have been broken by pain, it need not be inflicted anew to make you act against your will. The conviction that pain is ever behind the orders is very real. And the guards were always there to refresh our memory with kicks, smashes in the back with rifle butts, punches on the side of the head.

The second half of the apology concerned itself with the Korean

151

position toward us. First they had to make clear to the world that they did not hold us personally responsible.

Although our crime was serious enough, we are still hopeful that you understand that we only carried out the order of our superiors mechanically and it was by no means a deliberate, intentional act on our part.

We who were loyal to our military orders are stigmatized as criminals by having blindly joined in the tragic plot against the righteous Korean people. We are neither politicians nor military leaders and we are not well informed politically and know nothing at all on certain other questions.

We were not well aware why the U.S. government authorities and military leaders took so great an interest in the northeast coast of the Korean peninsula; further, the relations of our acts to U.S. policy and the use to which the data we had obtained would have been put were of no interest to us.

But now our eyes have been opened to the true nature of our crimes. We feel ashamed. We are sincerely apologetic for all our acts.

Then came the building of the case for an American government apology.

However, we must take note that the responsibility for the crimes belongs to those of us who committed them, and our government is even more responsible than us. The purpose of our armed forces is to carry out the policies decided by our government.

The contradiction between this and the statement earlier that "we are not mere prisoners of war" apparently did not bother the Communist author.

The responsibility for initiating this crime must therefore be borne by the U.S. administration authorities and military leaders. Sending the *Pueblo* into Korean waters is a completely criminal act of aggression. . . .

Our repentance for the criminal case of the *Pueblo* and our apology to the government of the Democratic People's Republic of Korea . . . can never be sufficient, because no matter how much we might apologize, it is an apology only by the members of the crew of the *Pueblo* and can never be an official apology on behalf of the United States.

Our fate depends largely on whether or not the government of the United States, which has forced us into espionage, makes public the facts of crimes to the fair world public opinion and apologizes to the government of the Democratic People's Republic of Korea. . . .

152

This document was not what we had written. They had used very little of our material. But because I could see no way out as I stood there looking at the handwritten apology on the table, and even though I knew I was again breaking the Code of Conduct, I signed it, as the camera whirred.

The crew, on the other hand, had little idea of what they were going to be asked to sign. In groups of about twenty they were called into the Big Room, where the *Pueblo* officers were already gathered. The Captain made a short and hopeful speech, saying that "the document I am asking you to sign tonight may help expedite our return." And, one by one, the crew members signed it. Most were thin and quite pale; a couple still limped from their wounds; none looked happy. Carefully, we counted them. Two were missing. Hodges, we knew, was dead. Woelk, Super C explained, confirming what Specs had told me, had been taken to the hospital for an operation. He was recovering nicely, and the Colonel planned to take the document to him for his signature. Later, the Captain said that he had seen the document after Woelk had signed it; he couldn't be sure, but he thought the signature looked real. Woelk did recover from his wounds after some harrowing medical treatment by the Koreans.

Back in my room, after the brief but intense reunion with the crew, the old loneliness flooded through me again. Yet I felt hopeful that we might get out alive, barring some drastic turn, such as the United States bombing Wonsan or Pyongyang. If that happened, we would have no value as hostages, and would probably be shot forthwith. That would be worth dying for, though. On reflection, I figured that since so much time had passed the U.S. was probably trying to solve the incident by negotiation.

There had been rumors from a couple of the duty officers of "talks" at Panmunjom. Judging from the apology we had just signed, I thought that the North Korean position there would consist of three A's: admit the espionage and intrusions, apologize for them, give assurances not to repeat them. I would have thought these demands were out of the question had it not been for a few passages in one of the pamphlets we had been given.

This pamphlet was entitled *Violations of the Korean Armistice Agreement by Imperialist Army of the U.S. Eighth Army*. It contained a reference to an alleged "intrusion into the air space of our side" by an "armed helicopter" of the U.S. Eighth Army. The helicopter, so the story went, had been flying an espionage mission when it deliberately intruded and was "shot down by the valiant self-defense forces of the Korean People's Army." The incident had taken place on May 17, 1963, and the two pilots, Ben W. Stutts and Carleton V. Voltz, were taken prisoner. Stutts and Voltz—who quickly became Nuts and Bolts as we *Pueblo* officers discussed the case in whispers whenever we found ourselves together—had been released. What gave me some hope was that the pamphlet said they were released after the head of the Eighth Army in Korea had admitted the intrusion and espionage, apologized for it, and given assurances that such an incident would not be repeated. The precedent boosted my morale even though the pamphlet also noted that Stutts and Voltz had spent a year and a day in captivity before their freedom was negotiated.

Super C let Colonel Scar introduce the next surprise all by himself. Gathered once again in that corner interrogation room, we learned of the next move, and it was a shock. "We think," Scar said, "that you should write a letter to your President informing him of the facts of the case. We would hope that this would help your plight and your fate. We think you should urge him to take the proper action." He paused, then repeated: "The proper action."

He had a few new tricks for this letter. First, he announced, we should "discuss the idea. After all, you are writing to your President. Of what concern is it to us?" And certainly, he said, we wouldn't mind if they made a tape recording and took some photographs. He then produced ten or fifteen letters supposedly composed by us. These were all addressed to our families. He was quick to point out, however, that some of the passages sounded quite sincere, and "possibly" we might be able to use them. Paper and pencils were quickly supplied, along with a couple of packs of cigarettes. The Captain asked for a typewriter, and Scar was more than pleased to accommodate him.

154

After the cameramen were finished, Scar announced that to make our job easier he was assigning us a room across the hall for our use, as well as one of his officers, to "assist" us. That officer turned out to be Silver Lips, a curly-haired major of medium height whose favorite, and apparently only, line was, "Ah, yes. I see. Well, if you will excuse me for one moment, I will ask my superiors." Unlike Max and Captain Nice, he did his job without interjecting his own personality or opinions. He was precise, refined, impersonal, and restrained, always courteous to us and respectful to his superiors. We were not surprised when he emerged as Super C's number-one interpreter.

We worked that night for a couple of hours, mostly regurgitating the apology we had just signed. The next afternoon Silver Lips picked up our papers, and that night Colonel Scar confronted us again. He had, he said, taken our various ideas and "put them together. Well," he continued, "I took some from here, and a little from there and some I made up myself." He was obviously quite proud of his authorship as he handed over a thirty-page typed letter for us to "approve."

The Captain read it aloud to the rest of us. The stumbling block was, of course, the alleged intrusions. Our government would know we had not intruded, and the Captain figured that the U.S. would not, and should not, humiliate itself by lying. We figured that the best angle was to contend that we personally had intruded—in direct violation of our orders. Then the U.S. could apologize for its overzealous captain, which would be a lot easier than declaring before the world that it had a policy of premeditated intrusion.

Scar's retort was, "But, if you did it on your own initiative, then you should bear all the blame and you would never go home." The Captain was quick to respond that that was exactly what he was proposing. Scar then said this was absolutely impossible. Our government was equally responsible and therefore should share the blame. We resigned ourselves and said the letter sounded fine. Scar was elated and sent us to bed.

The next morning we were again called out for a meeting. Before it got underway, Gene told the Captain that he thought the letter

155

to the President was in bad taste and that he had no intention of signing it. The Captain readily agreed.

Instead of Colonel Scar, however, Super C breezed in, obviously tense and nervous. He immediately addressed the Captain. "I have read your letter and want to know what you think of it."

This put the Captain on the spot, because, ostensibly, at least, it was we who had written the letter now in front of Super C. The Captain responded that he thought it was a good letter but hedged by saying that he wasn't sure it was the proper letter to send to a head of state.

Super C liked the answer and quickly agreed that "perhaps the tone is not quite right. And," he continued, "I am afraid that if you sent a letter that long to your President he would not read it." And then in a quiet voice he said: "I am afraid that my officers were carried away." He had rather definite ideas about how the letter should be formed. "As a military man, I do not like to waste words. Let us get to work."

So once more the process began. Our fumbling draft, again presenting the overzealous-captain theme, was presented; their censored version was returned. We told Super C that we wanted selected members of the crew to read the letter first, and he agreed. This would give us the chance to get eight or ten of the crew members together and obtain some sort of report on the crew's condition.

Hurriedly and in whispers, we learned about fierce eight-hour beatings administered to Marine Sergeant Robert J. Hammond, about the condition of the wounded Chicca and Crandell, and about the treatment in general. The crew, Chief CT James F. Kell told us, had heard the officers' confessions, had imagined how they were gotten, but had been noncommittal in their comments. So far, the questioning had seemed to be purely for propaganda; there had been nothing of any depth. The Captain told the men to consider the oceanographic cover of the ship completely blown and the specifics of the mission known. "No point in getting beat for that info. Anything else, lie like hell." At the conclusion of our meeting, after Silver Lips had left to "check with my superiors," Chief Engineman Monroe O. Goldman, the Chief Master at Arms and Chief of the Boat, leaned

156

over and said: "Don't worry, Captain. Anything you want to do is okay with us. We're behind you and your officers all the way."

Super C took our version of the letter and inserted the North Korean position. We had fought and lost again the battle for the over-zealous-captain theme, and were equally unsuccessful in trying to make the North Korean demands positive instead of conditional. We had written that "we will be returned when our government admits frankly, apologizes. . . ." Super C's version read: "We think we will be returned only when our government. . . ." All in all, I felt that the letter was about as clear a blackmail note as could be conceived without actually naming the ransom price.

After several days of waiting, on the evening of February 29 the officers and crew assembled to sign the letter. The cameramen were back to capture each signature for posterity as the men filed in one by one and signed the white paper. In the confusion, Harry Iredale had the boldness to lean over and ask me if I thought the letter would help our situation. I looked up at him quickly and answered: "Not a chance." He agreed.

The North Koreans obviously thought differently. So pleased were they with themselves and their deft diplomatic maneuvers that they started to loosen their grip on us. Super C received word via the International Red Cross that one of the men had just become a father. After a discussion with the Captain, he called the crew together and let the Captain make the announcement.

That was just the beginning. The next evening, to our great surprise, we were allowed outdoors to exercise for about ten minutes. After supper, and long after sunset, we lined up and moved in two columns to a dark track not far from the Barn. The air was icy cold, the sky clear and flooded with stars. There were, of course, snow and ice on the ground, but after so many weeks of isolation, the beauty of the night was overwhelming. All of us welcomed the opportunity to get some fresh air.

Exercise now seemed to be Super C's order of the day. Two ping-pong tables were set up. In the evenings the men were called out a room at a time and allowed to play for about twenty minutes. The crew asked, and received, permission to do morning exercises

157

in the hallways for about fifteen minutes. Law was named the "leader," and the officers were permitted to join in. Talking was forbidden, but these new exercise periods gave us the opportunity to pass notes and whisper. These periods were important, too, because they got the crew together again, if only briefly. The mind-spinning of solitary confinement slowed. We were gradually becoming a united Navy crew again.

The interrogations had virtually ceased, which was the biggest relief of all. It looked as if, for the moment anyway, the North Koreans were unaware of the vast knowledge and experience some of the members of the crew had; or else they had no further interest in our intelligence operations. Our value to them was apparently as propaganda pawns only.

The Barn was still a menacing place, however, and when the short periods of exercise were over, we had to contend with that empty room, that naked twenty-four-hour light bulb, and the unsympathetic guards.

The guards took all the liberties they could when out of sight of the day's duty officers. One Saturday, for example, the guard outside my door accused me of speaking to Hammond, who had been part of a work detail cleaning the hallway outside my open door. I had seen Hammond but we had exchanged nothing more than a quick glance. My claim meant nothing. The guard rushed me as I sat in my chair, pushed me down on the floor, then had me stand up and face the wall. He practiced his karate chops and kicks on my back for a while. When he turned me around, he delivered a roundhouse blow to my right eye. This session went on for a half hour, until he was relieved of his duty.

The reflex of a prisoner is to try to take such beatings without wincing. There is no thought of hitting back, or even of assuming a protective boxer's stance. It is best to take the punches standing relaxed. Rolling with them becomes a literal necessity, to survive permanent injury. But you have to give appropriate grunts and little cries of pain. Sooner or later while in the Barn we all learned the technique.

The next day the guard came by again, this time with some of his

158

fellow guards. He pointed to my injuries proudly and started at me again. Only the fortuitous arrival of the duty officer restrained him. He spit at me, shook his fist, and stomped out.

The next evening he came into my room for the third time, shaking his fist and growling. The Korean invectives seemed to be a threat to return tomorrow and finish the job. I went to bed that night feeling the old dread of the first days at the Barn.

Super C's Finishing School

All day Tuesday, March 5, I waited for the return of the guard. Nothing happened until late in the afternoon, when the duty officer we called King Kong strutted in. He was a very short junior officer with a large chest and flat feet. The skin of his round little moon face was stretched tight and was full of pockmarks. An early name for him had been Crater Face; but King Kong seemed to fit his personality better. He didn't walk; he either waddled or strutted.

With chest thrown out, head back, and short stubby arms swinging energetically, he entered the room. In very bad English, spoken as though his mouth were full of cotton, he instructed me to roll up my mattress. I looked at him as if he were crazy, but he persisted in his mumbling. Finally he gave up and did it himself, rolling up the mattress, blankets, and sheets into a big ball, and then he waddled out.

The door was flung open again, and two crew members rushed in, carrying a couple of buckets of water and rags. Without a word they marched to the end of the room and began scrubbing the deck. I asked them what was up, and they gave me the sailor's shrug of incomprehension. They did their work swiftly and thoroughly, and left. Two more crewmen arrived. Their mission, it turned out, was to take Kim's tome, the propaganda pamphlets, the soap and toothbrush; everything but the ashtray and the cup. They, too, had no idea what was going on. I gave them some cigarettes as they left. Another

160

team came in and removed the bed, then the bucket, then the wash-basin. The only items left were the table, the chair, the cup and ashtray, and an overlooked bar of laundry soap.

Dinner was served early, with no explanation—the same old turnips and water. After the meal I could hear the waitresses packing all the tin bowls and silverware. King Kong came back, and I asked him what was happening.

"You will know all in just a few hours," he replied, trying to be coy and clever.

I motioned to the bar of soap. "Should I take this, too?"

He then proceeded to blow the whole game by saying yes, "you will need at new place."

A little later the crew assembled in the hallway, as if to go outside for exercise. There was great excitement. We hoped this was the departure for Panmunjom. Silently, we filed out of the building and into two buses, the same aluminum-and-plastic kind we had ridden in so long ago.

The windows were covered, so we had little idea of where we were going. It was dark outside, and we saw only the light from an occasional streetlight. After about a half-hour ride over rough roads, we arrived at our destination.

We had no immediate name for the place; in fact, it was only after we were repatriated that we referred to it as the Farm. Our first look didn't tell us much. It seemed to be a more recent version of the Barn: three stories high, with square columns standing out from the entryway in the middle of two wings. It was completely devoid of architectural imagination. The floor of the front hallway was, to our surprise, made of highly polished marble. Quickly, we were ordered to remove our shoes and put on slippers. A rack was placed just to the right of the door for our shoes.

We lined up, as directed, for further instructions. The hall contained a couple of large green plants. Ahead, flanked by two huge columns crowned with red stars, was a wide staircase, also of marble, with a curving banister. To either side were hallways leading into the two wings. On the walls at each end of the hall were large portraits of Kim Il Sung.

161

Super C arrived importantly, bundled up in his gray overcoat. He was beaming, gloating over our reaction. "Welcome to your new home," he began. "I hope you will be comfortable here. Your Commanding Officer has requested better and more comfortable surroundings, and we have chosen this place for you. We hope that you will be able to exercise outdoors and take sun baths." Silver Lips fumbled over that one; perhaps what Super C was saying was that the next propaganda photos would be in color. "And," Super C continued, "you will have the opportunity to see films and to read books and to learn about Korea."

Silver Lips turned to the Captain and told him quickly that he should thank the Colonel. The Captain turned to us, and in unison he had us shout "Thank you, Colonel." About half the "thank yous" came out "Fuck you, Colonel," loud enough to be discernible. The Captain decided we needed a little guidance, so he stepped forward and thanked the Colonel on our behalf. Then, turning to us he said, quickly: "I caution you to never forget the difference between arrogance and pride."

My room was on the third floor and was about the same size as the one in the Barn. The uncovered windows were a big improvement, however. I opened them and breathed in deeply. In the room were a new round pine table, a pine chair, and a yellow-painted wooden night stand. My old bed was there, and neatly laid out on it were my sheets and blankets. Inside the night stand were all my possessions from the Barn. The room was in fine condition except for the floor, which was made of uneven, warped slat boards. The large pine door closed firmly and had no cracks in it. Yet I no longer felt as if I were in a closet lit by a naked light bulb. In fact, Super C had told us that the light, in a white globe, could be turned out at night. And, sure enough, just to the right of the door there was a switch, inside the room.

As I was completing my inspection the Captain and Super C walked in. Super C was out to get all the kudos he could and asked me solicitously if everything was all right.

"Fine, fine," I answered, as if complimenting a friendly hotel manager.

"Well, in just a while we will show you a movie," he said. "I hope you will enjoy it."

As it turned out, we spent a great amount of time in this new place watching movies. For the first couple of months, we were shown films twice a week. Occasionally we would be treated to a "special" showing: one of their six-hour, two-part films in one sitting.

Films were shown, we learned that night, in a large room on the third floor called the Club, invariably pronounced "Club-oo" by the Korean duty officers. The projectors, two bulky Zeiss 35-millimeter models, were part of the incongruity of North Korea—Zeiss projectors, Nikon cameras, Sony tape recorders, Mercedes automobiles. Why would a country that had clamored so hard and so long about independence and self-reliability allow these most conspicuous examples of foreign capitalistic trade?

A small, intellectual-looking Korean—the men referred to him as Plato or Fee-ture Feel-em—was in charge. He had curly hair, small beadlike eyes, and metal-rimmed glasses. His body was soft and rounded, not hard-looking like those of the tough military men he worked with. "Now to-nigh-et," he would intone in a nasal voice through a microphone, "we weel sho-ew yew a Korean fee-ture feel-em." The lights would go out, and we would become receivers, rather than transmitters, of their propaganda. The plot almost always consisted of the victory of the peasant in the land of Kim Il Sung— usually over the imperialistic warmongers of the United States. Because the movies didn't have English dialogue, Plato would summarize the story for us in the beginning and supply comments as it progressed. An example of his narrative, without showing his inimitable English, is the following:

"Just now, in this film, we will show you a true story about a country teacher. This teacher, Pak Hieeg, that is her name, is a teacher in a small mountain village. She works very hard to fulfill the teachings of the most glorious teacher of all, Marshal Kim Il Sung, our Premier. He has taught us that we must work very hard for the revolution. Comrade Kim Il Sung, the respected and beloved leader of the 40 million Korean people, ever-victorious, iron-willed,

163

brilliant commander, and one of the outstanding leaders of the international Communist and working-class movements, has made Pak Hieeg's life very good these days because of his Ten Point Political Program.

"Just now, there lives in the same village with the schoolteacher, the boy Yo Hong. Yo does not go to Pak Hieeg's school. He cannot go to school, for he was blinded by American aggressor bombings during the Great Patriotic War of Liberation. His father, Kim Hong, who fought with the Glorious Patriot, Marshal Kim Il Sung, was separated from his family while fighting the Japanese to gain his country's independence. Kim Hong was taken under the Japanese imperialists, who invaded and occupied our country before being thrown out by the glorious Kim Il Sung.

"Now, this film shows how the young girl goes to Yo's mother to find out why he isn't in school. Yo's mother works very hard in the rice fields to provide a living for little Yo, and tries at night to teach him. Pak Hieeg, she is the teacher, takes pity on Yo, and, together with the rest of the children, she tries to help him.

"You see, Pak Hieeg wants very much for Yo to get well so that he may go to school with all the other children and live and grow up in the great future of the revolution, but Yo is blind. So Pak Hieeg writes to her father in the capital city of Pyongyang, who is a famous doctor in the city. He arranges for young Yo to have an operation. Pak Hieeg takes Yo to the city to have the operation.

"Meanwhile, Yo's father, Kim Hong, is working very hard in Japan just to make a living. But, through the services of the General Association for the Korean Residents in Japan, he is repatriated to his country, the beloved Fatherland. In Pyongyang he meets Pak Hieeg's father, who tells him of the successful operation on little Yo. Kim Hong is very excited and asks to see young Yo Hong, who has just recovered from the operation and is about to have the bandages removed. And then Yo sees his father, and recognizes him, and together they go back to the small village to find his mother. The tears well up as the family is reunited in the warm bosom of the Fatherland, secure in their happy days, working hard for the revolution, always looking up to the Glorious Leader, Marshal Kim Il Sung, who

164

makes his happy face to shine upon all of the workers and laborers."

Obviously, the films, instead of accomplishing their intended purpose of making us think North Korea and North Koreans were not so bad after all, galvanized our resistance. Encouraged by the Captain's lead, we would whisper sarcastic or obscene comments to each other in the dark. It was easy to turn the propaganda into caricature, something the North Koreans never seemed to realize. The films gave us a way to put the overbearing Koreans in their place and get back our own nerve.

The predictable stories were played by actors and actresses distinguished from the general populace by their noses. It was a shock at first, for the usual Korean face seemed featureless. Anyone who had a nose apparently was made an actor or actress.

All the films contained key scenes: the peace and prosperity of the present; sun-flecked flowers in the meadows, babbling brooks, clean clothes, and a new schoolhouse; the arduous march made by the teacher over the mountain, through swamps and rivers, in driving rain, just to bring the blind boy a new lesson—symbol of the drive and determination all North Koreans must display in whatever they do; the bright, clickety-clack of a railroad train, the scenes from the windows of a new and prospering Korea (the train always seemed to pass through every industrial complex in the country), and the accompanying music, portraying hope and prosperity; the tour through Pyongyang, and, inevitably, a flashback to the bombing by the U.S. imperialist aggressors. A Korean boy would be playing contentedly by the side of the railroad track while the planes attacked a train several miles away. The antiaircraft guns of the train would swing into action, and six American jets would be blown out of the sky. One lone survivor would flee the scene and, idling down the track at 20,000 feet, would spot the small boy. With an evil sneer, he would swoop down and drop his entire bomb load on the poor child, only to be shot down with one shell from an old blunderbuss fired by the mother. The mother would throw down the gun and run through rubble and cinders to where the boy lay. "My son, my son," she would scream, "what have the Yankee imperialists done to you?" And then, as she picked him up, with blood running down his cheeks and tears flowing down hers, and cellos forming the musical back-drop, Fee-ture Feel-em would shriek at us: "They have blinded the boy." The Captain would yell back, equally loud, "Fuck you, fuck you."

Our new surroundings and slight freedom restarted life for all of us. The Koreans had taken everything from us in those horrible days of January and February, including a large part of our self-respect. Having lost it once, we knew the value of it, and got busy trying to rebuild it.

The new compound had only one bathroom available for our use, located on the second floor. It was large enough to be used for taking showers or washing clothes, and it was also large enough for ten or twelve at once. We weren't supposed to get together there, but for a long time we got away with it. This came about because of what happened when I was washing my extra pair of socks in a bucket of water in my room one day. The guard on duty was the Bear, or Half-Breed. Almost six feet tall, he had earned his nicknames because he spoke both Russian and Korean. He was mean, one of the three or four truly sadistic guards we ran into. Needless to say, he did not approve of my washing my socks in my room, and started to teach me a lesson. Fortunately, he hadn't done more than give me one black eye in his instruction when the duty officer appeared and restrained him. Then he quickly resolved the situation. "All right, you must wash your clothes down in the bathroom." That was the direction we needed, and every day for a while you could always find eight or ten crew members in the head "washing clothes."

These clandestine meetings gave us the opportunity to re-establish the old command and control structure. The Captain was definitely in command, and all information of any interest was to be funneled to him. Law had been elevated by the Koreans to a position where he was responsible for getting the whole crew to meals, to the films on time, and so on. Chief Goldman, however, was still the senior enlisted man as far as we were concerned. The senior man in each room, the Captain decreed, must take complete responsibility for the actions of the individuals in his room, and the senior enlisted men

166

were to keep a close eye on the junior nonrated men. "You guys are going to get out of here," he said. "Just make sure you get out in one piece."

The initial response to this was, of course, wildly optimistic. Gene summed up the thinking: "They won't keep us in a place this good for very long." Guesses ran from the end of March to the first of May—May Day, a perfect day for repatriation. All of them proved wrong.

During the nine months we spent at the Farm we learned a lot about North Koreans and the way they think. Their emphasis was always on propaganda; they were always showing us the unique and claiming it was the norm. The very building we were in was a prime example. "Most of the people in North Korea live as you do," they said, while out in the fields within our view were the thatched roofs and mud walls of a village. "Yes," we were told, "our country has television sets," and off in the distance was, indeed, the television transmission tower in Pyongyang. But early in September, when they set up television sets for us to watch a parade, we saw that the labels were RCA and Sony. They preached independence and self-reliance, yet drove German automobiles, flew Russian planes, and wore Japanese watches. "Ours," they would say expansively, "is a modern, highly technical country," while outside the ox carts moved slowly along. "Our agriculture is highly mechanized," proclaimed their literature; we watched for weeks as they planted and then harvested the paddy fields by hand.

In this nation of incongruities and lies, however, on one point they were consistent. "The U.S. imperialist aggressors, who are illegally occupying the southern half of our country, are responsible for all our suffering and unhappiness." That point was illustrated everywhere: in films, in newspapers, on billboards posted out in the fields, in public speeches, and in their literature.

Illustrative is one propaganda booklet, comparatively mild compared to the onerous writings of Kim, measuring five inches by seven inches, with a green cover, and entitled, in gold letters, *Among the People*. It is a collection of four stories illustrating the wisdom and benevolence of the great leader, Comrade Kim Il Sung, while among the people. One scene described a foot soldier's meeting with him while fighting the Americans in South Korea in 1950.

"You must not hope," Kim Il Sung told the soldier, "that U.S. imperialism will wash its hands of Korea and withdraw of its own accord. History knows no instance yet of imperialism quitting the arena of itself. Particularly, U.S. imperialism is the chieftain of world reaction, and its history is a history of aggression and plunder. . . .

"We should deal an annihilating blow to him at any cost and liberate the southern half of the country without fail. As long as U.S. imperialism remains in the southern half, our fatherland cannot be unified nor can our people enjoy a happy life. We must wipe out the U.S. imperialist aggressors to the last man. . . ."

In case the movies and booklets failed to make the point, the Koreans constructed a little picture gallery in the foyer of the second floor. During the nine months at the Farm, we saw three displays, each up for about ten days. The first had the theme of the propaganda pamphlets: violations of the armistice agreement by the American imperialistic forces illegally occupying South Korea. The retouched, out-of-focus photographs were pasted on a crude pink background. The idea was to portray American atrocities they claimed were committed during the war, and then to highlight some of the alleged later incidents. The technique was outrageously contrived. For example, there was a stock Army photograph—one the Pentagon passes out to anyone who asks—of an American tank. The caption read: "American tank used by Yankee Imperialists in Korea to run over women and children crowded together in a city street." A photograph of a dead Korean woman bore the caption: "Loyal servant of Kim Il Sung dragged through the street on a rope by American Imperialist soldiers until she dies from her agony." The other displays dealt with two other common myths of North Korea: "The Glorious Anti-Japanese Guerrilla Movement Led by Our Leader Comrade Kim Il Sung," and "How Glorious Is Our Fatherland," featuring scenes of steel mills and factories.

Each of the displays featured a "guest book," which we were to sign, making any comments we thought fitting. These ran from "No comment," to "I don't doubt that these photographs are real photographs," to "This is a terrifically swell display." The most exciting thing that happened to those displays was a large wind-and-rain storm that blew through the compound early in September. It managed to level all the billboards outside, then blow in the hall windows and flatten the display posters.

In the first ten days of October, we had four field trips. Evidently at that time the Koreans expected some sort of breakthrough in the negotiations and decided that we should see a little more than just the Barn and the Farm. The trips were propaganda for their presses, but they did give us a rare opportunity to see some of their countryside.

The first trip occurred on the night of October 1. We were taken by bus—this time with the windows uncovered—to the Grand Theatre, in Pyongyang, to see the musical spectacle "How Glorious Is Our Fatherland." The theme of the show was well known to us by then from the movies and propaganda booklets; seeing it in this form simply reaffirmed what a monotonous production it was.

Pyongyang looked worse to me than it had on the day of our arrival. Well escorted by the military, we breezed through the three checkpoints spotted along the seven-mile road leading to the city limits. The suburbs consisted of poorly kept slums, with thatched-roof mud shacks, scrawny dogs, rock-strewn yards. Farther in town were apartment complexes—row upon row of eight-story cement buildings lining both sides of the street. The city had been almost leveled during the Korean War; unfortunately, it had been rebuilt with little consideration paid to style or architectural beauty. The Daedong River flows through the downtown area, flanked by wide marble sidewalks and impressive street lamps. But the Ding Dong of Ping Pong, as we called it, was almost bone dry when we crossed it. The marble quays loomed incongruously. The Grand Theatre was rebuilt right after the war, with a nod to Korea's Chinese heritage. As a result, it features the curved roof and heavy ornamentation of an old Chinese pagoda.

The second trip was on the following Saturday night, October 5.

This time the journey was to see the Korean acrobatic theater, or, as we would call it, the circus. A circus is exactly what it turned out to be, complete with trapeze artists, tightrope walkers, dancing bears, and clowns. The clowns' routines were all directed against the U.S. military or the Japanese imperialists. The patient Koreans always managed to frustrate their enemies. The highlight of the evening was a mangy, moth-eaten lion. The lion was staging his version of a sit-down strike, much to the chagrin of the trainer. Finally, in response to a ferocious kick, the lion got up just long enough to lift his leg and relieve himself in the corner of the cage.

The next night we were treated to trip number three. We again traveled to Pyongyang, to visit the Moranbung Theatre and hear the Army Chorus. There was no getting around it, this was a grand performance. The voices were precise and clear. Humor was mixed with nationalistic numbers. And all of it was done with gusto and obvious enjoyment.

In charge of each of our field trips was Odd Job, a junior colonel of rotund proportions who did a little of everything and a lot of nothing. Odd Job did a good job, whether it was stopping the caravan to clear some peasants off the road or directing us to our seats. The audience consisted entirely of Korean Army personnel, who were curious but restrained. We were always the last to arrive and the first to depart.

Our last trip came the following weekend. The Koreans, I think, had fully expected that we would be repatriated at Panmunjom that weekend, but when the negotiations froze, they executed their alternate plan and sent us instead to Sinchon.

To a North Korean, Sinchon means roughly the same as Auschwitz must to a Jew. And it is *the* place to visit in North Korea to rekindle passion against and hatred for Americans. We had heard about Sinchon back in the Barn. Super C, in one of his first lectures on the Korean War, had mentioned it. After a half-hour description of American GI's cutting off women's breasts and driving stakes through their heads, he leaned forward earnestly and said, "Someday I hope you may visit Sinchon. Then you will really understand why we Koreans hate you Americans." It had been picked up countless times later. We had seen one wretched "documentary" film on the subject; we had read about school children making their annual pilgrimage to it; we had heard duty officers declare with some pride, "My family was at Sinchon."

And now, it was our turn. We took buses to Pyongyang, then an overnight train to the town, located about forty miles southwest of the capital. We arrived at 6:00 A.M., having spent most of the night waiting at the station, and boarded buses. This time the windows were covered. "We are afraid," explained one of the interpreters, "that if the people saw your faces they would want to kill you. That is how our people feel about Americans."

The grounds were immaculate. We entered a large stone building with a commanding view of the countryside. It was dark inside; the tones were reverently hushed. We took a quick look around this cathedral dedicated to hatred—the Sinchon Museum of American Atrocities. Here was supposed to be the documentary proof of American butchery during the Korean War. But again, as in all that we had seen, there was no proof at all, merely allegations made through captions on what could be stock photographs from the war.

A short, squat Korean woman in the building was introduced as our guide. Her voice was fast and impersonal; never once did she smile, so intent was she on her work. Silver Lips translated for her.

A picture of a group of American GI's standing around bore the caption: "American soldiers about to embark upon the notorious rape and killing of 13 November 1951." A lock of hair in a glass case, our guide explained, from the head of a "patriotic hero of the war who was brutally murdered by the U.S. imperialistic aggressors." A pastoral photograph of a river had become "the very spot where U.S. soldiers forced 3,000 pregnant women into the river to drown." Old shoes in a pile were "the very shoes the women dropped while fleeing from the U.S. soldiers." Some rosary beads in a glass case had belonged, the guide said, as she no doubt did to thousands of unskeptical Koreans every year, "to American missionaries in the nineteenth century." The number of beads revealed to American Intelligence the number of soldiers in the Korean Army. Evidently even American missionaries from years ago were on Kim Il Sung's list of the hated.

The props were really incidental to the captions. One glass case,

171

for instance, contained nothing more than an ordinary-looking nail. But it was, the guide told us, "the very nail" driven into a woman's forehead by the hated Americans. The caption said the same thing in Korean.

Just outside the museum building we were shown a small two-room cellar. "This," explained the guide, "is where the Americans placed nine hundred Koreans and then burned them."

The Captain became inquisitive and asked if all nine hundred had been burned at once.

"Yes" was the quick answer.

The Captain persisted, wondering just how they managed to get all nine hundred bodies into the small space. "Were they," he asked, "all short?"

"Yes."

"I suppose they must have stacked them, then," continued the Captain.

"Yes," she answered, looking around nervously, "they were stacked. Those on the bottom suffocated. Look closely and you can see still today the skins of the victims hanging from the wall." We couldn't see any skin on the walls.

Back in the museum, the Captain saw a heavily shadowed picture of an American military policeman, taken at Panmunjom. "Do American MP's always wear those masks?" asked the Captain.

"Yes, just like most bandits."

From the museum we were driven to two huge mounds of earth on a nearby hillside. "This is where the people of Sinchon, massacred by the U.S. imperialistic aggressors, are buried," we were told.

On another hill, we were shown two brick buildings. Our guide said the Americans burned Korean mothers in one of the buildings and their babies in the other. She noted "claw marks" on the walls made by the desperate mothers.

The whole display was ridiculous, in our eyes. But at the same time, it was depressing, because we knew that a visit was mandatory for thousands of children in North Korea. It was little wonder that they grew up hating Americans with such intensity. And I understood better why the guards beat us so savagely and with no provoca-

172

tion. Super C had been right. I did understand a lot more about hate after my trip to Sinchon.

When we returned to our compound, Colonel Scar was on the front steps to greet us. "Did you," he asked, "enjoy yourself?"

We made no response, but trudged back to the loneliness of our rooms.

Precisely at six o'clock each morning at the Farm, a guard would press a button in the first-floor guard headquarters of our building. He would press it twice, so that his comrades off duty would not mistake the reveille of the hated American prisoners for their later one. Shrill and resounding rings would come from the bells on the second and third floors. But the idea was to wake up before the bell. Otherwise it meant trouble, in this bizarre world we occupied, for the *Pueblo* man responsible for each floor.

Bob Hammond was then in charge of the third floor. At the first ring, the guard on duty would come to life and go galloping down the hall shouting, "Hammondie, Hammondie." Hammond was easily one of the gutsiest men in the U.S. Marine Corps, and certainly he was admired by all of us for the strong resistance he gave the Koreans. He was damned if one of those guards was going to have the pleasure of rooting him out of the sack. So he foiled them with his own game of psychological warfare. He got up a little early every morning and stood just inside his darkened room, all dressed and ready to go. As the guard reached his room, Hammond flung the door open and charged out, calling for the rest of us to assemble.

This would frustrate the guard, for his goal was, of course, to reach Hammond's room and find him still in bed. But Hammond was too shrewd for that. He knew the universal system of the military and how to make it work for him.

The day's schedule called for ten minutes for reveille, but he realized that no one got commendations for just meeting a schedule; praise came for beating it. As a result, we performed that ten-minute reveille in closer to fifty-four seconds, a worthy accomplishment in any man's army. This meant an awful lot of hustle early in the morning for us. But that was the military—hurry up and wait. The whole

173

insane routine symbolized the dreariness of our existence. The typical day started in stupidity, proceeded through boredom, and ended in stupidity sixteen hours later.

I remember one morning in particular. I came out as usual right after Hammond's call and met Gene. While the rest of the men lined up in the hallway, Gene and I went down to the second floor and fell in with the other officers. Then we six officers led the rest down to the first floor. There we exchanged our sandals for our green canvas, rubber-soled "shoes" and went outdoors for our morning exercise in a large cinder parking lot in front of the building.

The fact that we officers were kept separate, Super C had told us, was a privilege they were extending to us. Other privileges included being allowed to have our meals together in a separate "wardroom" and to spend fourteen hours each day alone in our own rooms. "Officers," Super C had said, "should not be crowded together like the enlisted men. They should have their own rooms. Well, I am not sure, but I think it is the same in your army, too, isn't it?"

On this one particular morning, the air was filled with a thick fog, almost like a cloud that had lost its bearings. The fog softened the outline of our building and yellowed its lights into a much friendlier glow. In the distance, where we knew the guard shack was, there was only a dim, diffused light. The fog wrapped itself around us and deadened the crunching of our boots on the loosely laid stones. And through the fog swarmed nostalgia.

I thought back to times spent on the bridge of the *Pueblo* at sunrise, about halfway through the morning watch. The sun, as it crept over the horizon, would try to bore through the thick fog, setting square miles of it aglow in rapidly whitening hues of gray. Fortified with a cup of hot coffee, to throw off the the chill, I used to enjoy the magic of those morning fogs.

In the land of Kim Il Sung, however, such moments of reverie were made impossible, even on foggy mornings, by the tireless monotony of the loud-speakers. At five-thirty every morning—four in the summer—they clicked on, and began dispensing their ceaseless barrage of propaganda. They played all day and most of the night in every village, seemingly in every rice paddy. We dubbed it the Rice

Paddy Network. Kim Il Sung was ubiquitous; he could not be shut up.

The guttural exhortations were diffused by the fog on this morning, so that they had no point of origin. We six officers did our deep knee bends while the crew, led by Law, ran a lap around the parking lot. The men were not in good-enough health to run hard, and he kept the pace easy. They trotted like tired dray horses—clomp, clomp, clomp—on the cinders. I looked at these once-strong men as they came toward us. They were gaunt shells of their former selves, wrapped like the mummies they almost were in Kim Il Sung suits of dull gray, their jackets buttoned all the way to the Adam's apple. Some managed to smile as they chugged by in front of us. "Good morning, Captain," said several. The men were not proud. The Koreans had taken away too much of them for that. But they had not given up either. They were going to endure. They made me feel proud of them and ashamed of myself.

I think I realized that morning our hidden strength: we were suffering together. All of us were in this thing together, for better or worse. In those few moments of silent communion we reaffirmed our common, mutual interdependence. Watching them run, I realized that we needed them a lot more than they needed us. Goldman had made their pledge for them: "Captain, we're behind you all the way." Could we fulfill our part and see them safely out of here? I offered a silent prayer that we could.

As in the Barn, we were supposed to sit much of the day and meditate on our crime against the Democratic People's Republic of Korea. The men were housed eight to a room; the officers were alone. I was supposed to read my propaganda booklets during the morning unless there was a lecture on the joys of Communism. The lectures were usually given on the second floor by Super C, and would often last from six to eight hours. He had a nimble intellect, and could take on all of us at once and easily hold his own. In his long lectures, without a single note in front of him, he could go from hyperbolic accusations against American imperialists to soft monologues on the natural beauty of Korean mountains, fields, and streams. I think he realized that the history of North Korea had been rewritten by the Communists, because he steered clear of history. He would never admit that his government was anchored in brute force, not intellectual choice. His line was that Communism is clearly superior to any other form of government if one will only be sincere and examine the facts.

Our occasional belittling made not a dent. I recall one discussion about the boring propaganda movies we had to watch— the same ones the North Koreans had to watch.

"We do not believe in art for art's sake," Super C said. "For us, films are used to educate. We learn from our films, and we think it is a very good way to learn."

Then one of his deputy officers—no doubt on the basis of what he had told them—would take up the argument. "In your country, films teach you how to murder and rob. The gangster films teach even your little families violence and crises. In our country, the films teach us how to live our lives, how to make revolution."

Super C had an answer for everything. Around forty years old, about five foot five, trim, erect, polished, and positive of movement, he was a consummate actor, politician, and a model soldier. He had fought in the Korean War, he told us. He also told me once that he was married and the father of two boys, aged fifteen and thirteen. When he ever saw his family I do not know. He seemed to arrive at the compound before seven o'clock every morning and leave no earlier than eleven at night. It seemed a tragedy that a man so skilled, so energetic, so devoted to a cause should have been blinded by the system he was willing to die for. He had no sympathy for human beings. He was coldly, cruelly efficient. We hated him, but at the same time could not help but admire his efficiency and dedication.

After lunch we went outside again for an hour of exercise. The rest of the day—except for the twenty-minute dinner period—was for self-appraisal. Lights-out was at 10:00 P.M.

Boredom was the big enemy. The waiting, the not knowing, the idleness combined to corrode the spirit. The Captain complained to Super C, declaring it would do no harm for the officers, who were in confinement alone all day, to get together in the evening for cards and chess. At the end of March, Super C approved. Steve, Tim, and Gene were allowed to congregate in Murphy's room for an hour after supper. I was allowed to go to the Captain's room to play chess during the same hour.

The chess games gave us an opportunity to ponder our chances of release and establish more direct lines of communication. I would bring any news I had managed to pick up; the Captain would issue any instructions he wanted passed on. It was informal, and normally we had little to pass, but at least it preserved a semblance of the old command structure.

The Captain doubted that the United States would ever apologize, because it had nothing to apologize for. He thought we would get out, but only if the U.S. succeeded in forcing North Korea's hand by military blockade, economic sanctions, or diplomatic pressure. I was more optimistic about the North Korean terms—thanks to my faith in the Stutts and Voltz precedent. But as time dragged by so oppressively, we stopped debating the point. We concentrated on living a day at a time, keeping ourselves rational despite the tedium, hunger, poor health, and overwhelming feeling of helplessness.

The Captain and I began to create for each other a chance to escape the cage of our most pressing thoughts. He was especially good at this. He made up mathematical puzzles and problems, which he would pass to the other officers at meals and to the rest of the crew during the exercise period. One of his favorites he had picked up in Washington while being briefed on the *Pueblo* mission. This was known as the twelve-ball problem. You have twelve balls—all the same size and color, but one ball is either heavier or lighter than the rest—and a balance scale. The problem is to determine in three weighings which ball is the odd one and whether it is lighter or heavier. It had taken the Captain twelve hours to figure it out; the brilliant Charles Ayling took about one hour.

The Captain also gave us word games: how many different words of four letters or more can you get from some specific word. This could occupy a morning or afternoon session in our rooms. Later on came crossword puzzles. CT 1 James A. Shepard originated them with CT 1 Donald R. Peppard, and then passed some around. This immediately stimulated others to create their own. At one time we had more than eight different puzzles in circulation.

The Captain and I played some pretty serious chess games, long and complicated. He was, and still is, a master at the board; I was a novice. After he felt that I had learned enough about the rudiments, we shifted to a "cut and slash" game, the Captain promptly trouncing me on most attacks.

When we tired of the game we would put the chessmen out on the board, hunch over the table, and just talk. For the most part, I listened while the Captain told stories. His career in the Navy had been varied and full, and he had a way, as do many sailors, of making a story come alive. He also talked about his youth, his college days, his wife and family, books he had read. And I can still remember sitting spellbound for hours as he described his arrival in North Korea and the treatment he got the first several days.

I remember asking him one night what he thought was the best thing about the Navy and what he thought was the worst. He had the same answer for both questions: people. The Navy both kept people in and drove them out. To the Captain, at least, it was not the security, the systematic, organized life, or the stability that attracted him to the Navy. And it was not the long nights at sea, the separation from home, or the lack of family life that detracted. It was the people who made the Navy what it was.

One time, just to relieve part of the monotony of our life, I tried an Edward R. Murrow approach when I walked into the Captain's room.

"Oh, good evening, Commander Bucher. We just thought we'd drop in to see how the Skipper of the *Pueblo* was getting along. I hope we haven't caught you by surprise."

"Yeah, I was wondering what all those trucks were doing out front, with all these cables and lights and people running all over the place," he responded quickly.

"Yes, sir. Well, we just wanted to drop in unnoticed to catch you at ease. My, this is an interesting room. I wonder if you could tell us about it."

"Why, yes, I'd be happy to. This is my living room, dining room, den, and bedroom. I've fixed it up rather plainly, as you can see, but I find it rather satisfying to be in isolation like this. Of course, my wife thinks it a little strange, but . . ."

178

"Well, yes, I see, it is rather . . . ah . . . comfortable. That looks like a nice bed you have there."

"Rustic."

"Yes, rustic. Tell me, Commander, how is your life these days?"

"Oh, I can't complain much. I just sit here all day. Not much to do. But then, my life isn't as hectic as it used to be."

After about two months, all the officers were allowed to gather together to play either cards or chess. This was a breakthrough, too. At first we experimented with hearts and poker, and then gin rummy. But none of them stood up. Only the Captain and I knew how to play bridge, and neither of us had played it for some time. But that didn't faze the Skipper, who had been "requested" to learn the game to satisfy wardroom requirements on one of his submarine assignments. He sat down and reconstructed from memory, and logic, all the bidding rules, using a combination of Culbertson and Goren.

The rules were perfect and rigid, and were passed around so others in the crew could learn. Tim and Gene became pretty good players, but Steve and Murphy never did quite catch on. Tim, Gene, the Captain, and I used to rotate partners to try to discover which team was best. Invariably, the Captain's team won, whenever he was able to put his keen mind fully to work on the game. Concentration became more and more difficult. All of us were suffering from general restlessness and tended to flit from subject to subject.

Super C occasionally, when he called the whole crew together for a group lecture in the Club, would pass on news about our prospects. He told us in April, for example, that negotiations between the U.S. and the North Korean governments were definitely underway in Panmunjom. "Your side will admit nothing," he told us. "When presented with all the evidence, they are backed into a corner but will admit nothing. They said they will not admit that the *Pueblo* was a spy ship and they will not admit the intrusions." He spoke with disgust about the impasse and predicted that the United States eventually would agree to the Korean demands and apologize. At least we now knew that negotiations for our release were indeed proceeding.

Our health deteriorated as the months dragged on. Almost everyone, as summer came, suffered from open running malnutrition sores and general infections. Lack of vitamins and proteins had shrunk everyone's weight, and some of the more unfortunate men had been attacked by bedbugs. Lean, gaunt, and weak, all of the men suffered silently, praying that they wouldn't contract any major infections or illnesses.

In June came the first big departure from what I had decided was their strategy: to trade us for an American apology. Super C called us together and said that they had decided to give us an opportunity to do some work. Work, he explained, was an honor in their country. Therefore we should be pleased that we were going to be given the opportunity to work. Then he asked us what work we thought we could do. The first response came from the Captain, who said that he could navigate and command ships and why didn't the Colonel give him a ship and let him sail it.

Super C laughed. "Well," he said, "I am afraid that if we gave you a ship you might sail away."

Some of the crew members thought they would be just perfect picking fruit in the orchards. "But," said Super C, "we are afraid you would eat all the fruit!"

"Wouldn't think of it, Colonel," was the prompt response.

Still others said they could drive automobiles and trucks, or fly airplanes. Tim said he could design buildings, and Russell said he could construct buildings.

"Well, Russell," replied the Colonel, "perhaps we could make a team, with Ensign Harris designing the buildings and you putting them up?"

"Yes, sir," said Russell. "I feel quite confident that I could build anything Ensign Harris is capable of designing."

Of course in the back of everyone's mind was a picture of back-breaking days in hot fields under driving guards, though we would prefer even this activity to the dull boredom of sitting in our rooms and becoming sicker by the day.

Putting us to work didn't seem to me to fit in with what I thought their strategy was. I figured it meant they didn't plan to release us soon. So I told myself that they wouldn't actually do it. And, curiously, that one lecture was the last we heard of forced labor.

At the end of June, when we had the next mass meeting with

180

Super C, he announced that our food rations would be increased. We had a long discussion about the quality of rice the workers received and the number of calories we received at home and the number we were then receiving. Suddenly, something apparently got mistranslated. Chicca was ordered to his feet for a forty-five-minute chewing-out by Super C for being "insincere." Upset, the Colonel then stomped out. But the food was increased, for reasons we could not divine at the time.

Two weeks later, Super C was back again, smiling and jovial. He announced that we were about to have a thorough medical examination, what he called their semiannual checkup. Equipment was moved in, and the place swarmed with doctors, who did, in fact, give us a pretty thorough going-over.

Super C also announced that some letters had come for us and would be distributed. This was great news, our first word from the outside. The letters were delivered open, but weren't censored. Most of them didn't say anything; they merely informed us that the grass was still green, the sky still blue, and everyone was fine. But at least the handwriting was familiar. Naturally, they took photographs of us opening the opened letters.

July 23 marked the end of six months in confinement. Spirits were again up. Everyone seemed to feel that the signs for getting home were favorable. But the beginning of the second six months was like being recycled back to the propaganda charades of the Barn. Somebody in Pyongyang—perhaps Kim Il Sung himself—sent the order to Super C to crank up the propaganda machine again; the Americans were taking too much time at Panmunjom. Super C apparently decided that more press conferences were what was needed. But his approach differed this time. He broke the crew into groups, assigned one of his officers to each as an "adviser," and charged us with the responsibility of suggesting ideas that might help get the Panmunjom talks off dead center. Directly ordering us to go through another press conference would have been too straightforward. Inevitably, one of the advisers suggested a press conference. Super C said he would put the suggestion to the *Pueblo*'s Commanding Officer. The charade continued, with Super C putting on a great performance of weighing all suggestions carefully. "Well," he said, referring to the press-conference idea later in a meeting with the *Pueblo* officers, "it seems that this is the desire of the crew members. We, for our part, will suggest this to our authorities. I cannot be sure of the results, but, as it is your desire, we shall try and assist."

We were ordered to prepare questions and answers for this second press conference much as had been done for the first one. Super C again assigned "advisers" to assist us. The focus for this midsummer propaganda barrage was to be on the humanitarian treatment we had received for so long from the Democratic People's Republic of Korea, and on our longing to go home. The North Koreans apparently figured that they had proved our crime to the world; the new emphasis would be on arousing sympathy for our plight.

The questions and answers duly memorized, August 13 was set for the conference. We were presented with new uniforms for the occasion. An outbuilding across the compound was our studio. To our surprise, a television van arrived. We were to go on camera live, which was not really much of a risk for them, because all the "correspondents" were under their control. This time, in addition to the six officers and Dunnie Tuck, eighteen members of the crew were added to the cast. The following excerpts from the press conference, which was televised within North Korea and broadcast by radio to the rest of the world, illustrate the new pressure tactics applied by Pyongyang on Washington in election year 1968.

COMMANDER BUCHER: . . . we wish to express our intense desire to be reunited with our families at the earliest possible moment and thereby to appeal to the people of the United States to urge our government to take appropriate action to enable us to return home. . . .

LIEUTENANT MURPHY: . . . I ardently desire to return home as quickly as possible to the United States of America where my wife, my baby children, my sisters, my mother, my aunt, my uncles, and other relatives and friends longingly await my return. . . . I am sure that those who know the grief of losing the father of the family can share with me my fervent desire to return home as quickly as possible and end this remorse. . . .

182

My role was to suggest that politics lay behind the American delay in apologizing. "... I must admit that I personally cannot understand why the U.S. government does not try to settle this issue with honesty and responsibility, especially when the details of our criminal acts of espionage against the Democratic People's Republic of Korea and intrusion into their territorial waters have been conclusively proven.

"I feel therefore that the only solution to this question is deeply influenced by political factors which have nothing to do with the actual facts of the case. Why U.S. political factors would delay our repatriation I do not know.

"But I do know that neither I nor the *Pueblo* crew desires to spend the rest of our lives in a foreign land. My appeal, therefore, is for the U.S. government to lay aside whatever political considerations it has and seek to realize our repatriation as early as possible by accepting full responsibility for our crimes and our fates."

Another exchange laid bare the Korean threat to put us on public trial if an apology was not soon forthcoming. Such a trial, with no recourse to an objective judgment, could end with only one recommendation.

"... there is a limit to the patience of the Democratic People's Republic of Korea. If the U.S. government does not admit, apologize, and insure that such acts will not be repeated again, the crew will be held responsible for them. We will be placed on trial in this country and punished according to their laws. ...

"We desire very much to be reunited with our families and parents to prevent any further grief that may come to them. I hope the U.S. government makes the necessary apology enabling the crew to return home."

As before, the correspondents had had to do as much preparation as we did. We marveled at the accuracy with which they proposed their "questions"; their memories were better than ours. To help himself, the Captain had written down all his answers, laid them on the table in front of him, and read from them. The Koreans seemed not to mind.

The press conference was followed by other demands, equally repulsive. Obeying them got no easier as the months dragged on. Each act sickened us, and led some of the men to take a stand. One such was CT 3 Earl M. Kisler, who rebelled when the Koreans ordered him to sign a letter of appeal to *Newsweek*.

Kisler's room was under the tutelage of Robot, one of the "room daddies" assigned by the North Koreans to "advise" us on the press conference and to answer any questions we might have about North Korea. Robot earned his name because of the mechanical and doctrinaire way he followed the Communist line. He was thirty-nine years old, lit one cigarette after another with his most prized possession, a gold cigarette lighter, and went into a rage whenever one of his "ungrateful, insincere American bastards" transgressed. His biggest desire, he once said, was to "return to the factory. But," he continued, "until my country is unified, it is my duty to remain in the Army."

Robot didn't much like Kisler's idea of not signing the letter. On the afternoon of August 30, he got his favorite guard, Bear, and called in Kisler, who recalls that he knew he was in trouble when Robot stood up and removed his wide leather duty belt and laid it on the table. He was right. Bear probably hit him first, from behind, a favorite North Korean move, but Robot issued careful instructions and personally supervised the beating. He wanted to teach the crew a lesson. Kisler, unfortunately, was his blackboard.

Bear used a wide board on Kisler; Robot joined in with his belt, then with his rubber-soled leather sandal. The forty-five minutes of savage blows ruptured blood vessels and caused a gigantic swelling of Kisler's head. His eyes were slits, and the imprint of the sandal marked parts of his face like tire treads on a dirt road. Finally satisfied, Robot sent Kisler back to his room, and carefully instructed the duty officers to make sure that he attended all meals, the movie that night, and the exercise periods.

One look at Kisler and we all got the message: behind every "suggestion" from one of Super C's advisers was brute force, which said, "Don't get fooled into thinking you ever have the option not to follow our orders." Miraculously, Kisler was still in defiant humor. "That's one more son of a bitch I put on my list," he muttered.

Kisler did sign the letter to *Newsweek*, rather than go through another beating. But we still resolved to defy the Koreans as much as we dared. We had come too far together in the last months to be scared back into our holes now. We saw the difference between having something or nothing to live for, between hanging on or giving up.

This new mood of comparative daring took over at the next press conference we were ordered to hold. So confident had Super C become that he decided to call in reporters from outside North Korea. No non-Communist newsmen from the United States would be permitted, of course. But they were taking a slight risk by inviting reporters they could not control completely. The conference was to be staged in September to coincide with the Twentieth Anniversary Celebration of the founding of the Democratic People's Republic of Korea. The reporters attending that celebration could easily travel the few extra miles from Pyongyang to the compound to see Kim Il Sung's trophies from his hunt off Wonsan.

Super C was visibly nervous about this international press conference. Besides the usual memorization of questions and answers, we had to rehearse our movements. We walked from the barracks to the press-conference building, practiced marching in and out, sitting down, answering questions. He warned us in a friendly way that the crewmen not participating in the conference would be under heavy guard in the Club. Any false moves or extemporaneous statements would bring immediate retribution on them—hostages for hostages.

The big day was Thursday, September 12. "This will be a big step toward your freedom," Super C told us. "You must make it a success." The foreign reporters started arriving early that morning in cars driven by Army men. To our surprise, an American showed up—Lionel Martin, billed as representing the New York *National Guardian*, which none of us had ever heard of. We filed into a crowded, smoky, hot, noisy room. Though not televised, the conference was video-recorded on a portable Japanese Sony set, and almost every reporter had a camera and a tape recorder. So we took our places before a barrage of microphones. There were probably seventy correspondents present, representing forty or fifty nations. The Africans were the most indifferent, and a couple of them fell asleep. The representatives from the United Arab Republic were the most intent; the Japanese the hardest-working. There were a couple of women—an overweight girl from the French Communist party and a slender one from Norway.

Robot, as he had done before, served as chairman. Super C flitted about in civilian clothes, sweating out this big production that could affect his future in the Korean Army. Unfortunately for him, Fee-ture Feel-em, rather than the trustier Silver Lips, served as interpreter. Stage fright hit him, making him stammer and cough from the outset. More than once, an Indian jumped to his feet, shouting, "I can't hear, I can't hear."

Each question and answer had to be translated into Russian, French, Japanese, and Spanish, which quadrupled the time required for the conference. Murphy wisely decided to go through the points of "intrusion" one by one, giving the latitude and longitude of each. Thus his answer alone took over two hours, and set most of the reporters to fidgeting and talking among themselves. One of the Russians leaned forward and said loudly in English: "How long is this shit going to last?"

The questions and answers followed the usual outline: the origins of the ship, its mission, details of the alleged intrusions, and emotional pleas for the U.S. government to apologize so we could all get back home. CT 3 Ralph McClintock had the best line of the day: "Oh, how I long to walk down the quiet shaded streets of my home town, to swim again in the rolling surf of old Cape Cod Bay, and to indulge in the sumptuous feast of one of Mom's famous apple pies." He gave this statement with a strong Boston accent, and had the East German delegate bursting with laughter.

The summation of the long, rambling, farcical conference was to be delivered by the Captain. It contained the same warning to the U.S.: either apologize or watch your men stand public trial as spies. The statement had been carefully worked out by Super C himself, and the answer had already been printed in the transcript to be handed out at the conclusion of the conference. But the

Captain never gave the full statement. Robot became so flustered over the way things were getting out of hand that he decided to cut the conference short. This prompted the Captain to jump up and start talking, as if misunderstanding, and answering his cue. The foreign reporters crowded around him, and he had to shout to make himself heard. He threw away his script and told the reporters in rapid English that the message they should convey was: resolve the issue. Eight months, he said, is long enough for the decision to have been made. The issue should be settled now, one way or the other. Our only desire now, he said, is that the U.S. take some action; either sign the document or take military action.

The press conference seemed to us to have been a disaster. We had the distinct feeling that most of the correspondents realized what a farce it was, though we doubted that this would get accurately reported. Super C, however, concluded that it had been a smashing success and rewarded all hands that night with a ration of beer.

We didn't see Super C for about two weeks. When he returned we knew why. In place of the four stars of a senior colonel, he now wore the single large star of a lieutenant general. We promptly gave him a new name: GG, meaning, depending on who you were talking to, Glorious General or Genius General.

GG, the Captain told us, also had some news. He thought the press conference had helped our chances for repatriation immensely and that, in fact, we might be able to go home "very soon." This was reflected in our treatment. The food was increased; meat and potatoes were added to our diet, cookies and candy were freely dispensed, and we received apples or other fruit with every meal. In addition, the doctor started issuing more than aspirin for our illnesses. Our health began to improve. Letters, which before had taken three to six months to reach us, now came through in less than eight days. And it was at this time that we were taken on our field trips.

Early in October, GG ordered us to submit a joint petition to the Korean people asking for leniency. "If the document is successful," he said, "it might provide the impetus to win your quick release."

187

This time he left it up to us, gave us a room by ourselves, several bottles of beer, and a typewriter.

The result was a petition laced with hyperbole and sarcastic comments. We termed ourselves "superspies" who "lurk in dark corners," guilty of "dark, nefarious and naughty" crimes. Our best paragraph concerned the alleged intrusions. "We, as conscientious human beings who were cast upon the rocks and shoals of immorality by the tidal wave of Washington's naughty policies, know that neither the frequency nor the distances of these transgressions into the territorial waters of this sovereign peace-loving nation matter because, in the final analysis, penetration however slight is sufficient to complete the act." We hoped that in the Pentagon they would recognize our paraphrase of the standard military definition of rape. And we had written in our concluding line that the entire crew of the *Pueblo* wished to "paen" (pronounced, of course, pee-on) "not just the Korean People's Army, not just the people of North Korea, but the Korean People's government, and most of all Kim Il Sung."

The tone was appropriately groveling, and our hard-core plea read: "Please accept, then, this heartfelt petition submitted humbly and entreatingly in order to convey that our intense repentance is forever unshakeable." None of us knew quite what that meant, but apparently the North Koreans loved it.

On Wednesday, October 9, about eight hours after we had submitted the petition, GG called us together to read the North Korean response. Movie cameras, tape recorders, and lights were at the ready, and GG allowed himself to be photographed for the first time. He had, he said, an important announcement. Nothing but home was on our minds, and his words were galvanizing.

"The Democratic People's Republic of Korea," he began, "has accepted your petition and decided to pardon the whole crew of the *Pueblo*. If the United States will sign the document the whole crew including the Commanding Officer and officers, and the body of the one dead crew member, will be returned." He was beaming as he put down his prepared statement and addressed us directly. "The way for your repatriation," he cried, "is now open. You will be going home not before Christmas, not before Thanksgiving, but this month!"

188

Triumphantly he strutted out, with a mission-accomplished look on his usually stern face. He had never committed himself before, and it was unlikely, we reasoned, that he would risk losing face, even to American prisoners. And repatriation looked a lot closer when we were told to write a final farewell letter of gratitude. "It will," Odd Job told us, "be your last letter while in Korea. You must make it a good one. And you must hurry! There is not much time!"

A group of us assembled that afternoon to write the letter, and GG sent in another case of beer. We worked through the night, and early the next morning GG read the letter and said that it was fine. "I will have my officers translate it," he said, "then you can all sign it." He was in a lighthearted mood, probably drunk with his own success, and not from the 18-per-cent-alcohol beer North Korea manufactures. He looked at his watch. "There is," he said, "much to be done and not much time. And I think you understand that I must do it all myself. My officers," he revealed surprisingly, "are not as good as I would like. And I myself am more accustomed to commanding field maneuvers than writing papers. But," he concluded, "this must be done." He started to get up, then stopped and looked at us carefully. "Your side," he said, "has agreed to sign the document. The next meeting will be at 11:00 A.M. I will let you know the results."

Elated, we went to have our breakfast. Robot had said long ago that when the day of our repatriation was near we would know it because "we will serve you fried eggs for breakfast." That morning we were served fried eggs.

The Captain

I had regarded Captain Bucher as a tower of strength since our first meeting back in San Diego. I wondered as Operations Officer on his ship whether I could live up to his expectations. I wondered as a prisoner in the Barn whether I could live up to his example.

I had no way of knowing in those first days of captivity what he was going through. I figured that the Koreans would work on him first. I didn't expect him to give in; but then, I didn't know the kind of torture the North Koreans were capable of. When they started working on me, I thought it was only because they couldn't get to him. The Captain must be dead.

I was quite unprepared for what I saw in that first meeting for our initial press conference. The Captain still looked strong physically, but his face had buckled under whatever version of hell he had gone through. He had aged ten or fifteen years in days. His dark eyes showed pain. His face had deep lines of worry and frustration. The muscles seemed to have sagged with resignation. At that first meeting we were not allowed to speak. During the next two days we had opportunity only for guarded, hurriedly whispered comments. I remember that he said once: "Don't cross these bastards, Skip. They're inhuman."

On the night of February 16, when we were gathered together for the painful experience of signing the letter of apology, the Captain knew he had to lead his men in a disgraceful act. Yet he knew the horror behind the order. There were two options for the crew: the Captain could order the men to sign the letter, or the North Koreans could torture them until they signed. The Captain chose the former.

While we were sitting with him watching the men file by to sign, I felt Murphy nudge me with his fist as he whispered, "Pass this to Gene." Casually, I covered his fist so that there would be no sudden movement to attract the eyes of Super C or the guards. I felt a ring and a piece of paper drop into my hand. I duplicated the maneuver with Gene. Murphy nudged me again. "This," he whispered, "is for you." I grabbed the folded piece of paper and managed to get it into my pocket unseen.

Later that night, in my room, I unfolded it. The Captain had squeezed a lot of words onto the small piece of white paper from inside a pack of Korean cigarettes. The note, as nearly as I can remember, read:

Skip—

I think you and the others have a good chance of getting out of here in a year or less. But there is *no way* they can let me go. I tried to commit suicide. Tell Gene to give my ring to Rose—she'll want it. Go and see the Hodges—I think they live up in Oregon—and tell them that I consider myself personally responsible for their son's death. When you get back, tell Mark and Mike [his sons] that I will miss them both. Tell them never to underestimate the value of a good education. Tell Rose that I loved her always and am sorry for dragging her into this mess. She's been a great wife.

Take care, buddy.

Pete

The note floored me emotionally. Here was the strongest man I had ever known giving up hope. Here was a man I thought could cope alone with anybody or anything writing down his last words. Feeling every blow that he heard hitting others; feeling personal responsibility for everything that was happening to his crew; feeling the burden of having lost his ship and its secrets—all this must have pushed him under; the beatings would not have been enough.

I realized, though, that he had reached out to me, that I must have lived up to at least some of his expectations, that I had a

191

chance to repay him for his trust and confidence, and that I not only needed him, but he needed me as well. I had an additional reason for living. I had a chance to help another man—to steady his balance at a precarious moment in his life. I had somebody besides myself to worry about and work for.

I sat down and wrote the Captain a note. I told him that I, too, had given up hope and had tried suicide; that it didn't work. I said that the worst was over, that he and everybody else were getting out of this place, that they wouldn't bother with all this apology business if shooting us was their intent.

I slipped this buck-up note to the Captain the next morning during the exercise period in the hall. The morning after that he nodded his thanks and slipped me another note. What evolved, through notes in February and early March, was a clandestine communication between the Captain and me.

Mainly, we traded ideas on the diplomatic options facing the United States and North Korea regarding our fate. He reported that a *Pueblo* seaman assigned to clean his room had learned from a Korean duty officer that talks about us were actually underway in Panmunjom. I argued that there was a precedent for the United States to apologize to effect the release of American military men. The Captain maintained that the United States would never lower itself to apologize for something it did not do. He did not believe it should, but he admitted that that seemed to be the only way out for us.

These notes laid a foundation for a close relationship when we moved to the compound at the Farm. I got to know the Captain much better. I found depth and cunning and intelligence and quick-wittedness. He used all this equipment, often at his own personal peril, to help his men. He pumped fight back into his beaten crew. By force of his own example, he restored their emotional life, their pride in being American Navy men.

The Captain knew how important little victories were. When the Koreans ordered us to walk at all times with chin on chest—a position of guilt and supplication—he bent down from the waist. I can still remember Specs' surprised question: "What is wrong with you, Captain?" The Skipper explained that the guards made his men walk this way. Specs made no further comment, but two days later Super C announced a new policy: crew members could walk with their heads held high.

The Captain backed his men, and they appreciated it. Super C periodically picked one crewman and grilled him for being "insincere" or for making trouble. CT 2 Anthony A. Lamantia, for instance, was once accused of laughing at one of the guards. Super C hadn't gotten two-thirds into his spiel before the CO was on his feet saying he would personally accept full responsibility for Lamantia's conduct. This happened many times. Hammond, Chicca, Law, CT 2 David L. Ritter, and I all were, at one time or another, accused. In each case the Captain was there by our side.

Out at exercise time or huddled in the head, the Captain would issue his "guidelines." "Be careful with these guys," he would say. "Don't try and argue with them. Just admit they're right, if you have to. But always leave them a way out."

The Captain enjoyed contesting the North Koreans. His whole life, in fact, had been one challenge after another to get away with as much as he could before he got caught. In North Korea it was no different. Time and again he would frustrate the guards. They would come in and tell him, in Korean, to do something. Naturally, he wouldn't understand, but, rather than just sit there looking stupid, he would do something completely ludicrous. One time, he immediately jumped up, grabbed his chair, and set it on his table. Then he grabbed his night stand and put that on top of the chair. He took his bucket and placed that on top of the night stand. The guard left as he was heading for his bed.

Another time, a guard came flying in and jabbered something at him. Without batting an eye, the Captain went over to his bed, grabbed his sheets, and threw them into his bucket. Dumbfounded, the guard got the duty officer. "I thought," explained the Captain, "that he said I should wash my sheets."

During the summer, a duty officer once came in and told him he should put on his jacket. "But," protested the Captain, "it is too hot. If I put on my jacket, I'll sweat." The duty officer repeated the order and left; the CO put his jacket on and then took it off again. The duty officer returned and again issued the order. "But I'm telling you, if I have to wear my jacket, I'll sweat." Again he put the jacket on. This time, as soon as the door closed he grabbed his pitcher and poured the water over his head. When the duty officer returned, he found the Captain, jacket on, sitting there drenched. "I told you I'd sweat," said the Captain.

After one of our first movies, Fee-ture Feel-em asked the Captain: "What is your impression of the feel-em?" The Captain jumped to his feet and answered with three words: "It was swell." That ended Fee-ture Feel-em's question-and-answer period.

In April, the Koreans returned to terror tactics. The guards took to raiding our rooms, looking for cigarettes. When they tired of that, they took to raiding our rooms to look for people. The duty officers pretended not to notice, and one by one the guards would try out their prowess on the defenseless Americans. As these capricious beatings continued, several of the duty officers joined in, even goading the guards into more savagery. The Captain complained to every duty officer who came by. Most just laughed at him. Finally he managed to corner Specs. "But," protested Specs, "in our country we do not believe in physical torture."

The Captain was seething. "Well, then, just take a look at my men. This senseless beating has got to stop."

Super C called a meeting and bawled us out for four hours for not being fully appreciative of the humanitarian treatment we were receiving. But that was just to save face. The next week the entire complement of guards was transferred—to Vietnam, we hoped— and more senior duty officers came to supervise. That ended the beatings, at least for a while.

When the Captain complained about the food and got no response, he went on a hunger strike. He contracted dysentery. This put him in contact with the prison doctor, to whom he pleaded the case. The doctor must have listened. Some fatty chunks of pork were added to our meager diet.

There were many little things the Captain did to raise our spirits. Told to prune a plant the Korean duty officers were trying to save, the Captain cut it to a stump—much to the Koreans' horror. "No," said the Captain to the protesting Koreans, "now it will sleep and conserve its strength." The Koreans watched, mystified, as the dead plant slept.

Reminded that Easter was approaching, he successfully persuaded the authorities that his vitamin-short men must be given an egg that day.

Weakened because his leg wounds had been aggravated by kicking, the Captain would smile and give the thumbs-up sign when he limped across the compound in sight of the crew.

He was a star at the propaganda meetings called by Super C. He would name comic-book characters as influential people in the United States. Asked once by Super C for names of people the crew could write to to bring pressure on President Johnson to apologize, the Captain said, "How about John Dillinger?" Super C looked blank. "He is," explained the Captain soberly, "one of the swell moralists of our times, an influential Baptist minister in Florida who baptizes people in the ocean." Super C wondered why the crew was laughing outright. Quickly, the Captain covered. "Come to think of it, though, maybe he wouldn't be so good. Last year he baptized three people so energetically that he drowned them." Super C was perplexed. He didn't understand the joke, but didn't want to find out if he had lost face. He never brought up that subject again.

Once, Super C got onto the subject of Marx and Engels. He thought he really had us, but then the CO stood up and delivered a thirty-minute monologue on how Marx had really been an outcast and had, in fact, stolen most of his philosophy from Hegel. Super C hurriedly backed off.

Another time, we got into a discussion of early-twentieth-century Korean history. The officer in charge was Artful Dodger, whom Super C had sent in because he didn't want to talk about history. Art wanted to talk about Kim Il Sung fighting the Japanese in World War II. Kim, he explained to us, hid out in China, building his army for the eventual "victorious march to Pyongyang."

"That's interesting," commented the Captain. "We were, as you know, actively supporting the Chinese against the Japanese in mainland China. I guess that made us allies?"

Artful Dodger, true to his name, quickly changed the subject.

The Captain also taunted the Koreans on nonpolitical subjects. One or our duty officers at the Farm was Bloke, so named because of his British pronunciation. He was, he informed us, not a regular interpreter or translator. He had learned English only by studying books and listening to the BBC broadcasts from Hong Kong. A large Korean, with a pronounced chin, he had a surprising twinkle to his eye, and his front teeth had all been capped with gold. Most of the time he wandered around with a big grin.

He was intensely interested in the crew, in America, and, most of all, in improving his English vocabulary. The Captain gave him a chance one evening when the officers were gathered in his room. Bloke came in, lamenting the fact that, though he could understand most English, he did not understand our humor. He wanted us, he explained, to teach him some jokes.

The Captain was most accommodating. He explained that some words in English had slang meanings. "For instance," he said, "the expression 'I want to go get a shack job.'"

Bloke looked puzzled and said that he didn't understand.

"Well," explained the Captain, "it means the same as saying 'I want a little tail,' or 'a piece of ass.'"

Bloke was still confused.

"But that," said the Captain, "is a joke. You can see from just looking at the others how humorous it is."

Bloke did not believe it. "I cannot," he said, "understand the humor. I think now you are try to fool me."

The Captain said that if he doubted our word, he should go down to Law's room and ask him. Bloke departed.

The next day Law approached the Captain. "Damnedest thing," he said. "We were sitting there playing cards when Bloke charged in and ordered me to stand up. Then he asked me if I wanted to go to the shack and have a piece of tail. What the hell were you guys up to last night?"

The Captain's sense of humor and audacity had an electric effect on the crew. Following his lead, they assumed the spirit and unity of men suffering together. This spirit was perhaps best summed up by Kisler, in a poem he wrote in early October. He called it "Bucher's Bastards." Part of it went:

196

Out of Japan on the fifth of Jan
The *Pueblo* came a'steaming.
Round Kyushu's toe, past Sasebo,
You could hear the Captain a'screaming.

"XO," he said, "full speed ahead,
We've got us spying to do.
Timmy be sharp," and with Charley Law's charts,
Away like a turtle we flew. . . .

If you're city pubs a'crawling,
And into gutters you're falling,
And in those gutters are 82 gaffers,
It's only the crew of the A-G-E-R two,
Better known as the Great Bucher's Bastards.

The poem, of course, was passed directly to the Captain. He enjoyed it so much that he had a couple of the crewmen memorize it, to make sure it wasn't lost to history.

That was the Captain's public face. He was always careful, no matter how depressed he might be, not to show any lack of confidence or hope to the crew. When he was really down, he wouldn't say anything. On a couple of evenings I spent with him, he didn't think we were ever going to be repatriated. There were, he pointed out, missionaries captured by the Chinese Communists in 1944 who had as yet to be released.

In early summer, he went through another trying period. Super C spent a session with the crew telling us of the activities of the Captain's wife, Rose. "Madam Rose," he said, "was in a parade on the Fourth of July." She had also gone to Washington; she had sponsored the "Remember the Pueblo" campaign; she was distributing bumper stickers. At the thought of his wife, the Captain unabashedly cried. Alone in his room, he faced a real dilemma. He did believe that Rose had become active on his behalf, but he was afraid that she would step on too many toes. If he ever got out, his career could be closed because of her activities. And yet, she was his wife, doing what many wives would do under the circumstances. He knew, too, that her activities re-enforced Super C's propaganda theme, and

197

yet he resolved to stand by her. It was a difficult choice, but even in North Korea he decided that his wife was more important than his career.

When the Captain wasn't suffering mentally, he was suffering physically. Wounded at the time of the capture, he went through several months of pain. And after being beaten ferociously in the Barn, it took, he said, "about three weeks for my insides to relocate themselves." Later, when he had dysentery, he passed out in the hall one day. Always a target for the younger guards, he once got kicked down a flight of stairs for no apparent reason. His leg, victim of an old football injury, started to bother him, and he limped during most of the eleven months. His eyesight got bad in September, and for nine months he was bothered by a rotten tooth.

But despite these problems, the Captain inspired a new attitude and frame of mind in all of us, and the men became increasingly receptive to ways to assert themselves against their captors. From the beginning, the Captain never let himself be photographed without giving the Koreans the finger, symbol in schoolyard circles for "fuck you." The crew, of course, picked this up as a visible despoiler of propaganda pictures aimed at the States. We realized that the Koreans did not recognize the symbol when a documentary film concerning the return of Stutts and Voltz featured a Navy officer turning around and giving the finger to the North Korean cameraman. From that day forward, we knew we had a great tool.

Friar Tuck immediately passed the word that, if questioned, the finger was to be described as an ancient Hawaiian good-luck symbol. All agreed. Led by the Captain, the crew became bolder. Law, closing an exercise period, held up his finger to the crew and yelled: "Good luck, everyone." The Captain figured the risk was worth the boost to morale and explained to Super C the good-luck meaning. Sure enough, right before our press conference in August Super C closed a meeting by holding up his middle finger, grinning, and saying: "Good luck! I wish you a successful press conference!"

King Kong, in Law's room one day, explained that, to a Korean, extending the little finger meant "no good," while extending the thumb meant "very good." The middle finger, Law said, must, therefore, mean "so-so." When inspecting the halls after cleaning, Law would whip around to King Kong when he discovered some overlooked dust, extend his middle finger, and say: "Only so-so."

Our greatest triumph came in August, when our rooms were photographed individually. The pictures, explained the room daddies, would be sent home to show everyone how well we were getting along. Of the forty or fifty pictures that were taken, better than 80 per cent, we figured, featured the finger.

Unfortunately, some of these photographs were picked up by the press. The Associated Press included this guideline: "Your attention is called to the possible obscene nature of the fingers in the picture." *Time* ran the picture, with the following story, in their edition of October 18: "The North Koreans are having a hard time proving to the world that the captive crewmen of the *USS PUEBLO* are a contrite and cooperative lot. Last week Pyongyang's flacks tried again—and lost to the U.S. Navy. In this class-reunion picture, three of the crewmen have managed to use the medium for a message, furtively getting off the U.S. hand signal of obscene derisiveness and contempt."

Seven weeks later the photo and caption landed on the desk of the Glorious General. It triggered a new reign of terror, which this time the Captain could not abate.

Hell Week

"You have ruined your own chances of repatriation," GG hissed at us at a December 5 meeting of the officers. He had called us together to rake us over for the finger gesture. On his desk was a thick envelope. Triumphantly, he spilled its contents onto his desk, then beckoned us closer. He held up, for our perusal, the *Time* picture. He was no longer concerned with what the gesture meant. "I think," he said, "that it is the lowest, the dirtiest gesture you can make." With that we had to agree. He had already forced admissions out of several of the crew members; Chief Goldman's split lip attested to that.

He was now probing a new angle: why did the crew members do it? "Perhaps," he said, answering his own question, "it is because they were ordered to do it." He made several observations, all ominous. "Well, Commanding Officer, you are in charge of the crew. We did not think that such a gesture would be lightly made. We think that it must have been ordered." He looked at each of us, and continued, "We have been watching and observing, and we begin to see concentric circles forming, from the crew to the officers to the Commanding Officer."

We sat mute. GG quite obviously was building up to something, trying to reshape the facts to fit his theory. His hand patted the photograph. "We have," he said, "the evidence. And we are reviewing all of the photographs, all of the moving pictures, to find out who are the insincere ones." He would, he said, let us know the results.

Alone, we pondered this new twist. GG's involvement showed that the Koreans' anger had escalated to the highest level of command. If there had been one picture published in the States, might there not have been others? And there were the petitions and letters. Downcast, we imagined the news media at home going over these sentence by sentence, carefully pointing out how the Koreans had been duped by the U.S. Navy. The height would, of course, be reached in our paraphrase of the military definition of rape in our petition.

"We never should have done it," Murphy said. "It will only mean more beatings for the crew." The Captain, however, was adamant. "Of course we had to do it," he said; "it was the only weapon we had to fight back with." And he put the word out to the crew that he was immensely proud of their cleverness. The North Korean aim was clearly propaganda, and, by their own admission, we had undermined it.

I wasn't sure what was going to happen. The North Koreans had known about the finger since early October. One of the room daddies had asked Berens about it. Berens had replied that it was a good-luck sign, and the Korean officer had indicated no, they knew what the symbol meant. At that time, when we were scheduled to leave shortly, they had been willing to excuse us. Now, almost two months later, they were in a different mood. Why?

The only answer we could come up with was that the North Koreans were only getting set for the coming winter. We decided that they did not expect an apology from President Johnson and needed a reason to tighten their grip for the next three or four months. The Captain feared the worst. He anticipated that we would be split up, the "ringleaders" going to some special prison camp, the others staying here or even going home. He thought maybe the North Koreans might start to release the crew a couple at a time. But for the short term, he saw nothing but carnage. "Tell the crew," he said, "to get set for a pretty rough time."

The period we called Hell Week began in painful earnestness on December 11. By this time GG was convinced that there was a master plan behind the almost universal use of the finger by us. He had earlier suspected the Captain of being a CIA agent, and these suspicions now resurfaced. He was determined to find out, at any cost to us, who had masterminded the use of the finger and why.

That Wednesday, lunch was served early, at about 11:30, a break in the rigid routine. After lunch, tables and chairs were set up in the hallways for some unknown purpose. Where before there had been eight crew members to a room, there were now to be twelve. The crew was concentrated in just two wings of the building, instead of four.

GG called the whole crew together in the Club at 1:30 for a short meeting. Silver Lips translated. GG was flanked by about ten officers. Present were two burly colonels we hadn't seen before.

"We know that you have been insincere," GG began. "We have learned all about your insincerity. We have information on the double meanings in your letters home, the obscene gestures in the pictures—all of which we have reviewed. Some of you have actively worked to discredit and heap dishonor on the Democratic People's Republic of Korea, which has treated you so leniently. You have been sending secret messages back and forth between you. We know all this.

"You know that our law calls for leniency only to those who are sincerely repentant of their crimes. The punishment is not meted out to the sincerely repentant. You have failed to show yourselves sincere.

"The Democratic People's Republic of Korea decided to give you humanitarian treatment because in the beginning we believed you had confessed all your crimes sincerely and honestly. But now we must go back to the beginning. All rights and privileges are suspended. There will be no more sports, no more entertainment, and you must ask permission from the guards for your every word and movement. No more mail will be distributed.

"I am going to give you one more chance to demonstrate your sincerity. You will write out complete confessions on three points: everything you have done to try to discredit the Democratic People's Republic of Korea, all you had planned to do in the future to discredit us, and what every one of your comrades has done and was planning.

202

"After we have read the confessions, we will decide whether you are sincere. Interrogations to test your sincerity will be resumed. Then we will know whether any of your rights and privileges should be restored.

"We have been watching the crew members closely for some time. We have observed circles going out from the Commanding Officer. We know"—he pointed his finger at the Captain—"there are those among you who are instigators and who work for the CIA. We will find out all about that very soon."

The Captain made a stab at our defense, but to no avail. He said it was true that some of us had transgressed, but now we had learned our lesson and were sincerely repentant. GG's only comment was a cold "We'll see."

Paper and pencils were then handed out, and each of the crew members was assigned to a chair and table. I was led back to my room, though the door was left open. The guard force was trebled, and the men were told to start immediately. A depressing silence descended on the building, bringing back memories of the Barn. We all hunched over and started to write. Another set of duty officers and translators had been brought in. Every sign was ominous.

I wrote for almost three hours, filibustering on paper about insincerity and true repentance, scarcely touching on the subjects GG had mentioned. I handed in my "final" confession to a duty officer at about 5:00 P.M. An hour later, it was handed back to me with orders to make it "more complete." This was a standard North Korean procedure, so I regurgitated what I had already written for another couple of hours, then handed it in. This time they accepted it.

The Koreans sent around a meager supper—turnips floating in oil—shortly before midnight. I was told to go to bed with the light on and to keep the door open so the guards and duty officers could watch me constantly.

About 2:30 in the morning, Silver Lips rooted me out of bed and said that my confession must be "more complete." "You must," he said. "tell about the others. We know from other sources," he said ominously, "that you are not sincere." He spoke to Tashi, a sadistic guard whose name meant "again." Tashi normally had the morning watch, and his favorite move was to inspect the cleaning details, then shout "*Tashi!*" and kick the closest crewman. Tashi looked at me now with evil interest, as if he had just been told to kill me. I sat at the table to write some more. Tashi gave me a couple of punches and slaps on the head as I sat there, but did nothing serious.

The next afternoon, Tashi sneaked up behind me while I was writing at the table. I never saw him coming. He kicked me from behind, in the rib cage, drop-kick fashion. The blow lifted me out of the chair and threw me into the table and the wall. I was still reeling when he came at me full force, using his fists and his feet, exercising his karate kicks. A right-hand cross landed on the left side of my face; a hard kick smashed into my shins; a knee drove into my groin. Having sent me to the floor, Tashi gave me a couple of kicks with his heavy boots and then waited while I slowly got up. Expecting his strong right jab again, I didn't see his boot coming. It caught me solidly in the chest, knocking the wind out of me and sending me crashing to the floor again. Satisfied, Tashi left.

The beating probably lasted a half hour. Muddy boot marks were all over my uniform, the chest pain made breathing difficult, and the left side of my face throbbed as it started to swell. I was dizzy as I tried to write something to get the Koreans off my back. I filled the pages with all kinds of insincere things I had done, from hidden meanings in letters to kidding the guards. I went into a long, rambling explanation of why I had been so insincere as to doubt their promises of humanitarian treatment. I discussed the petition for leniency at length, stating that publishing such a document was a generous act. We had been insincere in putting double meanings in the petition, but I had been solely responsible. I filled other pages with self-criticism of my previous capitalistic life, which had developed me into such a devious character. I put down everything I could make relevant about Western religion, and dwelled at length upon the significance of interpersonal relationships and how, through my insincere acts, I had displayed immoral dishonesty. It was the kind of thing you write in college when you don't know the answer to an essay question.

On Friday, Silver Lips was back. "Who is responsible? Who ordered these things? Your confession is not complete," he said, demanding that I write yet more. He brought along Tashi for further inspiration. I decided the only way out was to blame myself for every discreditable incident I could remember. I inspired, I wrote, the whole crew to use the finger gesture; I told another man to cut the plastic tableclothes; I instructed a certain room to disobey the guards—and on and on. Tashi came in to check my progress, decided I hadn't scribbled enough, although he couldn't read a word of English, and slugged me a few times. Both my eyes were now black, although not yet swollen shut. The left side of my face was continuing to swell.

Whether we were writing or not writing, the Koreans made us sit erect at the table all day, not even letting us cross a leg. Our heads were to be down on our chests, but no dozing was allowed. Going to the head required a formal request and escort by a guard. My chest felt as if it were collapsing. I had to roll in and out of bed because of pain whenever I bent over.

On Saturday, I waited in my room for the next move. The duty officer informed me that I could read the propaganda books. This at least gave me something to do, something to keep Tashi off me. My confession had not been returned, and I sat and waited for the coming of the next blows. Tashi only kicked me a few times. Disgusted, I could hear him working on other crew members. Their shouts and groans of pain were hard to endure. King Kong strutted in to gloat. One of the crew members, he said, had tried to kill himself. Two others, he informed me, were dead. But he never had been a good liar. He was being too pompous. I didn't believe him.

On Sunday, Tashi beat me twice, on each of his watches, for at least half an hour. The punching, kicking, and kneeing were savage and cruel, and he brought in an assistant to help. I was worried that one of them might misplace a kick and do some real damage. Inside, I went gray, trying to dissociate myself from the ferocity of the beatings so that fear would not mount inside me.

The campaign of terror was too obvious. I felt sure they were after something. Our position hadn't really changed much. We were still hostages, and therefore still had value to them. No one of us was yet being made an example for the others; so their campaign seemed to be individual terror, for some reason. If I could hang on, sooner or later they would tip their hand. The only thing I felt sure of was that our release couldn't be imminent. After all their propaganda about "humanitarian treatment," they wouldn't send us back with black eyes and bruises.

I waited in dread on Monday for whatever was to come next. But Tashi never laid a hand on me. I did receive one really hard blow from another guard, and the duty officer who witnessed it said that I was being insincere and would be shot. My left ear continued to swell and my chest bothered me a great deal.

On Tuesday Tashi was still restrained, and the other guards eased up. About 4:00 P.M. I watched as GG raced into the compound in his Russian-made jeep and screeched to a halt in front of the building. This was unusual; normally, GG arrived at one end of the building, not at the front. The duty officers were summoned, evidently for some emergency meeting. I thought I detected a sense of urgency. Perhaps GG had been given the order to shoot us. The Koreans, I decided, were thoroughly sick of us. It was probably just as difficult for them to maintain the charade of humanitarian treatment as it was for us to remain "sincerely repentant." Their attempts at brainwashing had failed, and, worse, we had made fools of them. But on the basis of our latest "confessions" they could justify our deaths. I tried not to think of Christmas, a week away.

The next day the duty officers returned without a word about their meeting, the morning went by without the sound of a beating, and no crew members were called out for "interrogation." Around four or five o'clock I heard someone coming up the stairs fast. As the steps approached my room, I tensed and rose. "Come out," an officer said. "You have meeting downstairs." I had to walk there as a penitent, my head down on my chest. I knocked at GG's door and entered the room. A single light illuminated it. At the desk sat Odd Job. Silver Lips sat at his right, looking tired, harried, stern. And no wonder—the majority of our double meanings had been translated and passed by him.

Odd Job told me to sit down. Another officer was present, also an interpreter, who copied down what was said. I held my head low and stared at the pine top of the narrow table in front of me.

"We have read over your confession," Odd Job said, "and it has many shortcomings. We know you have not written down everything. We know that from the others. Have you written down everything?"

"Yes," I answered. If I had left out something specific, I figured, they would tell me about it now. But, to leave myself a way out, I added, "I have written down everything that I can remember. But I am so plagued by my previous life that I probably could not remember all the times I discredited your government."

"I see," Odd Job said, with unexpected softness. "But you have left out very much."

Thinking that it was time to take a stand, I said: "I don't know what you mean. My confession is as complete as I can make it. But my crimes are so great that I cannot possibly remember all my insincerities. I should be shot. I have been so insincere."

"But you have left out the most important part," Odd Job replied, pointing to a stack of paper on his desk.

I was worried that he might know about the radio the crew had tried to make or about our various escape plans, concocted but never approved. Or possibly he was implying that I hadn't "squealed" on anyone else. Nowhere had I mentioned another crew member by name.

"You have not described those crimes which led you to be taken captive. You have not told in detail of your preparation for this mission and of your part in the crime. This is the most serious of your crimes against our country, and you haven't even mentioned it. Why not?"

"I have written that before," I answered.

Silver Lips droned on through all the old history of the *Pueblo,* the intrusions, the spying—all the old allegations, already published, broadcast, and filmed. "Can you write that for us?"

I sensed that something had changed their scenario. They were no longer looking for victims, for people to beat for conspiring against them. I decided to test this theory, and answered: "No, I don't think I can ever again write sincerely."

This caught them by surprise. They had no instructions to cover it. Odd Job and Silver Lips whispered for several minutes. I decided to keep stabbing at this chink.

"I am too insincere. My life has been so wretched. I have committed so many offenses. I should be shot for my crimes. Your government cannot tolerate my insincerity and transgressions."

"We know all about your trick writing," Odd Job said, with all the sincerity he could muster. "All about the double meanings. We just want you to tell the truth this time, straightforward, clearly, and with feeling. We do not want any more double meanings. We know what you are going through, but we think you are honestly trying to be sincere now. We could recognize much sincerity in what you have written."

It was true, then. They had changed direction. They were looking for a way to forgive me.

"What do you want?" I asked abjectly, to test my conclusion further. "I am so insincere I know I cannot be tolerated in your country. I tried to write sincerity into my papers, but I just cannot cleanse myself of all the sins of my past. I just don't think I could write anything more sincerely."

Odd Job and Silver Lips conducted another whispered consultation. They had to get me off the hook, whether I co-operated or not.

"We can recognize your sincerity," Silver Lips said. "We know you are trying to be truly repentant. We want you to go home. We will give you this one final chance to demonstrate your sincerity. We think you can do it. Will you?"

I clenched my fists on the table and shook my head. Then, after a dramatic pause, I said: "Yes. I can do it. I will do it."

"Look up," Odd Job said quickly. "Raise your head." The sight of my full face, swollen, bruised, and with one black eye, apparently startled him. He jumped back in his chair, rubbing the left side of his face.

"You must begin immediately," he said. "You must go back to your room and begin immediately. Are you sure you can do it?"

"Yes," I replied. "Yes, I can do it."

"Fine," Odd Job said with obvious relief. "We will give you

paper and pen. But you must begin immediately. Is there anything you need?"

"No," I answered. "I will begin now." I rose dejectedly from my chair, walked slowly out of the room, and then fairly skipped down the hall. We were going home! I felt sure of it. Something had been worked out. Hell Week, I was convinced, was over. This would be the "final" confession.

On the third floor, the Koreans had again set up the chairs and tables in the hall, and the men were sitting there writing their "final" confessions.

Further evidence of my hopeful theory came that night while I sat writing the rest of my confession at the table in my room. A concerned Odd Job appeared with the doctor. The doctor looked at my black eye and swollen ear and muttered in Korean to Odd Job. Then he handed me an egg and showed me how I must first heat it on the radiator, then rub it around my eye.

I took my confession down to the Club at about 11:00 that night. Many of the men were still working, but I was pleased that the guards had been called off. The duty officer was in a good mood. He looked at the stack of papers I presented to him, then at me, smiling. "It is good for you," was all he said.

Free at Last

The next morning—Thursday, December 19—GG summoned the whole crew to the Club. They were a shambles, with lumps and bruises prevalent. Several had black eyes, including Berens, Tuck, Iredale, and Law. Mack was walking hunched over, and he said: "It hurts to cough." He had, we discovered later, a broken rib.

GG was short and to the point. They had read the confessions and concluded that we were "sincere." "Some of you," he went on, "did not admit the intrusions." He had a few crew members stand up and say that yes, they had doubted the "evidence." Then he turned to me and said: "Well, you, Operations Officer, I think you know more about it than the others. Here, read them this." He handed me a secret instruction captured with the ship and indicated what to read. I rose and read the paragraph that stated that officially the United States recognized only the three-mile limit around North Korea and that "patrols to the three-mile limit are authorized."

GG had his evidence and turned to the men and asked them if they believed what I had read. They said yes, that now they recognized the truth. He then went on to say that because we had proved our sincerity in our confessions all our rights were being returned. And we would be permitted to go outdoors and get some exercise before lunch.

It was good to get outside in the fresh air. It was good, too, to unlimber sore muscles and to find out just what had happened.

Everyone quickly admitted that it had been pretty bad, but then we started to see the humor in it.

Tim and I ran around the field together, and Tim's comment was: "Fetch really blew it. He kept coming in and telling me what I should 'confess to.' They know about all the stuff we pulled, the escape plans, the radio—they know it all." Though we weren't sure what was going on, we felt certain that their plans had been interrupted.

At lunch the Captain asked what had happened to each of us. I was the worst-looking of the officers; my face and, particularly, my left ear were still swollen. Most of us had apparently been careful in our revelations, admitting only what they first mentioned, plus what we made up. Murphy, however, said that he had been quite sure that they knew everything and had confirmed it all for them.

"Even the radio?" asked the Captain.

"More than that," he answered. "They even know the nicknames."

"You're kidding, Ed. You didn't tell them those?"

Murphy said he had been convinced that the Koreans already knew all of them, and he had confirmed them.

"Jesus, Ed, you mean they know about the crew's nickname for Kim's mother? That's sort of like calling Martha Washington a whore."

"They know about that, Captain. They know about everything."

Thinking it was time to get off this subject, I told them what I had picked up from one of the crew: a duty officer had said that we would be going home before Christmas! And that was only five days away!

Later that evening, Captain Nice came into my room and confirmed the rumor. "Yes," he said, "our government is doing all it can to try to get you home by Christmas. We understand what that day means to you and we would like very much that you celebrated it with your families." I went to bed that night wanting to hope for the best, but not wanting to be disappointed again, as we had been in October.

On Friday we had another meeting with GG. The United States, he told us, wanted to apologize. He wasn't sure what would happen, but we must be prepared for any contingency. There would be another meeting soon; we must be prepared. He told us to finish our "final confessions." These would be used as insurance, in case the American authorities tried to get us to lie about our treatment when we returned home.

Later that afternoon I had a meeting with Robot concerning my "confession." I shouldn't, he said, use the phrase "Korean People's Army Navy." They knew, he explained, that this was not good English. He also said I should add more about what the other officers were doing on the day of capture. And then he rambled on. I had never had much to do with him, fortunately. He was one of the cruelest officers there. But now he was saying good-by, and he spoke of peace. "Just remember," he concluded, "that an officer in the North Korean Army talked to you of world peace and brotherhood."

Sure thing, Robot, I thought, but your version comes out world tyranny and slavery. I looked him square in the eye and said that when I returned I would try to tell only the truth about our capture and the detention period. "That," he said, "is all that we ask."

In a way, I was pleased that the North Koreans had discovered so much of what we had been doing. They seemed dismayed and angry when they learned the extent of our double talk and innuendos, and about the stunts we had pulled against them, the names we had called them behind their backs, and our attitude toward their "humanitarian treatment." No headway had been made by them against the unity and cohesiveness of our crew. Though not everyone could take the beatings Hammond and Kisler received, no one lost faith with our system or with the Captain. And the North Koreans knew it. They hadn't really hurt any of us, despite eleven months of hell. The real hurt was to come later—in our own country.

There was work to do, as GG had said. First, baths and shaves for everyone. Then all those confessions had to be read, translated, corrected, recopied, recorded, and approved. Because black eyes and bruises had to be taken care of, all the injured were put in one room, and Baldridge was assigned to administer a "hot wax" treatment. Preparations had to be made for a final press conference and a final letter of gratitude.

On Saturday, GG said we must be fully prepared, although he still didn't have any details. There would be another meeting the next day to "work out the details." I was selected, with Mack and CT 2 Wayne D. Anderson, to write the letter of gratitude. GG chose others to participate in an "impromptu" press conference.

Andy, Mack, and I worked all afternoon. We wanted to keep the letter short, and did. GG picked it up around dinnertime, and shortly after, we were called back together. We spent all night on reworking it, GG being very careful about the language. He called in two interpreters in addition to Silver Lips, and, at about six o'clock in the morning, was finally convinced that the letter was "Okay." He took off his glasses, leaned back, and turned to look out the window. I thought he was going to say something profound. Perhaps he was considering it. But he turned back to face us, looked at his watch, and said: "Well, I am afraid you did not get much sleep. I will tell the duty officer to let you men sleep." We mumbled our thanks. He got up. "There will be a final meeting at eleven. I will let you know the results."

I stopped by the Captain's room, figuring that we were back in their good graces now, it was getting-up time, and no one would notice. I sat down, had a cigarette with him, and told him what GG had said.

"He's been wrong before, Skip. I won't believe it until we actually cross the line."

"I guess you're right, Captain, but I think this is it. We're going home."

I went upstairs and toward my room. The duty officer stopped me and asked where I had been. "In the head," I answered. "I'm going to bed. Did the General tell you?"

"All right," he said, "you may go."

I slid onto the mattress and promptly fell into a deep sleep. Around ten o'clock Baldridge came in to put more hot wax on my black eye. I told him what I knew, after debating with myself whether it was right to get the men's hopes built up again. Finally I told him not to pass it on, knowing full well that he would.

A half hour later the doctor came in. He wanted, he said, to operate on my ear. I had been fortunate, I figured, to have gotten through these eleven months with nothing more serious than boils and bleeding rashes. But now my number seemed to have come up. A cyst under my left ear had become badly inflamed; it was a soft, infected mass about the size of a golf ball. Clearly, the North Koreans had decided that this would not do. It must be cut open and drained.

Down in his office, the doctor puttered around, finally asking me to lie down on his operating table. I was scared, but what could I do? He found a knife in a drawer, dropped it, then held it over an open flame for a few seconds. Florence Nightingale was there, holding a rag. Doc made a three-quarter-inch slash under my ear, and seemed happy with the result, though surprised by the amount of liquid that gushed out. He emphasized this with little grunts and whistles. The knife hurt, but it was a relief to have the pressure off my ear, and I thanked him.

Around 12:30, GG called us all together. He told us directly that the United States had apologized and that all the details had been definitely worked out. We would be released the next day, in Panmunjom, at 11:00 A.M. We applauded, the Captain got up and said thank you, and at some moment our letter was offered and accepted. The Captain, as I recall, signed it "on behalf of the whole crew of the USS *Pueblo*." Then GG said that we must be prepared to meet the press that afternoon.

This press conference was the usual sham. The correspondents had been primed, and so had we. I don't remember much about it; I didn't really care. About all we said was yes, it was nice to be going home.

We were fed early that night and sent back to our rooms to wait. I looked around my room. There was nothing to take with me, I knew, and not much I would have wanted. All papers had been confiscated, but if they were ever to tear up those floor boards on a systematic basis, as, indeed, Tashi had wanted to do, they might have found a few hastily torn notes from months past and a couple of packs of cigarettes.

214

Then, one by one, we were called out and taken into the barber-shop to change clothes. The new clothes were similar to the tan uniforms of July and August. The material was thin, the quality poor. In fact, of the three uniforms we had had while in detention, this one was by far of the lowest quality. We were also given quilted blue coats, sloping little hats, and black-and-white tennis shoes. And we were allowed to keep our watches and rings.

GG was quiet, reserved. He said that we were finally going home, that he was happy for us, and that he meant that sincerely. He flashed the finger at us, not appearing to realize what he was doing, but perhaps just to put himself into the joke. The Captain got up, thanked him, and paid him a compliment by saying that he knew that GG was a good soldier who was just doing his duty and that, even though he himself had no regard for their system, he had to recognize a fine officer. GG made no reply to this. Chicca asked if he could take any of the propaganda with him. GG said no, that was not possible. I asked why he thought the U.S. had waited until now to apologize. He grinned and said he thought it was perfectly clear. Then he looked at his watch. "Come," he said, "I don't want you to miss the train."

We boarded buses and rode to the Pyongyang railroad station. There we boarded a train, whose windows were covered. But it was warm and relatively comfortable. We six officers shared two little compartments. No one slept much.

The train left Pyongyang around 11:00 P.M. and jerked and poked its way down to Kaesong, at the northern edge of the demilitarized zone. We were served breakfast on the train—the same old turnips, fish heads, and bread—and then waited until about nine o'clock. Tashi was one of the guards on the train. I pointed him out to Tim, who shrugged and said: "No wonder he looks upset; he has to stay."

All of the duty officers had come with us, although most of the higher-ranking officers apparently had stayed in Pyongyang. We never saw GG again.

Finally, Bloke got us out and into four unheated buses, whose windows were covered by white sheets. After crawling through the streets of Kaesong, we sat and sat—10:30, 11:00, 11:30. Bloke popped in and said, "Here. It is signed. You can see for yourselves." He passed around a photocopy of what, he claimed, Major General

Gilbert H. Woodward had just signed. We looked at it in disbelief. They had eliminated the last sentence: "Simultaneously with my signature I hereby acknowledge receipt of 82 crew members and one corpse of the USS *Pueblo*." Without this last sentence, the statement was an "apology."

And then the buses started. "It is very near," Bloke said.

"How about a cigarette, Bloke?" we asked him.

He grinned at the nickname and gave us some cigarettes. "Well, you see," he said, "here is a Korean officer giving freely of his own personal cigarettes. Now what about it, huh?" He had a broad grin on his face. "I am," he said, "very happy for you. You see, we have kept our bargain. We are quite honest."

"Hey, Bloke," someone asked, "why don't you come with us?"

Bloke grinned again. "No," he said, "I must stay and work for the revolution."

When the bus stopped, Bloke explained what we were to do. He would call our names, we were to answer "here," then go through the sheet and down the steps of the bus. After giving our names again, we were to walk over a bridge, to freedom.

The officers, except for the Captain, who had gone first, were in the last bus, and we were called out in inverse order of rank, making me the third from the last. Rough hands grabbed me as I got off the bus and turned me in the direction of the bridge. At first my head was down. When I looked up, in front of me was the bridge—the Bridge of No Return—with a row of men spaced out about thirty feet apart on their half. Behind me, a loud-speaker was blaring out the Captain's last "confession"—"we humbly beg forgiveness and earnestly thank the people . . ." I didn't listen. Looking forward, I walked carefully, trying not to run. I saw Captain Bucher, waiting at the end. I saluted him, then shook his hand and mumbled, "We made it, Captain."

216

Epilogue   *by George C. Wilson*

Francis Gary Powers in his book, *Operation Overflight,* wrote:

"The U-2 incident was an almost classic textbook case of unpreparedness. . . .

"We manned the U-2 with pilots who had never been adequately briefed on what to do if captured. . . .

" 'You may as well tell them everything, because they're going to get it out of you anyway' [was the only instruction].

"I wondered how many Pueblo episodes would have to occur before we accepted the basic lessons we should have learned from the U-2 crisis."

Article V of the Code of Conduct for Members of the Armed Forces of the United States says:

"When questioned, should I become a prisoner of war, I am bound to give only name, rank, service number, and date of birth. . . ."

Commander Lloyd M. Bucher testified at the Court of Inquiry:

"Neither I nor any of my officers had any special training in the Code of Conduct."

Rear Admiral Joseph B. McDevitt, Judge Advocate General of the United States Navy, in 1969 told a special subcommittee of the House Armed Services Committee investigating the *Pueblo* disaster:

"The Navy certainly is obligated to train its people to face anything they are going to be faced with."

Lieutenant Schumacher, almost beyond his belief, was at last on the friendly side of the Bridge of No Return. He and his shipmates—after physical examinations at the 121st Army Evacuation Hospital, in South Korea—headed home for a tumultuous reception in San Diego, California, on the afternoon of Christmas Eve, 1968. Skip Schumacher heard the welcoming strains of "The Lonely Bull," theme song of the U.S.S. *Pueblo,* as he debarked from the plane in San Diego. He somehow kept his emotions in check as he spotted his parents, sister, and brother-in-law in the crowd of well-wishers. He was home.

This young lieutenant, along with his shipmates, had suffered a monstrous beating for his country. He had done his best in circumstances that offered no escape, no relief, not even death. He had, unexpectedly and without preparation, faced a vicious, relentless enemy. Defeat was unavoidable. Still, he had done his best. Was it enough? He pondered this as crowds cheered him and the rest of the crew on the drive fom the Miramar Navy field to Balboa Naval Hospital.

In addition to medical examinations there, Schumacher and the other crew members were questioned intensively by officers from the Office of Naval Intelligence. The officers wanted to know every detail of the ship's capture and subsequent eleven months of captivity. They asserted that the information would be kept secret—not used in any court or inquiry called to determine how and why the *Pueblo* was lost.

On December 27, 1968, the Navy announced that Admiral John J. Hyland, Commander in Chief of the Pacific Fleet, had convened a Court of Inquiry to "inquire into the circumstances relating to the seizure of the USS *Pueblo* (AGER-2) and the subsequent detention of the vessel and the officers and crew."

Hyland named Vice Admiral Harold G. Bowen, Jr., Commander of Anti-Submarine Warfare Forces in the Pacific Fleet, to be president of the Court of Inquiry. "The court is directed to inquire into all the facts and circumstances relating to the subject incident," Hyland ordered in his instructions to Bowen.

The court convened in less than a month, on January 20, 1969, in a small lecture room at the Naval Amphibious Training Base at Coronado, California, just across the harbor from San Diego. Commander Bucher was represented by E. Miles Harvey, a reserve commander in the Navy, who had served as legal adviser to Bucher's wife, Rose, during the *Pueblo* crew's captivity. Despite his naval reserve status, the Navy considered Harvey to be Bucher's civilian counsel. Assisting Harvey was Navy Captain James E. Keys, Bucher's military counsel.

Legal aide to Bowen and four other admirals, the full membership of the Court of Inquiry, was Captain William R. Newsome. Newsome was the nearest thing to a prosecutor in this Navy court, whose function and authority were limited to inquiry and to recommending further action; it was not empowered to impose penalties of its own.

The opening exchange that first day of the inquiry was surely unprophetic of its outcome.

HARVEY: Captain Newsome, I wonder if we might inquire whether at this time if Commander Bucher is suspected of committing any offense under the Uniform Code of Military Justice?

NEWSOME: No, at this time Commander Bucher is not suspected of having committed any offense under the Uniform Code of Military Justice.

In what soon proved to be a colossal error—an error his counsel might have avoided by more accurately gauging Bucher's visibly agitated emotional state—the Commander told the admirals that first day: "I believe that I have improved physically to the extent that I can fully withstand the anticipated length of time that this Court of Inquiry will take. . . . And mentally I feel that I am as sharp as I can be at the present time." Despite this assurance, Bucher broke down and cried, time after time, during the inquiry, which virtually amounted to a trial and, in unguarded moments, was called that by the officers conducting it.

Schumacher, sweating out the interrogation of his commander, felt as though he had been transported back to the Barn. Bucher leaned heavily on Schumacher during the interrogation under the admirals, just as he had during the trial under Super C. The implied crime this time was giving up the ship.

"At what point did you decide to surrender the ship?" Rear Admiral Edward E. Grimm, a member of the court, asked Bucher.

"I decided to surrender the ship after we had been receiving fire from the SO-1 and machine-gun fire from the four torpedo boats at point-blank range. I considered that any further efforts on my part to gain the open sea would only be futile and would result in the severe damage to either the ship, or, more importantly, the men on the ship."

As for using the two machine guns on the *Pueblo*, which the Navy had ordered him to keep stowed or covered with canvas to minimize the appearance of provocation, Bucher told the court: "Two P-4's [the North Korean torpedo boats] on my bow were playing porpoise with me. There was no hope in my outrunning these people. . . . I did not feel at that time or at any time thereafter that there was any point of attempting to go to war with this group of ships that were surrounding me.

"I was completely and hopelessly outgunned. And in order for me to man my fifty-caliber machine guns, which would have been the only effective weapon that we had at a range of fifty yards, I knew to send a man up to that gun would have meant certain death for him because he would have been walking to within thirty yards of a mount of machine guns which was already mounted. At that time we would have to have removed the covers to those guns, which were in fact frozen . . . and could not be easily removed. I felt that the minute that I sent people in that general direction they would be immediately shot, and I saw no point in senselessly sending people to their death. . . ."

Schumacher and every other officer of the *Pueblo* personally endorsed Bucher's command decisions when questioned in open session by the Court of Inquiry. Bucher had followed his orders as long as they were applicable. He had avoided provocation, had taken such evasive action as he could. Then, surrounded, outgunned, fired upon at point-blank range, vulnerable to additional attack, he considered the *Pueblo*'s situation to have outrun the scope of his orders. No one had seriously weighed the possibility of Northern Korean piracy; clearly the foe had departed from any script outlined by United States military leaders. Having disregarded the possibility of unprovoked attack, Navy operational authorities had designated no units on standby alert in case the *Pueblo* should need help. No advice—no countermand of standing orders or new orders—was sent by radio from higher authority. The Captain of the *Pueblo,* as he saw his situation, was on his own, with only two options: lose his ship and his men, or lose his ship and save his men.

He chose the latter.

The cause of the *Pueblo*'s plight was lack of preparation. This failure by the Navy, the National Security Agency, and the Defense Department might be understood and forgiven if the *Pueblo* was a first. It was not. This same lack of preparation marked the disastrous U-2 flight of Francis Gary Powers on May 1, 1960. Powers was the pilot of one of the high-altitude, high-speed reconnaissance planes then being used by the United States for observation and photography in overflights above strategic and often hostile areas. The Russians shot him down after the Central Intelligence Agency had assured President Eisenhower this could not happen. As in the case of the *Pueblo* seven and one-half years later, the United States government was humiliated and was confronted by an international crisis caused by miscalculation at the top.

Bucher told the court: "I never considered I would ever be attacked on this mission. . . . Nor had I received any briefings at any station along the way during my period as prospective commanding officer or after I was commanding officer that would indicate that there were any dangers of my ever coming under attack. . . . I did not consider, nor did it ever cross my mind, that I might be placed in the position that I found myself on that afternoon. . . ."

Gary Powers declared in his book, *Operation Overflight*: ". . . we blundered, and badly, not only during the U-2 'crisis,' but long before it became a crisis.

"We were unprepared for the possibility that a plane might go down in Russia. Yet that possibility had existed from the start of the program. A rocket wasn't needed. A simple malfunction could have done it. That possibility should have been taken into consideration. It wasn't.

"We used a plane of which almost every part carried some indication of national identity. We loaded it with equipment which, should even a portion be discovered, would constitute conclusive proof of espionage intent. And we placed aboard it an explosive device insufficient to the task of destroying all evidence. . . .

"A lesson learned? According to accounts of the *Pueblo*'s seizure, it carried 'hundreds of pounds' of classified documents, with no simple means of destroying them in an emergency. . . .

"I wondered how many Pueblo episodes would have to occur before we accepted the basic lessons we should have learned from the U-2 crisis."

President Eisenhower wrote in his memoirs of the White House years, *Waging Peace*: "A final important characteristic of the plane [the U-2] was its fragile construction. This led to the assumption (insisted upon by the CIA and the Joint Chiefs) that in the event of a mishap the plane would virtually disintegrate. It would be impossible, if things should go wrong, they said, for the Soviets to come in possession of the equipment intact—or, unfortunately, of a live pilot. This was a cruel assumption, but I was assured that the young pilots undertaking these missions were doing so with their eyes wide open and motivated by a high degree of patriotism, a swashbuckling bravado, and certain material inducements."

Bucher and Powers went into Cold War battle unprepared. The planners of the *Pueblo* mission assumed that the lightly armed old cargo ship would be safe as long as she stayed in international waters. The planners of the Powers mission assumed that Russian rockets could not reach the high-flying U-2; and even if one did, there would be nothing but fragments left to tell the story.

The planners and decision makers, who sent out Bucher, Powers, and men like them, were proved wrong. These planners—in the Navy, the Defense Department, and the National Security Agency in the case of Bucher, and the Central Intelligence Agency in the case of Powers—were not willing to accept their heavy burden of responsibility for the disasters. They allowed, perhaps encouraged, blame to fall on the men they had sent out to the Cold War. Powers, to be sure, had volunteered for a peculiarly hazardous mission. The men of the *Pueblo* had not. But the difference stopped there. The men who were under fire by the Cold War enemy, not the officials who

222

sent them out on their missions, were the same ones put under fire at home.

A sorry spectacle of the *Pueblo* inquiry came when the Navy admirals called before them one *Pueblo* crewman after another to ask why each had not been able to live up to the Code of Conduct for fighting men. Captain Newsome appeared to have forgotten that he had previously declared that the *Pueblo* men were not subject to the code, because they were illegal detainees rather than prisoners of war. (His exact quote is on tape: "The Code of Conduct is inapplicable to this present situation. We have an opinion that the crew members on the *Pueblo* were not prisoners of war. They were illegally detained, and when we don't have prisoners of war, we don't have use of the Code of Conduct.") Several of the *Pueblo* crew showed their dismay before the five admirals and broke into sobs as they told how the North Koreans forced them to violate the code by signing false statements. The fact that a U.S. State Department representative similarly signed a false statement—an apology for an intrusion into North Korean territorial waters that never occurred—did not receive attention. The "system" enjoyed special immunity; it was not asked why *it* broke the Code of Conduct.

Schumacher, in a relatively brief appearance before the court compared with the marathon questioning of Bucher, was asked why he had broken the code and replied that it becomes a matter of how much you can take before you find a way around the torture. He told the admirals that it seemed far more sensible to maintain his wits for frustrating his captors than to let himself be beaten into uncontrollable senselessness.

Seaman Edward S. Russell, a psychology major from the University of Southern California, probably told the admirals more than they wanted to hear when it came his turn to testify regarding the code: "I saw Kisler walking around looking like a pumpkin. I figured they meant business. . . . The only reason that I departed from the code was that I was afraid I would get worked over pretty well. When the code was first put out, it was my understanding that this was done to put a stop to a lot of collaboration that went on during the Korean War, where people would aid the enemy to benefit themselves. I believe that is the spirit of the code. . . . I didn't feel that I violated the spirit of it, because I never did anything for my own betterment. It was just to keep myself from being stomped on. . . . I think the Code of Conduct was originally made up for countries that follow the Geneva Convention—they follow the convention and you follow the code.

"This was a totally different situation. We weren't at war with these people, and we were not properly trained for the situation we were in. I think the whole crew was psychologically unprepared for what happened. These people were on top of us most of the time we were there. And they held all the cards. There wasn't much anyone could do. . . .

"I think the thing that kept the crew from cracking up was that we had faith in our country. We all had great faith in the Captain —that he was going to make the right decisions. I think every one of us would have followed and done what the Captain had asked of us. We knew that the people back home were behind us and were doing what they could to get us out. . . ."

While the five admirals on the Court of Inquiry, after the conclusion of the hearings, deliberated to determine their recommendations for Bucher and others, fresh testimony was taken by a subcommittee of the House Armed Services Committee, headed by Representative Otis G. Pike, of New York, a former Marine divebomber pilot. In addition to concentrating on the lack of preparation for the mission, the subcommittee focused on the Code of Conduct. Eighty-two men, of varied backgrounds and political persuasions, had found the code untenable under torture; not one of the *Pueblo* crew had been able to maintain it. The subcommittee asked the Navy spokesman, in view of that record, whether it was not time to modify the code.

Vice Admiral Charles K. Duncan, Chief of Naval Personnel, gave the Navy's position on the code: "In light of recent events regarding the conduct of military personnel while being illegally detained by a foreign government, a preliminary review was made by the Navy to examine the background and present application of the Code of Military Conduct. That review revealed no valid basis for either a modification of the code itself or its application. The code is simply a formalization of standards of military conduct which have been understood and accepted by fighting men since time immemorial. . . .

"The code is regarded as the bench mark which our personnel must do their utmost to achieve. If they are forced to depart from it under extreme duress, they are at least aware of the fact and extent of their shortfall. Additionally, the value and use of the code as a source of strength under these conditions has been validated by former prisoners of war."

The Admiral did not say who those prisoners were. No one in the Navy at the time had bothered to ask Bucher or Schumacher— two men whose deep concern to preserve the code prompted them to attempt suicide—how the code could be revised to make it more tenable. The Navy, despite the evidence of the *Pueblo* disaster, seemed interested only in rationalizing about and insisting on the code's theoretical value.

Nor would Duncan at the subcommittee hearing on April 28, 1969 concede that the United States, as a government, was equally culpable of breaking the Code of Conduct.

REPRESENTATIVE ALTON LENNON (North Carolina): You recall when negotiations were consummated that resulted in the return of Commander Bucher and his crew, and the body of the deceased, that we admitted at the national level that we were there illegally within the territorial waters of North Korea, that we were there to spy, and we did spy. You know what I am talking about. Now this statement was signed by the Assistant Secretary of State for and on behalf of the President of the United States and the American nation. Should a different degree of Code of Conduct be required of a serviceman than that of the Chief Executive of the United States or the Secretary of State acting directly for the President of the United States?

ADMIRAL DUNCAN: In my opinion, Mr. Lennon, there is not a direct analogy of a code that would apply—

REPRESENTATIVE LENNON: A lie is a lie at whatever level you find it, isn't it?

ADMIRAL DUNCAN: May I say, though, that a serviceman in these situations, under detention or captivity, undergoing very extreme conditions of duress, and the code is for him, to give him a moral standard which he should do his very best to live up to, that he should do his best to live up to it. This is my personal opinion, that this is not an analogy to what a nation would do.

Representative Lennon: I agree, but the average citizen doesn't agree. The average citizen is unable to rationalize the distinction of a man under torture and duress and pressure for capitulating as distinguishing between this nation's abject apology which we made to North Korea. . . . They say, "How in the name of God can you distinguish if this nation can get on its knees and apologize for an act which it was not guilty of, what do you expect of the human being?"

Admiral Duncan's firmness slipped momentarily when he said that, if the Navy changed the code at all, this would not be done until after American prisoners in Southeast Asia were released. He then added, without supporting his contention with any details, that former prisoners from World War II, the Korean War, "and a few from Southeast Asia" believed that the code should be left as is. "Naturally we rely on their advice," he said. He evidently was not interested in the advice of eighty-two recently released prisoners from North Korea.

If Duncan or anybody else in the U.S. Navy had bothered to ask Schumacher or Bucher or others from the *Pueblo,* he would have discovered that the men who had tried to live up to the code found it wanting. The "you've got to have something" argument made by Navy leaders who have never been in captivity themselves is hardly an answer to the obvious need for revision of the code. The open record of the Naval Court of Inquiry shows that at least three officers of varying backgrounds contemplated or actually attempted suicide. Marine Sergeant Hammond, the most defiant of the men held captive, inflicted a serious wound in his stomach as part of his resistance to the North Koreans. But he, too, broke the code. While the link between his final action and the code cannot be made with certainty, it is also worth noting that Engineman First Class William D. Scarborough committed suicide after returning to civilian life from his *Pueblo* experience. Lawyers on the admirals' side of the table during the *Pueblo* inquiry admitted in discussing the code outside the court-

226

room that it was a poorly written document. Yet the burden of the imperfections in the code is still just where it was—on the backs of the men who go out where the danger is.

One could fairly expect that the experience of the Vietnam war, if not of the *Pueblo,* would bring some realism into policy making. Not so with the code. One idea—proposed long ago but ignored by the Pentagon—is for the U.S. government to proclaim formally to the world that its soldiers, sailors, and airmen are free to sign confessions while in captivity. This announcement would detail tortures of the past and state that any signed confessions from Americans in the future would be assumed to be false and the product of inhumane torture. This policy would reduce the incentive to extract confessions from our fighting men in the first place. It should be admitted, if the United States intends to stay involved in the dirty part of warfare, that torture can make men do or say almost anything.

Gary Powers is a Cold War warrior who has been there. He knows. But until his book was published, his voice was unheeded— if heard at all. It is worth examining the parallels between the Powers and the *Pueblo* missions before asking why the lessons go unlearned despite all the pain suffered by the men involved.

Both missions involved complex, secret equipment for the gathering of intelligence, and each ran the hazard of that equipment falling into dangerously unfriendly hands.

Both dealt with operational personnel in possession of highly classified information, and each placed that personnel within border-line grasp of a Cold War foe.

Both were instituted on their planners' evaluation of dismissible minimal risk, and in each case those planners were grievously wrong.

In both instances personnel were profoundly ill-prepared for capture or interrogation, and equipment was inadequately designed for emergency destruction.

Both led to captivity, long imprisonment of personnel, and the concealment of much vital information by the determined evasions of the prisoners.

In both instances the planners remained anonymous and were relieved, at least publicly, of acknowledging their gross miscalcula-

227

tions and responsibilities, while the operational personnel were held strictly and openly accountable for all their actions.

Both resulted in one-sided inquiries that insidiously cast shadows of false guilt on good and brave men.

Francis Gary Powers had sought guidance before he took off in his U-2 on May 1, 1960. The question of what U-2 pilots should do if shot down or, through equipment malfunction, required to parachute over hostile territory had never been included in his Central Intelligence Agency briefings and was not specified in his contract with the agency. Powers, at the U-2 base near Adana, Turkey, about a month before his last flight, put the matter directly to his intelligence officer.

" 'What if something happens and one of us goes down over Russia? That's an awfully big country, and it could be a hell of a long walk to a border. Is there anyone there we can contact? Can you give us any names and addresses?'

" 'No, we can't.'

"While it was not what I wanted to hear, his answer was at least understandable. If we had agents in Russia, as we presumably did, release of their names could place them in jeopardy also.

"I persisted. 'All right, say the worst happens. A plane goes down, and the pilot is captured. What story does he use? Exactly how much should he tell?'

"His exact words were, 'You may as well tell them everything, because they're going to get it out of you anyway.' "

But, when it came time to testify to the Senate Armed Services Committee on what instructions it had given Powers, the Central Intelligence Agency made them sound well-thought-out, not spur-of-the-moment. If Powers' account is to be believed, and there seems no reason to doubt it, the agency tailored its after-the-fact instructions for its U-2 pilots to what Powers had actually done in captivity—used his own judgment. On March 6, 1962, the day Powers testified before the Senate committee, the agency released this set of instructions for U-2 pilots:

(a) If evasion is not feasible and capture appears imminent, pilots should surrender without resistance and adopt a cooperative attitude toward their captors.

(b) At all times while in the custody of their captors, pilots will conduct themselves with dignity and maintain a respectful attitude toward their superiors.

(c) Pilots will be instructed that they are perfectly free to tell the full truth about their mission with the exception of certain specifications of the aircraft. They will be advised to represent themselves as civilians, to admit previous Air Force affiliation, to admit current CIA employment, and to make no attempt to deny the nature of their mission.

The agency, at another point in its public statement, said of its instructions to U-2 pilots: "They were instructed . . . to be cooperative with their captors within limitations, to use their own judgment of what they should attempt to withhold, and not to subject themselves to strenuous hostile interrogation. It has been established that Mr. Powers had been briefed in accordance with this policy and so understood his guidance."

In his book, which the Central Intelligence Agency successfully delayed for almost eight years, Powers presents a decidedly different account of those instructions. He wrote: "As pilots, we were not only unprepared for capture, we were *ill*-prepared, in many ways a much worse situation. The advice 'You may as well tell them everything because they're going to get it out of you anyway' was, under the circumstances, bad. Perhaps the agency couldn't have foreseen this. Brainwashing, drugs, and torture having been the lot of prisoners in the past, it may have been wise to prepare for the worst. All I know, however, is that had I followed these instructions, the damage to the United States would have been monumental."

What Powers did instead was the same as Schumacher and the others of the *Pueblo* did. To establish credibility, he revealed what he figured the enemy already knew and then he held back on the really vital information. The improvised technique helped protect American security in both cases. Adherence to the Code of Conduct would not have worked in either case. Powers, had he initially remained mute, would have eventually yielded to torture, psychological pressure, or drugs. He, like the men of the *Pueblo* and so many other unfortunates, had fallen into the demon hands of experts.

When Powers was released from Russian imprisonment, he suddenly found himself tainted, despite the CIA's lukewarm approval of his performance. He listed the following as among his disillusionments: the Central Intelligence Agency had let him be severely criticized in public, his character denigrated, without attempting to set the record straight, even after he had been released from captivity; the Air Force reneged on its written promise to let him return to the service after his U-2 contract was fulfilled; the Air Force, further, withheld the Distinguished Flying Cross he had been awarded in 1957; and he was not included in the April 20, 1963, secret ceremony in which the Central Intelligence Agency awarded the Intelligence Star to pilots who had flown U-2 reconnaissance missions.

The Central Intelligence Agency, by its very nature, must avoid public exposure. The Navy, undertaking infinitely complex and hazardous tasks in a parlous world, is constantly subject to exposure and frequently to criticism from various sources; quite naturally, it prefers to avoid that. Both serve an enormous nation and properly consider its welfare of paramount importance. There is no question that these two arms of the United States government merit the admiration and gratitude of the citizenry, that they perform herculean and essential tasks day after day, and that they require authority and privilege to discharge their responsibilities. Yet when authority and privilege are used as a shield to mask incompetence or, worse, at the expense of vulnerable and virtually defenseless individuals, serious and ugly questions arise. They reach out to the mind and the spirit, the core of a free society.

The case of Francis Gary Powers raises such questions. Did the Central Intelligence Agency abandon him, cast him in the role of scapegoat? Did the agency mask its culpability in the U-2 crisis by letting the burden of blame settle on a man then incommunicado in a foreign prison and, after his release, by essentially gagging him for years through procedural delays in permitting him to reveal his experience?

Powers, with substantial evidence and persuasion, has indicted the Central Intelligence Agency. Several courses are open to the agency. It can, without detailed comment, simply validate the essence of his account and grant him long-overdue exoneration. It can, with whatever detail it deems feasible, attempt to refute his account. If the agency does nothing, Powers has not only the right to be heard, but also the right to be believed.

What of the men of the *Pueblo*? Where is elusive justice in their case? What happened to them?

Unlike Powers, who was debriefed in secret except for one short Senate hearing, Bucher and his crew in the public hearings in Coronado had said enough to spread the blame to other areas and personnel of the entire defense, security, and intelligence establishments. More than the *Pueblo* appeared culpable in the eyes of the public. This hard political reality must have played a significant role in Secretary of the Navy John H. Chafee's action after receiving the admirals' findings in the *Pueblo* matter. On May 6, 1968, he called a news conference at the Pentagon and issued a formal statement.

"The Court of Inquiry convened by the United States Navy to inquire into the seizure of USS *Pueblo* by North Korean forces on 23 January 1968 has completed its proceedings."

After a few paragraphs of background, Chafee continued. "As a result of my review, I have decided that no disciplinary action will be taken against any of the personnel involved in the *Pueblo* incident. I will first give you the conclusions of the Court of Inquiry, the convening authority and the Chief of Naval Operations, then explain the basis for my decision.

"Based upon its findings of fact and the formal opinions which it derived from those findings, the Court of Inquiry recommended that Commander Lloyd M. Bucher, U.S. Navy, the commanding officer of USS *Pueblo,* be brought to trial by General Court-Martial for the following five alleged offenses: permitting his ship to be searched while he had the power to resist; failing to take immediate and aggressive protective measures when his ship was attacked by North Korean forces; complying with the orders of the North Korean forces to follow them into port; negligently failing to complete destruction of classified material aboard USS *Pueblo* and permitting such material to fall into the hands of the North Koreans; and negligently failing to ensure, before departure for sea, that his officers and crew were properly organized, stationed and trained in preparation for emergency destruction of classified material."

Chafee further announced that the Court of Inquiry had recommended that Lieutenant Stephen R. Harris be tried by general court-martial for dereliction of duty; that Lieutenant Edward R. Murphy be given a letter of admonition for dereliction in the performance of his duties as Executive Officer; and that letters of reprimand be given to Rear Admiral Frank L. Johnson and Captain Everett B. Gladding. Johnson, the court alleged, failed to provide emergency rescue forces for the *Pueblo,* while Gladding, as director of Naval Security Group in the Pacific, was charged with failing to "develop procedures to ensure the readiness of *Pueblo*'s research detachment for the mission assigned and to coordinate other services and agencies to provide intelligence support to *Pueblo* during the mission."

"I make no judgment regarding the guilt or innocence of any of the officers of the offenses alleged against them," Chafee said. "I am convinced, however, that neither individual discipline nor the state of discipline or morale in the Navy, nor any other interest requires further legal proceedings with respect to any personnel involved in the *Pueblo* incident.

"In reviewing the Court's recommendations with respect to Commander Bucher, Lt. Murphy and Lt. Harris, it is my opinion that—even assuming that further proceedings were had, and even going so far as to assume that a judgment of guilt were to be reached—they have suffered enough, and further punishment would not be justified. . . ."

The sophistry squirming in those last two paragraphs may be startling, but it is surely not blinding. In three consecutive sentences, Chafee asserts that he makes no judgment regarding guilt, then opens the clear possibility of guilt, and then opines that, regardless of guilt, sufficient punishment has already been inflicted.

The implication of guilt in this presentation is unconscionable. The omission of the next—and vital—consideration is deplorable. *What if those charged are innocent?* Have they then suffered too much? *What of those who have not been charged?* Does their suffering merit concern, or gratitude, or even commendation?

232

Chafee, by letting the matter drift in the inconclusive, veiled area between indictment and trial, sought to sink the *Pueblo* incident once and for all. But this political decision did not stop the suffering of the *Pueblo* men involved. Bucher, after hearing Chafee's statement, wanted to demand a court-martial. His attorney declined to pursue that course. Schumacher, though not charged in any way, felt the Navy had been, at the very least, unfair; the system, it seemed to him, had determined to protect itself. He wondered what was the point, the value of his ordeal. He questioned whether there was even a remote understanding within his own Navy of what he and others of the *Pueblo* mission had undergone and with what intention. No one in the Navy seemed willing to hear him, perhaps to find some meaning to his experience. No one was even interested.

The *Pueblo* crew had done their best under extraordinarily brutal circumstances. Did the Navy mean to say their best had not been good enough? Yet no Navy official was even forthright enough to say that. The men—by Chafee's hopelessly inconclusive "decision"— were doomed to wonder for the rest of their lives what their service and their country thought of them.

An atmosphere of cynicism seems to pervade the *Pueblo* disaster. In that unhealthy climate, one can ask whether anyone involved had done his best and been recognized for it. The Navy hospital in San Diego that treated the *Pueblo* men received a Navy commendation; Captain Newsome, legal adviser to the Court of Inquiry, received the Legion of Merit; E. Miles Harvey, who lost the case for Bucher during the inquiry, will share in the earnings from Bucher's book; Admiral Thomas H. Moorer, Chief of Naval Operations when the *Pueblo* was seized, was promoted by President Nixon to the chairmanship of the Joint Chiefs of Staff; Robert S. McNamara, Secretary of Defense when the *Pueblo* was sent on her mission, became the head of the World Bank; Eugene Fubini, originator of the *Pueblo* concept, left the Pentagon for a lucrative business; Paul Ignatius, Secretary of the Navy when the *Pueblo* sailed, became president of the Washington Post Company. The ironies of fate and the vagaries of justice are endless.

As for the *Pueblo* men themselves, not one received any formal commendation of any kind from the nation that sent them into the dangerously uncharted waters of half-war, half-peace. Not even Marine Sergeant Robert J. Hammond—the gallant prisoner who took more beatings than anybody else for his near-incredible resistance in captivity—officially heard a kind word. In the face of the record, is it conceivable that not one man out of the eighty-three aboard the *Pueblo* had done something worthy of commendation by his country? In an offhand manner, comparable to the CIA's treatment of Powers, the court did utter some qualified praise for the conduct of Schumacher and eight of his shipmates in prison camp. No other official, including Secretary Chafee, said so much as "well done" or "thank you" to even one of the eighty-two *Pueblo* survivors.

Months after Chafee had quashed the *Pueblo* indictment, I asked Admiral Moorer at an informal gathering what he would have done that day off Wonsan if he had been on the bridge of the *Pueblo*. "I wasn't on the bridge that day," said the Admiral, "so I won't comment. But I don't give up easy."

Some months after his decision on the court's findings, I interviewed Chafee, a decorated ex-Marine and former governor of Rhode Island, and asked him what he expected the men of the *Pueblo* to have done under North Korean torture. He replied: "Every man has his limit." If that is the case, I asked, how is the Code of Conduct tenable? He said: "You've got to have something."

Whether that particular "something" is better than nothing is open to challenge, given the tragic experiences of the eighty-two survivors of the *Pueblo*. Powers agrees that "something" is needed to guide men sent out to fight the Cold War. But the present code is obviously inadequate and unfair to the men ordered to live up to it— particularly when their own government does not.

Beyond the need for a new code—and more important than any words put down on paper for servicemen to follow—is the need for a new spirit, a return, perhaps, to that traditional concept of Navy *esprit* expressed as "loyalty up and loyalty down." If the United States wants to send men out on perilous missions, then the leadership should be willing to share the blame when plans go awry. Or set the record right. Or, at least, say "thanks." Instead, the men of

234

the *Pueblo* have been left out in the cold. The Bridge of No Return turned out to be just that for Skip Schumacher and his shipmates.

What right has the Navy and the rest of the country to leave men like Schumacher unrepatriated spiritually? This book was written to ask that question. Now it is time for the country to answer it. The *Pueblo* men have already waited too long.

The Crew of the U.S.S. *Pueblo* (AGER-2)

The *Pueblo* crew was a cross section of America—geographically, politically, and culturally. A small ship, without the appeal of the destroyer or aircraft carrier to ambitious young officers, the *Pueblo* did not have a single Annapolis graduate aboard. Her crew of seventy-nine uniformed Navy men, two Marines, and two civilian oceanographers who worked for the Navy represented Main Street.

The *Pueblo* sailed off on her one and only mission from Sasebo, Japan, on January 11, 1968. Almost eighteen months later—as of April 1, 1970—about 60 per cent of her uniformed crew had elected to leave the service. The other 40 per cent, despite their ordeal, stayed in the Navy.

In this list of the men of the *Pueblo,* checked by the Navy's Bureau of Personnel in July 1970, ages and ranks are those on the day of the ship's capture—January 23, 1968; addresses are those of next of kin or parents on that date; Navy assignments are those of April 1, 1970 or later.

Commanding Officer and Executive Officer

Commander Lloyd Mark Bucher, USN, Commanding Officer, 40. Lincoln, Nebraska; born in Pocatello, Idaho.

Lieutenant Edward Renz Murphy, Jr., USN, Executive Officer, 30. McKinleyville, California; born in Berkeley, California. Resigned from Navy May 13, 1969.

Lieutenant Stephen Robert Harris, Research Officer in charge of the special detachment of electronic specialists under Commander in Chief of the Pacific Fleet, 29. Melrose, Massachusetts; born there.

Communications Technician Second Class Michael William Alexander, 21. Richland, Washington; born there. Left Navy.

Communications Technician Second Class Wayne Drexel Anderson, 25. Waycross, Florida; born in Alma, Georgia. Left Navy.

Communications Technician Third Class Charles William Ayling, 22. Staunton, Virginia; born in Syracuse, New York. Left Navy.

Communications Technician First Class Don Earl Bailey, 28. Ridgeville, Indiana; born in Farmland, Indiana.

Communications Technician First Class Michael Thomas Barrett, 30. Kalamazoo, Michigan; born there.

Chief Communications Technician Ralph Dalton Bouden, 40. Nampa, Idaho; born in Enid, Oklahoma.

Communications Technician Third Class Paul David Brusnahan, 20. Trenton, New Jersey; born there. Left Navy.

Sergeant Robert Joseph Chicca, USMC, 23. Chillum Terrace, Maryland; born in Washington, D.C. Left Marine Corps.

Communications Technician Third Class Bradley Reed Crowe, 20. Island Pond, Vermont; born there. Left Navy.

Communications Technician Third Class Rodney Harteman Duke, 25. Fayette, Mississippi; born in Mobile, Alabama. Left Navy.

Communications Technician First Class Francis John Ginther, 24. Pottsville, Pennsylvania; born there.

Communications Technician Third Class John White Grant, 21. Jay, Maine; born there. Left Navy.

Sergeant Robert James Hammond, USMC, 23. Claremont, New Hampshire; born there. Left Marine Corps.

Communications Technician Third Class Sidney Jerry Karnes, 22. Havana, Arkansas; born in Paris, Arkansas. Left Navy.

Chief Communications Technician James Francis Kell, 31. Honolulu, Hawaii; born in Peoria, Illinois.

Communications Technician Third Class Earl Murray Kisler, 21. St. Louis, Missouri; born in Bremerton, Washington. Left Navy.

Communications Technician Second Class Anthony Andrew Lamantia, 21. Toronto, Ohio; born in Steubenville, Ohio. Left Navy.

Communications Technician Second Class Peter Morton Langenberg, 22. St. Louis, Missouri; born there. Left Navy.

Communications Technician First Class James Dewar Layton, 25. Binghamton, New York; born there.

Communications Technician Second Class Donald Raymond McClarren, 32. Johnstown, Pennsylvania; born there

Communications Technician Third Class Ralph McClintock, 23. Milton, Massachusetts; born in Boston, Massachusetts. Left Navy.

Communications Technician First Class Donald Richard Peppard, 30. Chippewa Bay, New York; born in Barton, New York.

Communications Technician Second Class David Lee Ritter, 23. Menlo Park, California; born in Allentown, Pennsylvania.

Communications Technician Third Class Steven Jay Robin, 21. Silver Spring, Maryland; born in New York City. Left Navy.

Communications Technician First Class James Antwyne Shepard, 27. Williamstown, Massachusetts; born in Bennington, Vermont.

Communications Technician Third Class John Allen Shilling, 21. Mantua, Ohio; born in Cleveland, Ohio. Left Navy.

Communications Technician Second Class Charles Ray Sterling, 28. Omaha, Nebraska; born in Tyler Town, Texas.

Communications Technician Third Class Angelo Salvatore Strano, 22. Hartford, Connecticut; born there. Left Navy.

Communications Technician Second Class Elton Allen Wood, 21. Spokane, Washington; born there. Left Navy.

Operations Department

Lieutenant (junior grade) Frederick Carl Schumacher, Jr., USNR, Operations Officer and First Lieutenant, 24. St. Louis, Missouri; born there. Left Navy.

Hospital Corpsman First Class Herman Paul Baldridge, 36. Carthage, Missouri; born there.

Yeoman First Class Armando Moreno Canales, 34. Fresno, California; born there.

Radioman Third Class Charles Henry Crandell, Jr., 23. Kansas City, Missouri; born in El Reno, Oklahoma.

Radioman Second Class Lee Roy Hayes, 26. Columbus, Ohio; born there. Left Navy.

Quartermaster First Class Charles Benton Law, Jr., 26. Chehalis, Washington; born in Port Townsend, Washington.

Signalman Second Class Wendell Gene Leach, 25. Houston, Texas; born there.

Photographer's Mate First Class Lawrence William Mack, 34. San Diego, California; born in Cleveland, Ohio.

Electronics Technician, Radar, Second Class Clifford Clair Nolte, 22. Washington, Iowa; born in Adel, Iowa. Left Navy.

239

Quartermaster Third Class Alvin Henry Plucker, 21. Trenton, Nebraska; born in Gallup, New Mexico. Left Navy.

Deck Department

Boatswain's Mate Second Class Ronald Leon Berens, 22. Russell, Kansas; born in Hays, Kansas.

Boatswain's Mate Third Class Willie Columbus Bussell, 22. Hopkinsville, Kentucky; born there.

Seaman Robert Walter Hill, Jr., 19. Ellwood City, Pennsylvania; born there.

Boatswain's Mate First Class Norbert John Klepac, 34. Granger, Texas; born in Jerrell, Texas.

Seaman Roy Jay Maggard, 21. Olivehurst, California; born in Oklahoma City, Oklahoma. Left Navy.

Seaman Apprentice Larry Joseph Marshall, 19. Austin, Indiana; born in Scott County, Indiana.

Seaman Earl Raymond Phares, 19. Ontario, California; born in Waukegan, Illinois. Left Navy.

Seaman Apprentice Richard Joseph Rogala, 20. Niles, Illinois; born in Chicago, Illinois. Left Navy.

Seaman Ramon Rosales, 19. El Paso, Texas; born there. Left Navy.

Seaman Apprentice John Robert Shingleton, 20. Atoka, Oklahoma; born in Stillwater, Oklahoma. Left Navy.

Gunner's Mate, Guns, Second Class Kenneth Roy Wadley, 29. Carthage, Mississippi; born in Earle, Arkansas.

Supply Department

Ensign Timothy Leon Harris, USNR, Supply Officer, 22. Jacksonville, Florida; born in Oshkosh, Wisconsin.

Steward's Mate Rogelio Parel Abelon, 25. Bani, Pangasinan, Philippines; born there.

Steward's Mate Rizalino Lastrella Aluague, 28. Zambales, Philippines; born there.

Seaman Stephen Paul Ellis, 25. Los Angeles, California; born in Detroit, Michigan. Left Navy.

Storekeeper First Class Policarpo Pollo Garcia, 33. Cavite City, Philippines; born there.

Commissaryman Second Class Harry Lewis, ship's cook, 31. Chester, South Carolina; born in The Bronx, New York.

Commissaryman Third Class Ralph Edward Reed, 29. Danville, Pennsylvania; born there.

Seaman Dale Evans Rigby, 20. Centerville, Utah; born in Salt Lake City, Utah. Left Navy.

Seaman Edward Stuart Russell, 24. Glendale, California; born there. Left Navy.

Engineering Department

Chief Warrant Officer Gene Howard Lacy, USN, Engineering Officer, 36. Seattle, Washington; born in Omak, Washington.

Fireman Apprentice Richard Everett Arnold, 21. Santa Rosa, California; born there. Left Navy.

Engineman, Fireman Apprentice Richard Ivan Bame, 20. Willis, Michigan; born in Ann Arbor, Michigan. Left Navy.

Fireman Peter Milton Bandera, 19. Carson City, Nevada; born in Reno, Nevada. Left Navy.

Engineman, Fireman Apprentice Howard Edward Bland, 20. Leggett, California; born in Mesa, Arizona. Left Navy.

Engineman Rushel Junior Blansett, 34. Anaheim, California; born in Walnut Ridge, Arkansas.

Interior Communications Technician Second Class Victor Deleon Escamilla, 26. Amarillo, Texas; born in Rio Hondo, Texas.

Chief Engineman Monroe Onel Goldman, 36. North Little Rock, Arkansas; born in Pine Bluff, Arkansas. Left Navy.

Electrician's Mate First Class Gerald William Hagenson, 37. Stanley, Wisconsin; born there.

Fireman John Charles Higgins, Jr., 22. St. Joseph, Missouri; born there. Left Navy.

Fireman Duane Daniel Hodges, 21. Creswell, Oregon; born there. Died aboard the *Pueblo* from wounds inflicted by North Korean shell fire.

Fireman Apprentice William Thomas Massie, 20. Roscoe, Illinois; born in Freeport, Illinois. Left Navy.

Fireman John Arthur Mitchell, 20. Dixon, California; born in Woodland, California. Left Navy.

Fireman Michael Andrew O'Bannon, 21. Beaverton, Oregon; born in Portland, Oregon. Left Navy.

Engineman First Class William Douglas Scarborough, 25. Anderson, South Carolina; born there. Left Navy; committed suicide in 1970.

Fireman Apprentice Norman William Spear, 25. Portland, Maine; born there. Left Navy.

Fireman Lawrence Edwin Strickland, 20. Grand Rapids, Michigan; born in Petoskey, Michigan. Left Navy.

Fireman Apprentice Steven Eugene Woelk, 19. Alta Vista, Kansas; born in El Dorado, Kansas. Left Navy.

241

Engineman Third Class Darrel Dean Wright, 22. Alma, West Virginia; born there. Left Navy.

Civilian Oceanographers

Harry Iredale III, 24. Holmes, Pennsylvania; born in Goochland, Virginia.

Dunnie Richard Tuck, Jr., Chief Oceanographer, 30. Richmond, Virginia; born in South Boston, Virginia.